Vigilance

Vigilance

A defence of British liberty

Ashley Mote

TANNER PUBLISHING

British Library Cataloguing in Publication Data
A catalogue record for this book is available from the British Library

ISBN 0-9540124-0-2

Typeset by Amolibros, Watchet, Somerset
This book production has been managed by Amolibros
Printed and bound by Porfessional Book Supplies, Oxford, England

"The condition upon which God hath given liberty to Man is eternal vigilance", which is usually misquoted and attributed to Thomas Jefferson as: "the price of liberty is eternal vigilance".

John Curran, 18th-century Irish judge

"[We are] unwilling to permit the slow undoing of those human rights to which this nation has always been committed...[and] to assure the survival and success of liberty."

John F Kennedy, 1961

Contents

Acknowledgements

A great many people have contributed to the evolution of this book over several years. They have researched particular aspects of this huge subject, and made that work available to others, often via the internet, and with no other motive than to see the truth unveiled. I hope this humble effort of mine will provide some satisfaction to them, and with it goes my sincere thanks.

The euro-realist movement is now a large one, and it goes on growing as we gradually overcome the obstacles of a pro-European Union BBC (now known contemptuously as the Brussels Broadcasting Corporation), a press that is often sceptical but never manages to reach a logical conclusion, and an opposition in parliament that has the same difficulty.

In that environment, the instigators of internet websites seeking the truth about the EU, and the subscribers to the numerous euro-realist e-groups, have been a priceless source of help, and I salute and acknowledge every one. In a sense, this book is as much theirs as mine.

In these circumstances, I hope they will accept my not attempting to name every individual and I ask their indulgence when I pick out a small handful of people whose contributions have been truly exceptional.

I am particularly indebted to Torquil Dick-Erikson and Lindsay Jenkins for their research and commentaries on *corpus juris* and Europol. Their work has been extensive and freely quoted on the grounds that it is impossible to improve on the best. Likewise, great credit goes to three hard-working researchers – John Hurst, Mike Burke, and David Bourne – who provided much of the raw material for *Defence of the Realm*, which now forms the appendix to this book.

My good friend Idris Francis has not only fed me continuously with information, but he has also driven me many hundreds of miles to private meetings with others of like mind, and to a few that were more public, lively and controversial. At the end, he even volunteered to read the manuscript and made many improvements, corrections and perspicacious comments. This is a better book for his input.

Tony Bennett and Greg Lance-Watkins both kept up a constant supply of ideas and facts, despite being fully occupied with their own commitments in other corners of the battlefield. Towards the end of a long journey, Jane Tatam and her team at Amolibros, and my editor Peter Cowlam, have been valued allies as this book finally came to life.

But perhaps *Vigilance* belongs above all to the countless people at meetings and elsewhere who encouraged me to write it. Without that support and enthusiasm this book would never have reached completion. To them, and to everyone else who helped and encouraged me, I hope *Vigilance* proves an acceptable and tangible thank you.

Introduction

One day this book may be banned. One day, to express these views may be illegal. The British right to freedom of speech will have been abolished.

One day, perhaps soon, the United Kingdom of Great Britain and Northern Ireland will cease to exist as a free and sovereign nation. Some will tell you it already has.

But if it hasn't happened yet, it will, unless a majority of British subjects is prepared to stand up and say "No" – loud and clear. I believe that majority is there, waiting, perhaps puzzled by what has been going on over the last 30-odd years.

In 1975, as new members of the EEC, we thought we were voting for a free trade area. What we have today is an undemocratic, unaccountable police state that makes laws behind closed doors and seeks by stealth to destroy the UK as an independent nation. The EU is being increasingly rammed down British throats in pursuit of a dream we never voted for. That dream has become a living nightmare. Silent discontent is no longer an option.

❖

So if you are concerned, or merely doubtful, about the EU and its endless interference in the UK, then this book is for you. *Vigilance* is not a book about politics, at least not in the normal sense. Nor is it academic. It has no endless footnotes. It is as simple and clear a message as I could write about what is being done to our country as it is integrated into the EU, why it matters, why it must be stopped, and the huge benefits of leaving.

This book is a call to all men and women of good will, who care about the country they love – a country presently being dismantled by stealth. It is a call to them to stand up and be counted.

I belong to no political party. In fact I am as sceptical of politicians as I am of the EU. Far too many have no experience of running an enterprise, don't know what it is to take tough day-to-day business decisions, and think wealth grows on trees. For what it's worth, my instincts lie towards the Old Whig end of the spectrum.

Like most widely travelled Britons, I like Europe. Many of the people I met and did business with across western Europe over many years became good friends. So did numerous other people I met socially. I am not anti-European.

In any case, there are almost 50 countries in Europe. The EU isn't "Europe". It is less than a third of Europe in terms of nations. My opposition is to the system of government being created by the EU.

My father's generation, and his father's generation, fought and died in two world wars to defend this country and its way of life against tyranny. They were obliged to use the traditional weapons of war. They fought to preserve our essential liberties, particularly during 1939–45.

My own generation is now faced with a war of equal importance. Once again it is about the preservation of our essential liberties. But this is not a war of weapons. This is a war of ideas, and of words. It is a war in which our opponents use weapons of cunning and disinformation.

To win that war, the EU and all its works must be expelled from the UK. Nothing less will do. Neither should we harbour any aggressive intentions. This is purely a defensive war.

We should seek no political influence over Continental Europeans. What they finally make of their dream is a matter for them. They are free to get on with it.

Euro-sceptics (euro-realists is a better phrase) are criticised as "little Englanders". Such epithets are both offensive and petty, particularly since quite the reverse is true. If the EU has its way, we shall become "little Englanders" in a giant Europe.

One day, I hope to see a prosperous, democratic, open, dynamic, flexible, responsive, outward-looking, competitive, successful Europe trading freely with us and the rest of the world. A Europe thriving on enterprise, and with a prosperous and independent Britain close by. We must live in hope.

Meanwhile, these are deeply worrying times. We need to ask ourselves some basic questions about the way we wish to be governed – about the constitution we wish to live under – and about the powers we are prepared to give to others.

We should not just consider the personalities visible today, but those unknown and quite possibly ruthless individuals who might follow. However Europe evolves, politicians must be kept in their place. Otherwise, what Charlemagne, Charles V, Louis XIV, Napoleon, the Kaiser and Hitler all failed to achieve by force could yet be achieved by stealth.

In recent years we have seen a helter-skelter destruction of our birthrights of freedom and self-determination. It is essential – and overdue – that we turn back the tide.

The present debate about the EU is of monumental proportions. When everything else is stripped away it is about liberty itself. Four goals are paramount: restoration of the sovereignty of the UK; protection and preservation of that constitution in perpetuity; re-establishment and subsequent maintenance of the rights, liberties and customs of the subjects of this realm; and a preparedness to challenge all attempts to subvert, compromise or overthrow the constitution.

One of the most extraordinary features of the battle between pro- and anti-EU campaigners in recent years has been the replacement of genuine political debate with what can be described only as a dialogue of the deaf. When europhiles are asked: "So, what, precisely, are the benefits of the UK's membership of the EU?", the question is never answered. Indeed, no government, nor any politician of any persuasion, has ever given accurate, clear-cut and straightforward answers to that question. Instead they speak pathetically about "avoiding being isolated", about "gaining influence", about "protecting our trade with the EU". As we shall see, all these statements are spurious, and we are right to be suspicious of them.

The British public knows perfectly well that we have been invaded from within. Today we live under a government of occupation, and it is more and more deeply resented. People are incredulous that their way of life is being destroyed, they are increasingly frustrated by it, and they will no longer tolerate such ruination.

Deep in many hearts, and in their heads, is a smouldering conviction that, free of EU interference, the recognisably British sovereign nation will quickly re-emerge from the ruins of the EU disaster - a thriving, wealthy, confident and outward-looking independent country once again.

❖

Opinion polls make it crystal clear that some 40 per cent of the people of the UK want us to leave the EU. That figure rises to over 60 per cent when they realise that we will be free to trade with the EU afterwards…and for three crucial reasons:

1   Trade agreements made between countries under the auspices of the World Trade Organisation (WTO) and the General Agreement on Tariffs and Trade (GATT) are binding on all signatories and ensure that trade is conducted freely between them all.

2   We buy far more from the EU than they do from us, and we have done so ever since we first joined what was then called the Common Market. They need our trade far more than we need theirs.

3   The Germans will still want to sell us their cars, the French their champagne and wine, the Danes their bacon, the Mediterranean countries their tourist destinations. Our markets are essential to them. So they must keep their markets open to us – whether we're in or out.

The proof is staring us in the face. The Americans now export more to the other 14 members of the EU than we do. Non-members Switzerland and Norway trade freely with the EU and – would you believe – so does Mexico! And they all pay less for the opportunity than we do. They are not leeching out over £1.3 million every hour of every day in membership fees, nor are they burdened with 30,000 directives.

So the situation is this – there is a clear majority, and good reason to leave – but no major political party offers the choice. The honest choice, which should be placed before the British people, is complete integration or complete withdrawal. EU leaders have repeatedly made it clear that major renegotiation of either their current powers or ultimate objectives is not an option. As we stand, the final building blocks of complete integration are already within sight. Yet politicians on all sides still duck the issue, despite the smouldering anger in Great Britain at the increasingly powerful and arrogant "government of Europe" — as Mr Prodi chooses so grandly to call it.

Many euro-realists argue that the UK's membership of the EU is illegal, and always has been. They claim that the signatories to all the treaties — Rome, Maastricht and Amsterdam — exceeded their powers.

Our freedoms, rights and customs have long since been guaranteed under common law by Magna Carta, the Declaration and Bill of Rights, and by the coronation oath. Yet they have, in recent years, been placed in jeopardy by the very people who sought the trust of the British people and were elected to power.

This book is one small step on the road towards the restoration of those freedoms, rights and customs, not just for this generation but for future generations.

Chapter One

Clearing the Smokescreen

Are the Swedes like the Portuguese? Are the Finns like the Irish? What do Italians and Danes have in common? Do they want the same things? Do they want to live by the same laws? Do they want to live in the same way? And what about the British, who feel far closer to Australia and North America than to France? Mileage has nothing to do with it. What matters is lifestyles, customs, history and attitudes.

The essence of Europe lies in its diversity.

This part of the world is the cradle of modern civilisation. For thousands of years it has thrived on the richness of its diversity. Competition and different ways of life, different ways of thinking, different ways of doing things have thrown up such a treasure-trove of successful human endeavour that it is now quite beyond comprehension that anyone might wish to stifle these differences.

Across the generations, Europe has given the world a cornucopia of breathtaking music, soaring architecture, stunning art, stimulating literature and theatre, imaginative inventions, revolutionary ideas, discoveries that have changed attitudes and behaviour, and much, much more. In modern times, Europe has created and contributed hugely to the worlds of pop music, film, television, advertising, marketing and fashion. It makes some of the best cars and aircraft, and the whole world enjoys its food and drink. The inventiveness, ingenuity, creativity and sheer enterprising drive in and around Europe are long-standing, well-established and ongoing.

And all of this richness of thinking and activity was, and is, as different and distinctive as the people and places from whence it came.

Europe now boasts more than 45 independent nation states, the precise number depending on where the line is drawn in the east. Each has its own culture, its own lifestyle, its own traditions. Each has its own laws, its own coinage, its own army – in short, its own way of doing things. The great majority have their own language, or at the very least a dialect that is different from that of their neighbours. These are the factors that make each country a nation state.

This rich diversity has also served as a seedbed for many more, newer, younger nations around the world. The USA and Canada both emerged from European emigration, while colonisation of parts of South America, Africa and Australasia has also left lasting and distinctive marks. Europeans as a whole, and the Anglo-Saxon British in particular, have spawned all over the planet.

Yes, sometimes – perhaps far too often and more than once with catastrophic consequences – the nation states of Europe have squabbled to the point of war. Competition for space, competition between ambitious rulers and governments, competition for assets, competition between political ideas, have all caused wars in Europe over the centuries, and the more humanity has improved its ability to move quickly and increase the fire-power of its weaponry, the progressively worse these wars have become.

Into that melting-pot of turmoil must be added the greed, corruption, deceit and ruthlessness of a few power-mad individuals, who would stop at nothing to achieve their personal goals, regardless of the consequences for millions of other individuals and their families, sometimes regardless of the well-being of their countries, and often regardless of their own personal survival.

Not that war is confined to Europe. The wars here have been no different, no worse or more agonising, than those that have been inflicted on peoples living in every other corner of the globe. And war still goes on today. It is an appalling fact that there are more – admittedly localised – wars being waged today than at any time in history.

Only one thing is certain about war. War is the privilege of the powerful. Never, in the history of humankind, has war been started by ordinary people. And in more modern times, no two genuine democracies have ever made war against each other. War is also the privilege of the unelected tyrant – the pursuit of political ends without the bother of political debate.

This is one of many reasons why the original invention and current development of the system of government known as the EU is so potentially dangerous. It has deep within it the seeds of tyranny.

It is a profound mistake to attempt to detail on paper what the vast, awe-inspiring potential of an entire continent should be; especially in the futile belief that more than 360,000,000 people can best be organised, directed and controlled by a tiny handful of puny officials, whose only idea of leadership is regulation and whose only claim to power is a misguided conviction that they know best.

History is against them. It will end in tears.

❖

Look back over aeons of time and consider evolution itself. The one common thread that runs through evolution is that there is no common thread. Life has evolved, often with limited success, sometimes without much success, and occasionally with great success – the dinosaurs and humanity being just two of the prime examples on land, and the dolphin at sea.

Every species that faces a changed environment, whatever the reason, adapts to maximise its chances of survival. It has a built-in mechanism, requiring no conscious effort. Over time, perhaps, it may become quite unlike the original species from which it came. Failure to achieve this change and diversity from the original form can lead directly to extinction.

If the scientists are right, the dinosaurs that would have evolved after another 65,000,000 years might still be ruling the world today, and we would possibly not exist, but for the asteroid that landed in the Mexican Gulf. It changed their environment so completely, so fast and for so long that they had no opportunity to adapt, and the evolution they had achieved up to that time was not equal to the threat. Indeed no such threat had ever faced them before, so there had been no evolutionary drive to deal with it.

The point is this: nature and life itself teach us that the greatest risk to any species at any time is to lack diversity. The greater the diversity, the greater the chance of survival – by some if not all – when, metaphorically, the asteroid lands.

Add to that the fact that there is not a single example in history of humans tolerating an imposed system of government or regulation for more than a few generations. From ancient Greece to 20th-century communism no voluntary or dictated system of government that sought to regulate ideas and lifestyles has survived. It may have left its mark, it may still influence thought today, but it has had its time, passed away, and humanity has moved on.

The present attempts at the globalisation of government and commerce may also have their day. But one thing is absolutely certain – they will not last. Evolution and humanity's deep instincts to survive, by being diverse, will prevail in the end.

The fundamental case for diversity is valid in both commerce and politics. It is powerful, positive and overwhelming. It stems from our deepest instincts. Everything we see and know – from the past as well as the present – tells us that we need all the variety we can get, at every level and in every nook and cranny of our lives.

Our whole thrust must always be to maximise competition – of systems and ideas – because the law that governs us all ensures only the survival of the fittest. Coming back closer to home, so to speak, by the same reasoning we can see that history has already condemned the EU to its doom. By definition, it cannot last.

❖

"The further you look back at the past the clearer you see the future." Those are the words of Winston Churchill. It is a total myth that we need the EU. When attitudes are stripped to the bone, the EU is seen to be hostile towards sovereignty and the nation state. It seeks to establish laws that bind its successors and cannot be repealed – in direct contradiction to the British parliament's power to repeal any laws at any time. And that is something no parliament has the power to give away, abolish or dilute, and that no political party in the UK has ever proposed or included in its manifesto at an election.

The British people have never been asked for – nor given – their consent to the loss of such powers.

Free of the EU's cloying bureaucracy, and the undemocratic nature of this unaccountable and extravagant institution, the UK would do rather well. We are ideally placed to become Europe's very own offshore island.

We are one of the world's great international trading nations. There are well over 150 countries around the world, mostly smaller and poorer than the UK, who all have their own currencies, and many of them are getting on just fine.

How can a nation of over 55,000,000 people, with the fourth largest economy in the world, seriously ask itself if it can survive independently?

Does Canada survive next to the USA? Canada has its own currency, its own independence and belongs to the North American Free Trade Area (NAFTA). Its trade with the USA exceeds 80 per cent, far beyond the UK's trade with Europe. But no one seriously suggests it should submerge itself and become the 52nd American state and adopt the US dollar.

South Korea thrives next to Japan, Chile next to Brazil. Even little Iceland, a country of a mere 275,000 people, is doing fine. They have total control over their own fishing grounds and a thriving tourism industry, among other things, and they have lost nothing by being outside the EU. Neither has Greenland, which had the temerity to resign – which demonstrates that leaving the EU is possible, and sets a precedent. Switzerland and Norway are two of the richest countries in the world, both are smaller than the UK, both refused to join, and to this day neither is part of the EU. Both are doing very well, thank you.

Here, the City of London alone is more wealthy than many successful independent nations, including Norway and Switzerland. As it happens it is also more wealthy than several states in the EU, Austria and Belgium among them. Over the generations, Britain has built up wealth and global influence far beyond the norm.

As part of a huge free trade area where enterprise can thrive – reinforced by strong links with North and South America, Africa, Australasia and the rest of the English-speaking world – and with London as one of the great international financial centres – what else do we need?

The repeal of all UK legislation empowering EU control over our affairs would enable us to recover our fishing rights, free our farmers from the Common Agricultural Policy (CAP), and allow us to retain in the UK huge sums of public money exclusively to fund the things we need, and to benefit the people in our society who really need it. And abolition of all European directives would release a vast new store of enterprise, nationwide.

Compare that with the situation today. The French and Germans tell us how to run our lives. Our industries and businesses are hamstrung by regulation. We are lied to, and fed a diet of distortion, evasion and weasel words by our own government.

And for what? Almost 100,000 pages of laws, directives and regulations in nearly 30 years, every one of which we previously managed perfectly well without.

The EU has taken upon itself the roles of legislator, enforcer, investigator, prosecutor, judge, jury and executioner, all in one – as clear a case of violation of the rule of law as you could ever imagine. Furthermore, none of these functions is undertaken by elected representatives of the people, and none can be held directly accountable to them.

The EU is an affront to democracy, fundamentally unconstitutional, irredeemably flawed, and endemically corrupt. None of the politicians running the European Commission (EC), the bank or the judiciary has been elected, nor ever will be.

Yet the EU assumes the right to interfere with every aspect of our lives, makes decisions in secret, takes no account of the best interests of the people, and has set out to establish a United States of Europe that scarcely anyone in Britain wants, nobody voted for, and that ignores the huge differences in culture, history, tradition, language, lifestyles, global ties, methods of government, jurisdiction, economic cycles, and just about everything else that matters to every man, woman and child in Britain.

The EU has stolen our fishing grounds, ruined our agricultural industry, destroyed whole sectors of industry, put tens of thousands of small entrepreneurs out of business, and for good measure attempted to steal our gold, dollar and oil reserves.

Essentially, the case for the UK leaving the EU is based on three great issues:

1   Constitutionality – or, rather, the lack of it.
2   Commercial and economic realities.
3   History, culture and tradition – theirs and ours.

All of these add up to a fourth – the huge benefits of our leaving.
It is common knowledge that EU ministers have considered plans for

the eventual withdrawal of the UK. It is not high on their list, but it has been considered. Indeed, it would be surprising only if such an eventuality had not been considered. It seems the EU is quite aware of the possibility that the UK might leave.

While not wildly enthusiastic about it, the EU would be bound to accept a UK withdrawal on negotiated terms. But it much prefers the UK inside because of a virtually perpetual trade advantage for western Germany, Benelux, and eastern France, and the second-largest contribution to the EU's budget.

It's only in the UK that the "inevitability" threat is used, and then almost always by professional europhiles with the most to lose by our withdrawal. UK membership suits our politicians and bureaucrats. It offers them access to many permanent benefits. In the EU, as in much of Continental European government, the political classes are difficult to dislodge, they enjoy cosy coalition arrangements, the distinction between the elected and non-elected is seriously blurred, real power usually lies with the unelected, and countless levels of pseudo-democratic administration – from the most local to the supranational – offer endless career opportunities.

Politicians also enjoy the dubious benefits of proportional representation (or PR), which – contrary to popular belief – are not primarily to do with reflecting the will of the people. PR offers professional politicians a permanent hold on government and greatly reduces the risk of their being turfed out at the next election, especially if the particular form of PR used is based on the party-list system.

All of that is in sharp and chilling contrast to the UK's preference for total accountability every five years at most, no guarantee of future employment, and what has been described as the "chilly uplands of less government and lower public spending".

❖

In the latter part of the 19th century the distinguished biologist and explorer, Alfred Russel Wallace, found two islands in Indonesia that were only 15 miles apart. But they displayed totally different flora and fauna. He wrote in his log that these islands must once have been far apart. It was an astonishing statement for those days and he was much ridiculed for it.

By the end of the 20th century he had been utterly vindicated. Those two islands are on different tectonic plates, one moving north and the other south.

Our relationship with Europe is like that.

Great Britain is on an Anglo-Saxon tectonic plate, with North America and much of Africa and Australasia and the rest of the English-speaking world.

The original purpose of Anglo-Saxon government was to protect the liberty of the individual from sovereign power. Restraint was achieved by dividing power up.

Even that did not overcome the fundamental and permanent flaw in democracy, namely that the majority will always think of themselves as the "have nots", and seek to coerce those they see as the "haves" to share more of it. Sadly, it was inevitable that universal suffrage would lead directly to social and economic engineering and the creation of the nanny state.

Today, virtually every Act of Parliament involves confiscating property (money being the usual form of property in this context) and giving it to others. That is how pro-active social and economic engineering works.

And that is bad enough.

But at least we have a regularly elected parliament. It passes all our laws – or at least it did until recently. With a few minor exceptions, the executive (the cabinet and ministers) are all elected to parliament before they become ministers. Any laws passed by one parliament can be repealed by another, at any time.

And the whole parliament can be dismissed – lock, stock and barrel – by the people if they fail to retain the approval of the country. At most – and at worst – a parliament can govern for a maximum of five years.

Meanwhile, the judiciary – responsible for enforcing the law – has no legislative or executive powers. Its powers are limited to attempting to interpret what parliament intended.

So there are checks and balances. It is not a perfect structure, but generally it can and does work. It also takes account of the Anglo-Saxon dislike of government generally, and its particular dislike of being told by others what to think, and what to do.

Continental Europe may be only 22 miles away at its nearest point, but it is on a totally different tectonic plate. It is different in culture, it has a different style of government and follows different economic cycles. It has been said that an "Englishman is never at home in continental politics".

French President Charles de Gaulle understood the British perhaps better than we understood ourselves when he vetoed the UK's application to join what was then the Common Market, in 1963: "England, in effect is insular. She is maritime. She is linked through her trade, her markets, her supply lines to the most distant countries. She pursues essentially industrial and commercial activities and only slightly agricultural ones. She has, in all her doings, very marked and very original habits and traditions. In short England's nature, England's structure, England's very situation differs profoundly from those of the Continentals."

Europe is – and always has been – moving in a different direction. Its idea of democracy is not our idea. In Europe, government by bureaucracy has been the norm for generations. The electorates in most European countries have been largely impotent for centuries. They are used to the idea that unelected bureaucrats run their affairs.

On the other hand, British parliamentary democracy was based on the idea that representation mattered at least as much as legislation. The passing of new laws was intended to follow debate and discussion, and a search by elected representatives for genuine understanding of the needs of the people who elected them. That was the intention, and the practice, at least until recent times.

Even today, it is still true that:

> In Britain the state is the servant of the individual. In Europe the individual is the servant of the state.

> In Britain all people are free to do all manner of things unless forbidden by law. In Europe no person is free to do anything unless permitted by law.

> In Britain our parliament, and the party that forms the government of the day, draws its power from the electorate, to whom it is fully accountable. The electorate can throw the parliament and the government out and elect another. Every minister must answer for his own and his department's actions at any time.

Every word spoken in parliament is recorded verbatim and published immediately for all to see. All legislators and law enforcers are themselves subject to the full rigour of the law. No parliament may bind its successors. No parliament may legislate to limit or prejudice the rights and freedoms of the electorate.

In the EU (and much of Europe) none of these things is true. There, parliaments are at arms-length from their executives. Ministers do not have to answer for themselves or their departments. No verbatim records of proceedings are published. Law enforcers are not accountable for their actions under the law.

So there is a curiously simple dichotomy here. The founding fathers of the EU assumed that it was necessary to write down how it shall operate. That is, and always has been, the Continental way of doing things. Once started on that road, however, they and successive generations of bureaucrats have inevitably found comfort in writing everything down. Otherwise, if something was not written down it was not permitted. This foolish logic has ultimately obliged them to legislate on literally every speck of trivia, every possibility however remote, and every contingency. Thus, the EU's directive on duck eggs contains 26,911 words!

Yet great truths can be simply stated. The Lord's Prayer contains 56 words, the Ten Commandments required 297 words, Abraham Lincoln's immortal Gettysburg address was about the same length, while the American Declaration of Independence – which created the most powerful nation the world has ever seen – took all of 1,300 words.

In the UK we have never written our constitution down, except in part, and then only when it proved necessary to clarify issues of great moment – Magna Carta and the Declaration and Bill of Rights. But the drafters of those great documents were clever and insightful enough to realise that the protection of rights did not require their definition. They established principles, not details.

This may be only a simple difference between us, but it lies at the very root of our problems with the EU. As a result, an unbridgeable incompatibility exists between Anglo-Saxon government and the Continentals' system based on Napoleonic and Justinian law.

Speaking at a meeting in the House of Commons, in December 1999, the leading constitutional lawyer, Leolin Price QC, asked a meeting of euro-realists: "How did we ever come voluntarily to join this most selfish, protectionist, secretive, inward-looking political body the free world has ever seen? It is an organisation which steadfastly fails to define any benefits it might have claimed for itself, and which defiantly ignores the injury and damage it does. From Brussels and Westminster we are now being governed by constitutional illiterates."

He was right, of course. So much so that, in recent years, when both the Belgian and French governments suspended parliamentary democracy and openly ruled by edict to meet the Maastricht criteria, hardly a word of protest was to be heard anywhere in Europe.

Their parliaments and elected representatives were simply ignored, and nobody cared.

The warning was there, right at the start, if only we had seen it. When the Treaty of Rome was signed in 1957 it was not actually signed by all six founding states. The ministers representing Germany, Italy and Holland signed blank pieces of paper, because the translations of the French original were not completed before the meeting broke up. Again, nobody cared.

The charade that passes for democracy in the EU went even further in Denmark in 1993, when the Danes rejected the Maastricht Treaty. They were obliged to vote again, in a second referendum – and threatened with more – until they gave their government the pro-European result it wanted. It might have been a referendum, but – as in the Soviet Union in previous times – only one result was acceptable to their political leaders, and they would stop at nothing to get it.

Despite Denmark's constitution saying that sovereignty cannot be devolved to any other body, the second referendum went ahead.

It was structured so that the Danes were asked to vote "yes" for four opt-outs to the Treaty. They did so. Then, afterwards, the result was interpreted by the government as a "yes" for the Treaty itself! They claimed that a "yes" to the opt-outs implied a "yes" to the Treaty in its revised form, while a "no" to the opt-outs was a "yes" to the Treaty in full. In other words, there was no way of voting "no".

The result, and the way the Danish government manipulated the result to give them the authority to ratify Maastricht, produced riots in the streets.

Students barricaded themselves in EU-free zones and, for the first time in Danish history, Danish police fired at Danish citizens.

The government of Denmark and supporters of the "yes" campaign in the second referendum later admitted that they had lied to the people.

What sort of democracy is that? The answer is very simple. That is European democracy. And these fundamental differences between Anglo-Saxon and European democracy should have sounded deafening alarm bells long ago on this side of the Channel.

The inescapable fact is that an unelected minority executive governs the 15 countries of the EU today, and it is rampant. European hostility to the Anglo-Saxon system of democratic government is ingrained in Continental European culture, and it stems from their deep well of government by bureaucracy. It is their system, not ours, that rules the EU.

Even the Council of Ministers is a mere fig leaf. It is not a single body. It functions by areas of responsibility, and draws together all the ministers from member states who are responsible for particular portfolios. So, for example, all the home affairs or interior ministers meet as a Council of Ministers. So do all the foreign ministers. And the agricultural ministers, and so on. There is no such thing as the Council of Ministers. There are as many as there are government portfolios. They meet rarely.

But what happens when they do finally meet? The short answer is "very little". These meetings are never in public, and are tantamount to political horse-trading behind closed doors. No advocacy and opposition, no proper debate on issues, no close examination of detailed draft legislation, and no verbatim record of proceedings. Not even a summary. Just a bland public announcement of the decisions taken. But virtually all those are taken by officials beforehand, not by ministers at all.

One Conservative minister, writing about his first visit to an EU ministerial conference, remarked that on entering the conference chamber he was given a copy of the final communiqué. When he pointed out that the subjects had not yet been discussed he was told: "Oh no, sir, the decisions have already been made. You are here only to sign the communiqué."

There is a built-in assumption among European bureaucrats that the Anglo-Saxon system of accountable democracy will simply have to be abolished. It is in a minority, and must go. European politicians prefer to do things their way.

And what a way it is! In 1993, some 57 French members of parliament (MPs) were under criminal investigation for corruption – a record even in Europe. The new president of the EU, Romano Prodi, was under investigation for corruption even before he took office. So far he has survived four separate fraud investigations in Italy – but the saga goes on to this day.

So the European's version of politics is not our version – in fact, it's not politics at all. It is merely the bureaucratic administration of society and the economy – a system of patronage that positively encourages corruption. The process of argument and debate, of getting all the pros and cons out in the open, of risking dissent and inertia as part of the process of making the right decision and being seen to make it – these are anathema to European bureaucrats.

They want secrecy, not public debate, and no danger of their being held accountable afterwards – let alone losing their jobs. The differences between us are fundamentally about differences in our perception of the rule of law, the role of the nation state, and the ultimate freedom of the people – the freedom to choose, the freedom to do, say, and think what we like. The freedom to say no.

Precisely because of this profound gulf between the British and Europeans over their respective perceptions of government, and the way it is conducted, it will be in Britain that this great debate about the nature of the EU will finally be resolved. The differences are greatest here, and so is the need to decide.

❖

Right-wingers tend to think of the constitution of their own country as something precious, to be protected and preserved. Many left-wingers, on the other hand, regard the constitution as something to be used to assist them in meeting their own political objectives.

So it was little wonder that many socialists leapt at the idea of a European superstate after Mrs Thatcher unwisely fobbed off Jacques Delors at a Trades Union Congress (TUC) conference in 1988. Suddenly the left wing thought that here might be a back-door route to a European-wide socialist state.

The long overdue debate about Europe in the UK was finally sparked off by the prospect of the pound sterling being abolished and replaced with a new currency to be called the euro. But the debate itself clarified that the underlying issue was not money at all. It was fundamentally about the creation of a profoundly undemocratic European superstate. Since then the debate has broadened as the EU began to talk openly about many of the other trappings of a superstate.

Having created its own parliament, flag, anthem, passport, driving licence (which is intended to double as an identity card), supreme court, central bank and frontier, it now wanted – in addition to its own currency – a constitution, its own embassies around the world, a single system of taxation, a single army and defence policy, a single police force, a single legal system, a single foreign policy, and the power to enforce all its laws via its own network of regional assemblies across the EU.

Worse, this European superstate has developed an insidious language, all its own. Officials attempt to downplay each step along the road. First, we hear: "It's only an idea, it isn't happening…yet". Or: "It won't happen." Later, the emphasis changes: "It's already happened…but it doesn't matter." Finally, the crunch: "You ought to have realised… ."

In reality, the constitution of the EU is soviet in style. We have a Council of Ministers (ruling clique), the EC (politburo) and a powerless European parliament (supreme soviet). Like the former communist states of eastern Europe, the government of the EU – the Council of Ministers, the EC, and the European Central Bank (ECB) – are not only all unaccountable to the people, but at times appear utterly contemptuous of them.

The EU shares many other obvious characteristics with the former communist states of eastern Europe – its power base cannot be dismissed by the people, it seeks to establish laws that bind its successors and cannot be repealed, it creates law by directive, and it often does so with a breathtaking disregard for the consequences to the livelihoods of ordinary people. Some critics now detect signs that the EU has ambitions to rival – if not threaten – the USA as a world power, just as the Soviet Union (or USSR) did in its day. And how much more like the former USSR can the EU be if it turns itself into a two-speed state, with an inner core (the soviet republics) and an outer protective ring (the satellite countries of the Warsaw Pact)?

Is it any wonder Gorbachev was less than heartbroken when his regime collapsed? As he later commented, he saw a bigger and better version developing in the West.

Meanwhile, no elected legislature has the power even to consider the torrent of new EU law, let alone amend or reject any of it. Their directives pry into every corner of our lives, and more often than not it quickly becomes apparent that they have been introduced without thorough consideration or understanding of the consequences.

Worse, they are then enforced on a partial and haphazard basis.

Here in Britain, as law-abiding people, we obediently and – it must be said – stupidly observe them all, while the rest of the EU picks and chooses what suits them. That is the norm in Europe. It's their way of coping with bureaucratic stupidity. It's a long-standing way of life, particularly in France, which has by far the worst record of adopting the attitude: if you don't like a law, ignore it! They ridicule the British behind our backs when they see us enforcing everything coming out of Brussels regardless of its destructive nature or idiocy.

So where is the constraint? Where is the dynamic, healthy, and open debate? Where is the acceptance of responsibility and accountability in Europe? Where is the nation state seeking to generate law by consent, stopping to ask itself from time to time if a new law on this or that is necessary at all?

None of these essentials exists in the EU today.

Yes, we have an elected European parliament. But it is a mere talking shop, a paper tiger, nothing more than a sop to the people. It is certainly not a legislature, and can scarcely bring itself to use its limited powers of sanction over the executive. When, after nearly 40 years, the first opportunity arose for the European parliament to exercise what limited powers it had, the members fudged even that – and appointed a commission of enquiry instead.

Members of the EC, who are the real source of power and decision-making, are appointed by governments. Even if the governments that made those appointments are subsequently elected out of office, their appointees continue in Brussels as if nothing had happened.

Most of them are political failures at home, or opposition politicians that governments want to push aside to make their own position at home more secure. The appointment of Neil Kinnock by the British Tory government and the subsequent appointment of Chris Patten by Tony Blair's socialist government are classic examples.

The same pattern emerged with the appointments to the ECB. They are not even bankers. The ECB is largely peopled by second-rate European political failures. Records of their meetings and the reasons behind their decisions remain secret for 16 years. Yet these individuals have the power and capacity to destroy Europe's economy if they make a major error of judgment at any time.

The European judiciary is also unelected, also unaccountable, and has long since empowered itself to create law as well. The idea of judicial restraint is lost on the European Court of Justice (ECJ). Like Alice in Wonderland, the judges will make the law mean whatever they want it to mean, whenever it suits them and the political masters they serve. It is merely an engine of the EU, specifically charged with making decisions in the interests of the EU, regardless of what might be regarded as the "justice" of each case.

Even as these words appear on the page they look incredible. The great minds who, over the centuries, have helped to structure Magna Carta, the Declaration of Rights, the Bill of Rights, the American constitution, the Declaration of Independence and the USA's Bill of Rights, must be spinning in utter disbelief at our pathetic acquiescence to the system of government we permitted to emerge from Europe at the end of the 20th century.

Government by the EU offers no mechanism for restraint. It shares with Burma, Cuba and North Korea the doubtful distinction of being one of the tiny handful of governments on the planet who rule by decree and make laws in secret. The EU has no checks and balances. That is doubtless why the British, having ceded some power to Brussels, continue to deny the EU any claim to true authority over us.

It has been suggested elsewhere that our relationship with the EU is rather like the attempts made by the Saxon kings of England, who paid Danegeld to the Vikings, to persuade them not to loot, pillage and burn. But the more Danegeld paid, the more the Vikings wanted.

Today, the same situation exists with the EU. The more we concede the more their bureaucrats demand. They seem never to be satisfied. They truly believe they have the power to impose and demand whatever they want.

The inmates are not only running the asylum, they built it. They even admit it themselves.

When the European parliament is invited to vote on resolutions – not laws – the voting procedure is completed at breakneck speed. Members of the European Parliament (or MEPs) pack the chamber, so that they qualify for their daily allowances. The minute the voting is over most disappear again. Absentees are presumed to have voted in favour of every resolution, and their "votes" counted in support of the motion – whatever it is. On one occasion, 287 votes were taken in just over an hour. On another, 65 votes were taken in 20 minutes, so quickly and without any proper introduction or explanation that few, if any members were left with the faintest idea of what they were voting for or against. They merely pressed whichever button their party bosses instructed. *Corpus juris* (which we will come to later) was approved in this way, when UK members voted in favour and subsequently said they had made a mistake. It was a mistake they could not rectify, and their votes stand to this day.

During voting on an EU budget of over £65 billion, the UK's MEP Roger Helmer felt that the voting was so disorganised and dishonest that he called for "a point of order", protesting: "None of us has a clue where we are. The paperwork in front of us bears no relation to what is going on. The lunatics have taken over the asylum."

Support for his interjection came in the form of loud applause from all areas of the vast parliamentary chamber.

Yet this incident did not happen – officially. No record of it appeared in the European parliament's version of *Hansard*. Yet the censorship and deliberate corruption of parliamentary reports are most serious matters. Such interference with the records indicate quite clearly that the parliament itself is regarded as a tool of the executive, even to the extent that its proceedings can be used as a vehicle for propaganda.

A verbatim record of this charade of parliamentary democracy is the very least the hundreds of millions of EU taxpayers have a right to expect.

❖

The next step is already clear. The inter-governmental conference during 2000 was due to culminate at the end of the year in a new EU treaty – in Nice, France – which will extend majority voting into virtually every aspect of EU influence.

It was intended to establish even closer integration within what effectively becomes a single European state. As a result, the member states, Britain included, will be left with less self-government than Delaware, USA.

The conference was tasked with introducing fundamental changes in the EU and with the construction of a new EU constitution. In future, the majority will prevail on a wide range of community affairs, regardless of the objections from, or damage to, any minority. These issues, of major constitutional importance, directly threaten our rights and freedoms, and destroy the oaths of loyalty to the Crown sworn by privy councillors, British armed forces and the police. Such fundamental matters cannot be considered merely the stuff of day-to-day politics. They concern every British subject, and generations yet unborn.

Even if the proposals for Nice were watered down before the final wording was agreed, at the end of 2000, they clearly reveal the way the EU intends to go. If any of these components are lost this time, we can be certain they will re-emerge at some later date. So, to that extent at least, it matters not whether they were agreed at Nice. These proposals are the EU's signposts to the future.

The EU wants to:

➢ Ban political parties and political dissent of which it disapproves, including opposition to the EU itself.

Its plans to finance political parties of which it approves carries the plain threat to crush those of which the EU disapproves. This must include all those who seek its demise. How can political parties be "suspended", as the proposals put it? A weasel word – "suspend" – which can mean in this context an intention to outlaw or ban or abolish political parties of which the unelected EU disapproves.

So will the EU order armed police, who will already have power to act above the law, to raid the offices of a political party? Will they be under instructions to arrest everybody in the building, and remove files, membership lists, printed pamphlets and other literature? What other means of enforcement are there?

This is not freedom and progress. This introduces two particularly abhorrent propositions – taxation without representation and the use of state power to suppress public opinion. This takes us back to the 1930s in Germany. This is no different from Russian communism. But the most dreadful aspect of all is the fact that it is being proposed in our name, in all seriousness, here and now by a political union of which we are currently members.

Elsewhere, the proposals talk of cracking down on racism and xenophobia, without defining either. Is this book racist? Am I being xenophobic? Is it either of these things to want to live in what is recognisably your own country? Is to loathe the EU the same as loathing all Europeans? This is not so in my case. But outlawing political parties and personal opinions disliked by a ruling clique is tyranny and dictatorship.

Abolish national borders and you abolish nations. Abolish the natural human process of debate – politics – and you abolish freedom. To achieve debate, you must have dissent. Conflict is an inherent consequence of liberty. We can't have one without the other. Politics is, by definition, the process of resolving dissent. War is merely the failure of politics. So, far from abolishing war, the abolition of politics may ultimately lead to its replacement by war.

➢ Impose direct rule from Brussels if member states fall out of line.

If a member state is held to have breached EU law, or its future constitution, the EU will remove its voting rights, and impose direct rule. It proposes that it "shall lay down the regulations governing" what politicians may or may not do in that country until the EU bureaucrats subsequently decide otherwise. Meanwhile, that same country will still have to pay its financial contributions to Brussels as if it were a full voting member. In a nutshell, taxation without representation.

➢ Enable the EC president to rule absolutely.

By giving the president the right "to determine the political orientation of the commission" – the words originally proposed for Nice – we see as clear a statement of intent as there can be that the president ultimately shall have absolute power – and the basis for a political dictatorship is established. What else can the words mean?

➢ Start abolishing the essential cornerstones of English criminal law, including trial by jury and *habeas corpus*, replacing them with Napoleonic law that has no such safeguards.

This aspect of the EU's future plans will be covered in the next chapter.

➢ Introduce qualified majority voting (QMV) on a wide range of topics, including economic and monetary policy – effectively giving the EU the power to force the UK into the euro, and control our taxation, whether we like it or not.

QMV will also be imposed on fiscal and budgetary decisions, internal affairs and the free movement of people (including visas, immigration and asylum), agriculture and fisheries policy, competition and environment policy.

In future, constitutional matters only will still require unanimity. All operational matters will not.

➢ Give the highly politicised ECJ jurisdiction over British courts with "no restrictions whatsoever".

The draft "proposes with a view to the establishment of an area of security, freedom and justice that no restrictions whatsoever shall henceforth be placed on the jurisdiction of the Court of Justice".

This is unconstitutional in the UK. It will have the effect of removing the Queen from the throne, removing our sovereign right to govern ourselves and placing all British subjects under the jurisdiction of a foreign power. Jurisdiction means the power to give coercive orders that the police are bound to carry out. So to grant unrestricted jurisdiction in the UK to a foreign court is clearly and unmistakably treason.

If our parliament were to ratify a treaty containing this measure it would be signing its own self-destruction. The ECJ would have the power to rule on any pretext that the British parliament at Westminster was illegal, and order it to be dissolved.

The EU also wants to establish fully that it "shall have legal personality". This means that the EU can in future conduct negotiations in its own right and sign treaties that will bind member states. The governments of member states will have no power to influence or stop such treaties. Thus the state of Europe comes into being and all power and control passes to Brussels. The purported notion that we were created citizens of the EU by the Maastricht Treaty will finally become a reality by this declaration of "legal personality".

Meanwhile, this same step will allow the president of the EC, as Mr Prodi put it, "to speak for member states on the world stage".

Many other ideas for further integration were mooted for inclusion in the Nice Treaty. They included the EU establishing itself in a coordinating role for what it chose to call "international and civil crisis management". This means the control and deployment of troops at times of war and rebellion, so that the cost of any military action will fall on the member states taking part, despite their having no control over the orders given to their troops. This proposed combination of open-ended financial liability and utter lack of control in times of armed conflict is unique in military history.

Economic, social and employment policies will be "coordinated" still further. In future, the emphasis will be on applying what the EU chooses to call "social justification". The generation of wealth by free enterprise will take a back seat to equality and the abolition of competition. According to EU logic all competition is by definition unfair!

Of course none of these ideas or intentions is hidden from the people of the EU, except in Britain. In the UK, politicians are desperate to keep the cat firmly in the bag. But occasionally it just pops its head out:

"The European parliament and the commission are allies against the member states. Together we have to prevent the member states from taking back power" – the words of the president of the European parliament, speaking on BBC Radio 4, in July 1999.

"When we build the house of Europe the future will belong to Germany" – Helmut Kohl, speaking in Germany, unaware that reporters were present.

"Germany as the biggest and most powerful economic member state will be the leader [of Europe] whether you like it or not" – Theo Waigel, former German finance minister, 1997.

"The top priority [is] to turn the EU into a single political state" – Joshka Fischer, German foreign minister, quoted in *The Times*, November 1998.

"Never again must there be a destabilising vacuum of power in central Europe. If European integration were not to progress, Germany might be called upon, or tempted by its own security constraints, to try to effect the stabilisation on its own and in the traditional way" – German CDU Party parliamentary committee on European affairs, September 1994.

"After the common market, after the common currency, after Schengen [the EU's open-borders agreement], we have started the long march towards common justice and common security" – EC president Romano Prodi, October 1999. "We are here to take binding decisions as an executive power. If you don't like the term "government" for this, what other term do you suggest?"

"Why does Europe need fifteen foreign ministers when one is enough? Why do member states still need national armies? One European army is enough" – Hans Eichel, German finance minister, November 1999.

"I am not embarrassed to suggest that, sometimes, the answer to the concerns of a disillusioned European public is not less Europe but more" – Mr Prodi again, this time in *Die Welt*, 22nd July 1999.

Other, wiser persons spoke another truth many decades ago:

"Experience should teach us to be most on our guard to protect liberty when the government's purposes are beneficial. Men born to freedom are naturally alert to repel invasion of their liberty by evil-minded rulers. The greater dangers to liberty lurk in insidious encroachment by men of zeal, well-meaning but without understanding" – Justice Louis Brandeis, Olmstead *vs* US 277, US 479, 1928.

"I do verily believe that...a single, consolidated government would become the most corrupt government on the earth" – Thomas Jefferson to Gideon Granger, 1800.

❖

"Europe has never existed except as being the totalitarian ambition of dictators like Napoleon, Hitler, Charlemagne and Charles V. It is an area open to the admission of a few madmen with no unity of any kind – no linguistic unity, no cultural unity, no common view of things, no common destiny – it is a total mystery" – Jacques Attali, principal adviser to President Mitterand of France.

At least one of the motives behind the EU's headlong rush to establish its own supremacy and create a single superstate across the whole continent is a profound fear – loathing, even – of Britain and the Anglo-Saxon world in general, and the USA in particular. French and German political leaders see their EU superstate as a bloc big enough to compete with the USA and the rest of the Anglo-Saxon world. Swallowing Britain doubles their chances. It switches the British to their side, and divides and weakens the Anglo-Saxon world at the same time.

Democracy is dying in Britain as it is trampled into the mud. Our constitution and our common law, rights, freedoms and customs, ours for centuries since Magna Carta, are simply ignored by politicians and judges alike. Today, these declarations are reduced to little more than illusions.

The House of Commons is almost a sham, an empty charade, as container-loads of EU rules pour through it in such volume that there is not the slightest possibility of any genuine parliamentary scrutiny, let alone the opportunity to reject any of it. Most of this so-called law goes straight from Brussels onto our statute book. It dominates parliamentary time, generates more than 90 per cent of all new legislation in the UK, at a rate of some 3,000 new laws, directives and regulations a year, about which parliament can do – or chooses to do – virtually nothing.

Meanwhile, the creation of an EU army is a clear threat to the North Atlantic Treaty Organisation (NATO) – a view loudly expressed in the USA. In Britain, it is plainly against the constitution to pass military power to a foreign government, especially if one of the consequences is to provide the otherwise unremovable so-called government of Europe with the military means to hold on to power.

President Prodi has already gained the support of member states, including Britain, to set up a 60,000-strong European defence force. It is the embryo of a future European army that will one day be responsible for defence across the continent. It will be commanded by senior officers drawn from all over the EU. The UK's armed forces will no longer be under sole British command, and may eventually no longer be free to defend the security of this nation unless the bureaucrats in Brussels agree.

This development holds two big dangers, of course. First, the very existence of a European army undermines and fragments NATO, as France has long sought to achieve, and with it the long-standing and special relationship Britain has enjoyed with the USA on matters of defence is similarly undermined. Second, the European army could one day be used to suppress internal dissent within the EU – not least to prevent Britain exercising its right to leave the EU at any time by passing or repealing an Act of Parliament. This same army might equally be used to deal with civil disorder when, for example, the stresses and strains caused by the failure of the EU start to spill over onto the streets.

Is it not entirely possible that, when the whole idea of one country is seen for the folly it is, those driving the EU will become even more ruthless than they are already? Do we expect them meekly to admit defeat? Or will they use all the force they can muster, including threats? What is to prevent them from declaring a state of emergency, mobilising the armed forces as a show of strength, and making a claim on the assets of the Bank of England?

There is an incalculable risk attached to the armed forces of Britain becoming more deeply tied to those of the EU. Ultimately, a country's sovereignty depends on the freedom and strength to defend itself.

In the UK, the sovereignty of the people, free speech, free association, the right to petition the government for redress of grievances, the right to due process according to law, the right to a public trial in front of an impartial jury of our peers, the right to travel freely, and recognition that the monarch, no less, is subject to the law – these are the essences of the constitution of the UK, and they subsequently became the basis of the constitution of the USA, which refers specifically to Magna Carta in Section 9 and several later amendments.

US Senator Gordon Smith, speaking to a British audience in 1999, asked why Britain, which for centuries had stood as a "bastion of liberty", and had always looked with caution, sometimes even with hostility, on concentrations of power on the Continent, now seemingly wished to turn its back on all this by ceding power to Brussels, and by losing its unique national identity in a new European state.

This is precisely the question that the British people should be asking themselves. And is it not extraordinary that it should take an American politician to put the all-important question that no government – indeed no leading British politician – since the 1970s has dared ask in public? Yet we are now within sight of living in a small part of a vast new state, under a political system as undemocratic as any in the world.

When the Americans achieved independence and wrote their constitution they were shrewdly careful enough to recognise that the greatest risk to the people flowed from the corruption of government. To minimise this risk they invented a government structure that continued the separation of executive from legislature that then applied in the mother country.

Back here, Crown (government) and Commons were separate bodies. The American version separated elected executive government (the president and his appointees) from the two houses of the legislature – the House of Representatives and the Senate. To give legal status to the wishes of the executive, congress had to debate and approve. Happily, the USA president (the executive) and congress (the legislature) still operate the system they originally borrowed from Britain at the time of the War of Independence. We, on the other hand, have abandoned it.

Today, the role of executive and legislature has blurred in the UK to the point where they are, and have been for some time, one and the same. The original system of checks and balances in the UK worked well. Today it is out of kilter. Once the Crown was the executive. Now it is not. Now the executive is the cabinet of elected MPs who also have a majority in the legislature. This change has been a clear erosion of the essential checks and balances needed in any genuine system of democratic government.

Ultimately, all government – however well intended – is about coercion. The basic objective of law is to enforce behaviour that might not otherwise have occurred, and that is deemed to be in the overall public interest. So any acceptable system of government that seeks the power to coerce the people must be subject to adequate and effective checks and balances, again in the overall public interest.

Accountable democracy works best in practice when the elected executive has no legislative or judicial powers; the elected legislature has no executive or judicial powers; and the judiciary has no legislative or executive powers beyond enforcing the law created by the other two acting together.

The EU, of course, has never made any pretence at establishing anything so genuinely democratic, accountable and balanced. What we see in the EU is a bizarre parody of such a structure. The executive is not elected and has all the power. The legislature is elected but has no power. And the judiciary is free to make the law up as it goes along.

Nigel Farage MEP, after a few months in the European parliament, described it as "far worse than I ever imagined". He had come face-to-face with what he called "a megalomania complex which is totally out of control".

He, with all other MEPs, represents a cost of £1.2 million a year to the citizens of the EU, and he may be allowed to speak for 90 seconds a week at best. If he exceeds the time limit his microphone is simply cut off, even though he might be talking about an issue that directly affects the lives of millions.

Furthermore, MEPs have no control whatsoever over EU law. Law is created by the 23,000 unelected and secretive bureaucrats of the EC, whose sole job is to create new law, which becomes effective in the member states when the EC says so, whether or not the parliament in that country has approved it. This was determined by a ruling of the ECJ, who said that a directive must come into force on the due date even if it had not been transposed into national law. EU laws can even be enforced after a national parliament has rejected them. On one occasion at least, in Denmark, their national parliament rejected an EU law, but it was then imposed anyway.

Even within the EU parliament the charade goes on. In the unlikely event that a resolution is voted down, under a procedure known as "conciliation", the vote is overturned and the original reinstated. The parliament itself has no legislative powers whatsoever. Jeffrey Titford MEP has described his experiences in the EU parliament: "Individual MEPs are not an essential, nor even an important, part [of the EU]. We are interchangeable bit-part actors, spear-carriers, participating in a mockery of the parliamentary process. Oratory plays no part. Reason plays no part. Conviction plays no part. Our votes cannot change a directive. We are there merely to furnish an illusion of democracy, providing a veneer to conceal what is a fundamentally undemocratic process. The cast may change, but the show always goes on, with the actors collecting their wages at the stage door."

To our shame, democracy is threatened by much else besides.

When tax is taken from me to pay for things that are illegal (teaching school children to support the EU), that is tyranny. When innocent people are harmed by government officials who abuse their authority (the enforcement of metrication), that is tyranny. When people are told by government bureaucrats that they can't use their own property for legitimate activities (shooting for pleasure), that is tyranny. When government intrudes into the lives of law-abiding people who simply want to be left alone (Inland Revenue and VAT inspectors telling people they are guilty until proven innocent), that is tyranny. When gangs of youths are permitted to assault innocent people (enjoying a fox hunt), while the police look on and liberal judges protect the rights of their assailants, that is tyranny. When innocent people walk in fear in their own area (in many inner cities), that is tyranny. When the government wants to intrude on the constitutional rights of people opposed to them (by threatening newspapers in an attempt to limit free speech), that is tyranny. When the government takes it upon itself to decide which political parties and views are acceptable (part of the Nice Treaty), that is tyranny.

Supposedly, we live in a free country. But the UK today is a country where stable family life is under threat – where political correctness is a substitute for moral values – where criminals are free to terrorise whole areas in our cities and countryside – where the lazy are free to rob the productive – where the government seeks to have unlimited freedom but ordinary citizens feel increasingly helpless.

In modern times, politicians have happily paid lip service to our rights and freedoms, but then carried on constraining them.

Today we have a government that funds projects that offend our sense of right and wrong, confiscates hard-earned cash from working people and squanders it on people who want a free ride, subsidises people from abroad who take our welfare and then deride the source of such generosity, positively encourages racial and minority discrimination, and turns over our birthright to foreign powers.

Yet a nation is not defined by its government. It is defined by its people.

In his book *The New World of the Gothic Fox*, published in 1994, Claudio Veliz developed Isaiah Berlin's observation that likened some people to the hedgehog – they know One Big Thing – while others were like the fox – and know Many Things. Veliz used this metaphor to compare the "Baroque Hedgehogs" of Spanish-speaking societies with the "Gothic Foxes" of English-speaking societies. He contrasted the Baroque Hedgehogs' obsession with unchanging unity with the passion for diversity, change, and heterogeneity found in Gothic Foxes.

Veliz says: "There can be no doubt that, from a cultural vantage point, all the world's English-speaking countries are islands off the coast of Kent. The cliffs of Dover can be seen as clearly from Cincinnati as from Edmonton, Wellington, and Ballarat. They all share a profound and irreverent distrust of bureaucrats, bureaucracy, and regulations that would be out of place in France, Turkey, or Mexico. They exhibit a propensity to volunteer that Greeks, Paraguayans, and Hungarians would find decidedly disconcerting."

That is, perhaps, why we loathe a system of government that, within ten years of our joining, had doubled the number of laws governing the UK. By the mid-1980s, the laws created by Brussels exceeded in bulk all those passed in Britain in the first 700 years of parliamentary democracy!

On its own, the Treaty of Amsterdam introduced more far-reaching changes in the UK than anything since the arrival of William the Conqueror. It effectively abolished the nation state and the monarchy. It purported to drive a coach and horses through what was left of Magna Carta, the Declaration of Rights and English common law.

It established the concept of regional councils appointed from Brussels, sowed the seeds for the destruction of the parliament at Westminster and authorised the creation of regional assemblies with less real power than a county council. And all of these new bodies will be in place merely to do the bidding of the ECB who hold the purse strings, and the EU commissioners who hold the power.

Real power lies in the hands of the president and a few others. "It's a very small circle where the decisions are taken", according to Hubert Vedrine, head of the French negotiating team at Maastricht.

Yet the big international issues such as the environment, pollution, Third World poverty, security, drug trafficking, shipping, aviation and so forth can all be dealt with perfectly well by negotiated agreements between sovereign states. Being outside the EU wouldn't change those opportunities one jot – indeed it would ensure that the British voice was heard and not drowned in a collective EU voice that takes little account of the British view or British interests.

Over the generations, Britain has built up a wealth and global influence far beyond the norm. We have developed a system of government that has been copied and modified for local circumstances all around the globe. It is not perfect, but it has served us well. It has avoided dictatorship and violent revolution for hundreds of years. Why discard that now – or ever?

Meanwhile the European system of government has generated tragedy after tragedy, provided vehicles for dictatorship and revolution even as recently as the second half of the last century. It is conceivable that, even now, the present EU debacle is another such dictatorship in the making, which will eventually be followed by revolution.

The real issue for the UK is not "how much" Europe, but "in or out" of Europe. We are still trying, and have been ever since the Second World War, to find the right role for a post-imperialist power. Our geography, history and traditions all direct us towards being an internationally-minded, outward-looking, free-trading country, making our own decisions, judging ourselves what is in our best interests, tied to no one, but happy to do business whenever and wherever we can.

Compare that with tying ourselves exclusively, closely and – so they would have it – irrevocably to an inward-looking, protectionist, highly regulated trading bloc with which we have very little in common apart from geography.

British MEP Jeffrey Titford asked a "priority" question in the European parliament in November 1999. "Priority" questions are supposed to be answered within three weeks. He asked for a "complete list of powers the EU has specified shall remain with member states and not be transferred at any time to the EU". As Mr Titford remarked after several months of waiting: "Why does it take so long to write the single word 'none'?"

When the answer finally arrived, it answered another question altogether. Romano Prodi eventually replied: "The only powers the Community has are those conferred on it by Member States in the Treaties." The answer to the opposite of the question actually asked. That answer also disguised a deeper truth. President Prodi wants to stop member states from repatriating powers. He dislikes the idea of subsidiarity. But what, exactly, is subsidiarity? The German Ambassador, Dr Jurgen Oesterholt, speaking to the European-Atlantic group of the British Data Management Foundation (BDMF), 12th June 1996, said: "Subsidiarity is meaningless to all EU officials and politicians except the British. It was conceived to disguise the word 'federation'...for fear of upsetting people in the UK." He added that British negotiators of the Maastricht Treaty, which invented the word, were aware of this linguistic device and were content with it, provided the sceptics "back home" didn't get to hear of it.

At a seminar just before negotiations were complete, European jurists were told that the word "subsidiarity" had political meaning, not judicial. It did not fall within the competence of the ECJ. Yet...the treaty itself says that subsidiarity applies only to those areas that do not fall within the "exclusive competence" of the community. As everything is taken to be within the competence of the EU, this makes the whole concept fraudulent, toothless and meaningless.

Reality is quite different. The Amsterdam Treaty gives the ECJ the powers to interfere with national jurisdiction and the right to override any Act of Parliament. This raises the question of their reaction if parliament were to repeal the 1972 European Communities Act. It also means that the Amsterdam Treaty attempts to abolish the UK parliament's absolute right to change its mind.

Article 189 of the Treaty of Rome allows no negotiation, no debate. Once the EU has established what it chooses to call "competence" over a community interest, all the laws, regulations, directives and judicial decisions are binding on all states, and that area of EU "competence" is held to have passed permanently to Brussels. This is known as "acquis communautaire". Every member state is then bound by every decision, and that area of "competence" cannot subsequently be legislated on separately by a member state. The driving force behind the EU is the ambition to extend "acquis communautaire" into every corner of our lives.

The recently released records of Sir Con O'Neill, who led the Heath government's negotiations in 1972, has proved what many suspected – that there was no real negotiation on this or any other aspect of the Treaty of Rome before the UK signed up to it.

It also destroys William Hague's promise to renegotiate the Treaty of Rome if the Tories win power. "Acquis communautaire" won't allow such a proposition out of the starting blocks. It is bound to fail on two counts. First, Hague has revealed a fatal weakness before he starts by declaring that he would "never" leave. His ultimate bargaining chip has already been thrown away. Second, the EU simply won't agree to discuss major renegotiation, let alone embark on what – for them – must be a destructive exercise, and they will use the Treaty of Rome as justification, as that treaty specifically forbids it.

(The cynic might point out here that the Bill of Rights specifically forbade the UK from passing power to a foreign entity – but that did not stop Mr Heath from signing it away.)

The Common Market has become the EU, but nobody asked the British to agree to the change. No government has ever fought a general election on that basis, nor sought a mandate from the people by a referendum or by any other means. We, the people of the UK, can argue that we are not a party to these treaties because we have never given our consent.

In any case, the Common Market was nothing to do with markets or trade. The whole thrust has always been to create a single European state. The Continentals always recognised that. Only British politicians couldn't bring themselves to say so because they knew very well that the British would never tolerate it.

❖

After more than 25 years as a senior corporate lawyer, working extensively in the EU, a friend of mine finally concluded that the UK should leave. He had seen enough of the "endemic corruption", the making of law "on the hoof" by the ECJ, and the highly selective enforcement of laws in various parts of the EU, depending on what suited and what didn't. He described the situation to me as being "beyond redemption".

The facts are on his side. The three most recent architects of the EU, Mitterand, Kohl and Craxi, have all been proved criminally corrupt since leaving office. So have many hundreds of minor officials and MEPs. The present head of the EC, Romano Prodi of Italy, a Blair nominee and an avowed federalist, has been investigated more than once for criminal corruption in Italy.

Over £5 billion a year is "lost" in the EU's black hole from corruption. It simply disappears, unaccounted for, unsigned for and not in the audited accounts, which have been heavily qualified every year since an independent audit was introduced in 1994.

The European Court of Auditors said that 4.25 billion euros were misspent in 1998 alone – five per cent of the entire annual budget. The following year the figure rose to seven and a half per cent. Worse, the EU's only parliamentary committee on budget control could not get at the facts. Other departments deliberately obstructed their investigations with misleading information and delayed the answers to questions.

Today, many hundreds of ongoing enquiries into fraud among EU officials, involving billions of pounds and going back over more than a decade, are still unresolved. Meanwhile, all the committee can do is refuse to approve the EU's annual accounts.

Instead, they are described as "incorrect or incomplete" and "refused a positive statement of legality and regularity". This has now happened five years in succession. The EC has also been condemned for its high-spending attitudes, and lack of control over bureaucrats who fling money away on badly thought out projects simply to ensure that their budgets are not cut at the end of each financial year.

In 1998, fraud in the CAP totalled 20,000,000 euros. The biggest problems were in research investment, then under the supposed control of the notorious commissioner Edith Cresson. Two-thirds of her spending was wrongly accounted for, either by deliberate false accounting, demonstrable waste, apparent errors or incomplete information. The expenses incurred by her department and the recipients of funding authorised by her department were routinely overstated by more than 30 per cent. A sizeable chunk went to her live-in dentist!

In spite of the highly publicised resignation of the previous commission president Jacques Santer and 22 commissioners in 1999, fraud and mismanagement was still rife in the EU, the auditors complained in their report for the following year.

They criticised inconsistent and inadequate day-to-day accounting records, tardy and incomplete documents, haphazard and wildly inaccurate estimating, vast sums disappearing without trace, assets and liabilities understated, hopelessly inadequate credit and cash control, regular payments made without regard for need or purpose, commitments made to spend non-existent funds, money paid to intermediaries that subsequently took years to reach the intended beneficiary, and – if all that were not more than enough – the total lack of a unified accounting system across all directorates and institutions.

In such a climate can we be surprised when, in February 2000, several MEPs went to the ECJ to stop the EU's own anti-fraud watchdog poking into their finances. "Offence against parliamentary immunity," they said. What is worse, the ECB, and the European Investment Bank have also refused to open their financial records to the EU's anti-fraud investigators, nor will they cooperate with them.

If no other reason for leaving the EU existed, and there are many, this indictment of scandalous corruption should be enough on its own. The EU has been systematically stealing and squandering vast sums of taxpayers' money that could have been put to infinitely better use back here in Britain.

❖

A great majority of British politicians, like politicians all around the globe, are classic examples of the "law of unsuitable attraction". This says: "People most unsuited to a career are most drawn to it." We all know accountants who can't manage their own affairs, the human resources managers who find difficulty in dealing with people, the public relations managers who can't communicate, the publicans who can't stay sober. The list is endless. But in the case of politicians the consequences can be catastrophic for the rest of us. That's what makes the problem much worse.

Today, so many are in politics for their own benefit. They want the money, the prestige, the opportunities for sex, the excitement of power, and the paraphernalia of being in government. Few, especially these days, enter parliament solely because they want to contribute, to serve, to make the world a better place.

They are not all corrupt. But they are cynical – about the world, about themselves and their motives, about making the most of the opportunities for their own benefit. For most, if not all, these objectives take precedence over working for the public good.

And these weaknesses spawn others. Politicians are not courageous. They are not natural leaders. They want to strut on the world's stages, but they lack the knowledge and understanding of the role. A psychiatrist friend of Norris McWhirter suggested that all politicians are failed Thespians who want to play to an ever bigger audience.

These people seek the glory, and the power, but without any underlying sense of true responsibility. Most have little personal experience of it. Few have ever run businesses, few understand the importance and attitudes of entrepreneurs. Few have ever staked all their worldly goods on a new commercial enterprise, and made daily decisions when survival is at risk.

Today's politician has usually gone from university to become a re-search assistant in a political party, or into the law, or teaching, or trade unionism, or the civil service. Scarcely one has been through the hard-ening process of running a business on his or her own. Collectivism, not individuality, is the culture that breeds today's politicians, and we are much the worse for it.

They seek safety in numbers. They cling together. They've joined the club. And the bigger the club, the safer they'll be. At a personal level, this is the mindset behind the drive towards a single European superstate. Its roots lie in weakness, inexperience and a mind-boggling arrogance that their political objectives must be imposed on the rest of the population, regardless of the consequences.

This inexperience is revealed all the time. Our political leaders, almost to a man, do not understand how a small island like Britain can remain successful and independent in the modern world. They truly don't. They cannot imagine a case for withdrawing from the EU. They may not like everything that emanates from Brussels, but they genuinely cannot see any alternative.

The new and inexperienced Tory MP for Chichester, Andrew Tyrie, is a former civil servant. Writing about the EU in a letter to a constituent (me) he said: "I would vigorously oppose any attempt to absorb Britain into a European superstate." It was pointed out to him that the use of the word "would" implied that he regarded this as merely a theoretical proposition. Yet the process was well under way, with *corpus juris*, tax harmonisation, Europol, common defence policy, and the establishment of spurious regional governments, as well as the euro and an EU army.

Mr Tyrie was asked precisely how he was "vigorously opposing" this trend and the specific aims and objectives of Prodi and his unelected, unaccountable, corrupt bureaucrats. That raised a second question: precisely how was this "vigorous opposition" squared with the Tory Party slogan about being "in Europe but not run by Europe", which seemed to be recognised for its demonstrable absurdity by all but the Tory shadow cabinet and Mr Tyrie himself.

Many former Tory voters have despaired for years about the European fence-sitting their party has indulged in since the Thatcher era. Typical of the complaint is a letter written by Idris Francis to the chairman of the Tory Party in May 1999:

"I doubt that any party in the long history of British political life has ever campaigned on a slogan more asinine than 'In Europe but not run by Europe'. Every day brings further confirmation that whatever mirage of a 'positive, modern, competitive, flexible Europe' you may aspire to, the reality of the EU's intentions is the precise opposite, the very antithesis of everything that Britain needs to prosper as a free and successful people.

"We now know that, regardless of the shameless lies that we were told in the 1970s, even then the intention was to impose by stealth a single European state."

Asked about the alleged benefits of membership of the EU, Mr Tyrie was invited to set them out in detail and to explain the reasons for the UK continuing its membership. The MP's reply was short and simple. He noted the points raised.

He could not or would not answer the question. Neither would Mr Tyrie accept a challenge to debate in public the issue of Europe at any time and place of his choosing, and with any supporting speakers he wished to employ in his support. Again, he merely noted the points raised!

Of course he is not the only politician to generate contempt for himself.

According to a discussion between a well-informed eurosceptic and the German correspondent of a pro-EU newspaper, reported on the internet, Tony Blair is personally loathed and despised by the German government. A planning paper, supposedly written with Chancellor Schroeder, was effectively repudiated by the German government. Schroeder did not read it before he signed it. When his party aides and advisers read it thoroughly they realised that it conflicted with much of what they had been elected to do – and it contradicted their plans for unity with France. As a result, Blair is now undermined at every opportunity in the European Council – and so are most UK ministers. Special scorn is poured on the UK's foreign secretary Robin Cook, whose linguistic shortcomings are legendary.

This same discussion also supported the view that the most serious opposition to UK withdrawal is in the UK itself. It is embedded in the Foreign Office (FO) and in the Department of Trade and Industry (DTI). It is also to be found in importers from euroland, and – to a lesser extent – among exporters.

Their logic says that a duty of about three and a half per cent may be imposed on trade with euroland if we left, with no counter-balancing savings to them. Companies trading with the EU believe their import costs will rise, making imports more expensive and giving negotiating scope to UK unions again. There will be a saving of 5.7 per cent on total UK costs, but this saving will not directly benefit the companies concerned. It will – in theory at least – benefit individual tax-payers, assuming the government of the day passes the savings on by cutting taxes.

Another point highlighted during these discussions on the internet related to the UK's present position outside the eurozone. The German correspondent suggested that EU ministers knew that sterling inside the euro at present would wreck it, or possibly turn it into a new sterling area, given the disproportionately large amount of UK trade with the rest of the world.

In any case, the Germans do not want any UK accountants scrutinising the loans made by Germany to the former USSR. There are reportedly "absolutely enormous liabilities" that have been swept under the euro-carpet. They were originally guaranteed by the Bundesbank, now by the ECB (after a fierce internal fight). The level of liability is said to be about US$200 billion. And any upsets in these cosy arrangements might result in a nasty interruption of the natural-gas supply from the former USSR to Germany.

❖

"The State is only people. And, generally, the least competent of people. They are the ones who cannot innovate, only steal. They cannot reason, only kill. They are brutes who see the greatest efforts of mankind as loot to seize and control" – *The Kings of the High Frontier* by G K Chesterton.

The people of the EU cannot change their government. The commissioners are totally secure. Even when they were sacked *en bloc* in early 1999 for corruption they remained in office for six months, kept their pensions and four of them were re-appointed. One of them (Neil Kinnock) was even promoted to vice-president and put in charge of rooting out corruption. Poacher turned chief poacher.

There is no European-wide political thought among the general public, and as yet there are no international political parties. European consensus is found only among the politicians themselves, whom the public loathe and despise.

They claim that the EU, and its predecessors, have kept the peace in Europe for 50 years – a travesty of the truth. NATO has kept the peace in

Europe over the last 50 years, mainly through the active and substantial contribution of personnel, money and materials provided by the USA, Canada and Britain. The EU's only contribution so far has been to stir up the Balkan war for the benefit of German economic interests and political ambitions.

The ECJ is lauded as a great source of new wisdom at a European level. Yet it is populated with non-judicial appointees, some from countries with appalling records of injustice. It is a blatantly political court whose remit is not justice but the pursuit of "ever-closer union" by the generation of case law.

The EU is not just undemocratic. It is positively anti-democratic. The evidence continues to pile up with every new revelation about its activities and organisation. It is institutionally corrupt and incapable of fundamental reform.

The Common Market was "sold" to the UK in 1972 and again in the referendum in 1975 as a cooperative free-trade area. It was well known at the time by the government of the day that it was no such thing. It has now virtually become what was always intended, a unitary state. If such monumental switch-selling were to occur in the commercial sector, the perpetrators would be in jail for fraud so fast their feet would not touch the ground.

When did any of us vote to give up the sovereignty of this nation? When did we vote to become citizens of another country? When did we vote to join the EU? When did we vote to accept the laws of a foreign government? When did we vote to have unelected officials making and enforcing laws on us? When did we vote to give up our rights, freedoms and customs? When did we vote to devolve the UK into 12 regions of a new European superstate? When did we vote in favour of sending over £1 million pounds an hour of taxpayers' money to Brussels?

In 1972, when the idea of joining the Common Market was becoming a reality, the Heath government talked in terms of a huge free-trade area, and being part of an alliance that would stand as an equal with North America and the USSR.

We were also led to believe that we would have influence when we joined, which we would not have outside. It was suggested we would make a difference to the way the Common Market was run. We would be the honest broker between those traditional foes – Germany and France.

All of this was a tissue of lies, as we now know to our considerable cost.

The single market was merely the first step on a long journey in another direction. We do not significantly influence the way decisions are taken, nor the way they are implemented and enforced. Nor shall we ever. The private battle between France and Germany to carve up the spoils goes on unabated. Under the terms of the Treaty of Rome they have an exclusive right to meet before each Council of Ministers' meeting to decide what shall be decided at it.

And, by way of an encore, since the USSR doesn't exist any more, Germany is free to increase its sphere of influence to the east, as it has always sought to do.

We were told our economic future was bound up with our near neighbours. But our share of trade is now worse than before we joined. Then, we had a positive balance of trade with the countries of the Common Market. Within a year of joining we were in the red, and we have been in the red ever since.

Meanwhile, the sacrifices we made, and the sacrifices we forced on other Anglo-Saxon countries with whom we had deep family ties, have all been for nought. We turned our backs on New Zealand and its meat, for example, and forced them and ourselves to change the trading and eating habits of generations.

Our proximity to the continent of Europe is utterly irrelevant. In attitudes, history, traditions, language, way of life, we have far more in common with the English-speaking world, scattered as it is around the globe. We go on holiday to the continent of Europe precisely because it is different.

And the world today is such a tiny place anyway. Physical distance is almost irrelevant. The internet, low-cost phone companies and cheap fast air travel have seen to that. Going to New York is not the big decision it once was. Getting a message to Sydney takes a few pence and less than a minute. Ironically, the cost of getting from London to Paris, and the delays when trying to phone Italy, have not improved to the same extent.

Meanwhile, the "distances" between attitudes have assumed immense importance. The English Channel may be only 22 miles wide, but it is an ocean away in terms of attitudes. The Atlantic may be 3,000 miles wide but the phrase "across the pond" reveals the closeness we share with the USA and Canada.

By ignoring or forgetting these great truths, we have arrived at a pretty pass. Many unexpected, curious and deeply worrying effects have flowed from the UK's membership of the EU.

The EU has built up great trade barriers against the import of food from non-EU countries. But such protectionism is not aimed solely at non-EU producers. Farmers in Britain are discriminated against as well. They are prevented from producing all the milk we consume, so that farmers on the Continent can sell us theirs. The rest must be imported from other member states. It is also illegal for us to produce all the meat and eggs we eat.

Worse, as a direct result of EU policies and because of the CAP, each family pays on average an extra £1,000 a year on food, of which £800 goes to subsidise Continental farmers. It is used to pay the Spanish to grow unwanted flax, the Italians for surplus wine, and the Greeks for poisonous tobacco that generates terminal diseases and that cannot be advertised. Meanwhile the British shopper pays more for milk and sugar than if we were outside the EU.

Today, our levels of food production are lower than they have ever been in modern times. Yet breaches of the regulations controlling food production result in severe financial penalties. As the whole world knows, our fishing industry has been discriminated against, systematically and from the first day of our joining, while our merchant shipping fleet is now a fraction of its former size.

Taken in combination, the bald fact is that we have reduced our ability to produce and import food to the point where we are now reliant on the rest of the EU. The UK was once one of the most successful food producers in the world. We have allowed ourselves to be deprived by others of our own self-sufficiency. That's a very strange thing to do.

Meanwhile, our electricity industry has been damaged as well. Once we were self-sufficient and led the world in generating technology. Our nuclear research was years ahead. No longer. Today, we have ditched coal and nuclear fuels and rely on gas-turbines. Security of supply is no longer a legal requirement. We import electricity from France, where early British nuclear technology has been developed further. Meanwhile, our research teams have been broken up by successively politically correct weak-kneed governments. The only completely successful fast-reactor generating plant in the world at Dounreay has been shut down, and our capacity to generate our own power has been reduced to below-danger levels.

Given that it takes many years to build generating plants, the UK's dependency on the EU for energy is now complete. Again, very strange. And why should all this have happened? When we look at the EU, we see an agenda they are reluctant to discuss in the UK. But is there another agenda buried deep below even the one we can see?

A successful society thrives on free and responsible choice. Central planning is the threat. Yet under the Maastricht Treaty, on behalf of the people of the member states, the EU takes upon itself "the right to intervene in common commercial policy, social policy, education, vocational training and youth, culture, public health, consumer protection, trans-European networks, economic and social cohesion, research and technological development and the environment". What other human activities are there?

The EU is about creating barriers. It is essentially an inward-looking trading bloc. The bureaucrats who run it have a siege mentality. Everything outside is a threat. So they use regulations and taxes to manipulate and protect what they perceive as the assets they have. And if those onerous regulations and high taxes obstruct economic activity, then so be it. They have achieved the protection they sought.

And this perception of assets worth protecting is highly selective, even within the EU itself. The French wine industry is worth protecting, but the British fishing industry is not. The Continental system of high social security and unfunded pension rights is more important than low taxation and flexible labour.

The income of supposedly impoverished artists and their estates is more important than the international fine-art market. A "withholding tax" on savings is more important than having a free movement of investment funds.

The EU claims to be in favour of fair trading – a level playing-field. Yet we have French and Spanish farmers, and Spanish fishermen, gaining hugely from the CAP and the Common Fisheries Policy (CFP) while our farmers and fishermen go out of business. The Germans and Spanish produce subsidised coal at twice the price of ours while our mines close. The French and Belgian airlines get huge handouts to compete against our airlines who receive none.

Integration has gone so far already that a nightmare scenario looms. When the EU eventually controls our finances, it will have command of our military forces too. The EU has merely to manufacture an "emergency" to justify – in its eyes at least – direct intervention in the UK, backed by paramilitary forces. Consider Article 224 of the European Treaty, which states that member states shall:

> "consult one another with a view to taking in common the necessary steps to avoid the operation of the Common Market being affected by measures which a Member State may be called upon to take in case of serious internal disturbances affecting public policy or the maintenance of law and public order, in case of war or serious international tension constituting a threat of war, or in order to carry out undertakings into which it has entered for the purpose of maintaining peace and international security."

Hostility towards the EU has risen dramatically in the UK in recent years, following a succession of disastrous high-profile events.

If the EU had set out deliberately to anger the British they could not have done a better job. Over the years the list has become a very long one. It all started with the destruction of the fishing industry. Then the effects of the CAP brought farming to its knees. The cataract of regulations has since drowned tens of thousands of previously successful businesses and made potential criminals of millions of law-abiding people, including market traders who just want to sell apples by the pound. The social chapter – which we thought we had escaped with an opt-out – was foisted on us through the back door and welcomed by the Blair government, adding millions to the costs of small businesses. Then our gold was sold to prop up the euro, which we don't want to join anyway. And so it goes on – relentlessly. Every day brings something more. The consequences must eventually come as no surprise to Brussels. We have had more than enough of this nonsense.

The opinion polls show an interesting and potentially significant split between those for and those against membership of the EU. People who grew up in the 1950s, and in the 1980s, tend to be more eurosceptical. Their formative years were years of growth, enterprise and success. Others, whose formative years were the 1960s and 1970s, tend to be more sympathetic to the EU. Their first understanding of government was socialist in nature and bureaucratic in style. Those decades spawned what we now call the nanny state. They saw the development of the idea that government knew best, that government was responsible for just about everything, and that government must take the risk out of everyday life.

But what happens when a nanny state assumes it has the right to do anything it likes? What happens when it never stops to ask itself the question: do we need to do this?

The Blair government has attacked and undermined every aspect of the British constitution. Most of it has been ignored by most people, and each element has been introduced and put into effect with the minimum of fuss. But the sum of the parts is all too clear.

Richard Littlejohn, writing in *The Sun*, in April 2000, said:

> "To the Prime Minister, like the Mad Hatter, words mean whatever he wants them to mean. In Blair's book, a xenophobe is someone who wants Britain to remain an independent nation, with its own laws, own parliament and own currency."

Blair said in an interview with an American journalist: "If that's the sort of country people want to live in, then f*** them."

Littlejohn, quoting the comment, went on: "What we have in those few words is not so much a throwaway remark as Blair's entire political philosophy. This is the F*** You government."

The monarchy is humiliated by involvement in midnight parties held to glorify politicians, while the prime minister struts about like a republican president. The House of Commons is carved up into a long-term left-of-centre coalition. The hereditary peers are kicked out of the House of Lords and replaced with Blairite apologists. The union of England, Scotland, Wales and Northern Ireland, making up the UK, is split into its component parts as a prelude to creating the 12 regional assemblies required by the EU – which in turn will render the sovereign parliament at Westminster redundant. The first-past-the-post voting system is under threat from forms of proportional representation that will disconnect the elected from the electorate and leave selection in the hands of the party bosses.

All of that reinforces control at the top, and has given the Blair government the confidence quietly to move the UK's levels of taxation closer to levels throughout the rest of the EU. The tax burden on individuals and businesses is growing faster here than anywhere in the developed world, including the rest of the EU. The Blair government inherited a strong vigorous economy that was already generating more tax revenue from growth. But that was not good enough. They wanted more – so up went the levels of taxation. Now, the tax burden in the UK, as a total percentage of Gross Domestic Product (GDP), is growing 30 times faster than in France. Of course, France is already so heavily taxed there is little room for tax growth, but the UK is in danger of catching up fast. According to figures from the Organisation for Economic Co-operation and Development (OECD), the UK tax burden grew by six per cent in the first year of the new Labour government, which was the fastest rate of increase for 16 years.

And all this when increased regulation and taxation have been proved beyond doubt to slow down economic growth and the creation of new jobs. It is so simple the proposition hardly needs proving. Look at what happened in Soviet Russia from state regulation. Look at what has happened in France and Germany, to say nothing of the rest of the EU, as taxes have been increased to pay for extravagant social security schemes and regulations on every conceivable aspect of everyday business life have been added almost daily.

Compare those countries and their stagnant economies with the USA and the UK. Compare Canada and the USA. Politically speaking, Canada is much where Britain was in the 1960s under Harold Wilson. Almost every other person seems to be on the state payroll and those who aren't are taxed to a standstill. Yet they share the same continent as the USA, and foolishly encourage entrepreneurs to migrate south to set up businesses and create new jobs. The only way Canada will ever stop that drain on their resources is for its government to change their attitudes and regulations.

Cheap air travel, instant communication across the globe, the internet, vast capital sums available for investment...all of these recent improvements in the quality of business life should be accelerating growth. And they are, despite the social and national borders that remain.

Does the internet need the euro? Within a few years it may have its own currency, completely bypassing all national and international borders, and all attempts at governmental regulation. In the context of modern business, the euro is a dinosaur already. As so often with politicians, they have invented a device for their own purposes, sold it as a solution to what will prove to be yesterday's problem, and ignored the needs of tomorrow. Will they ever realise how much more might be achieved if officialdom got out of the way?

The economists David Osborne and Ted Gaebler mapped out the right attitudes for governments to adopt if they were to get the most out of their economies. They included being committed to an "enabling" agenda, community-"owned", competitive, results- and market-oriented, customer-driven, enterprising, anticipatory and decentralised. That's much more a list of the qualities required to make a business successful. And many would argue that government should be minimalised, anyway – undertaking only those responsibilities that lie beyond the capabilities or resources of even large groups of individuals.

Certainly there is a powerful case for governments to stop legislating on everything and everybody in sight, and trying to nanny the risk out of life itself. They should not promise what is not possible, they should occasionally stop and ask themselves if legislation is required at all, and they should consider the other options more fully – the most obvious and least used being the involvement of private enterprise to solve problems. That way it will be done faster, at lower cost, more responsively and almost certainly better. It will also take politics out of the equation.

The Common Market – had that actually been the purpose of the EU – could have been created by simply removing government interference in trade between companies and individuals anywhere in Europe. Even the best-intended regulation by officials with no experience of trade is going to foul up. But pro-active regulation that seeks to interfere and control every transaction is little short of lunacy.

On the whole, businesses ignore government and just get on as best they can. They seek and find the most appropriate suppliers and the most suitable customers wherever and whenever they come to light. It is that very diversity of thinking and relationships that makes enterprise and trade what it is – the engine of growth and wealth-creation.

❖

Today, our aim is simply stated: to withdraw from the EU and re-establish the UK as an independent sovereign nation. The problem is how best to achieve it. There are several means, some easier than others. And the political timetable is unfortunate.

By legal means, it should be possible to make the case for the constitutional repudiation of the UK's membership of the EU. But that will take time, cost money, and will be vigorously opposed by the entrenched vested interests in the government, the judiciary and parts of big business.

There are, of course, at least two easy and quick routes to the exit. The government of the day might withdraw our ambassador. Or we could exchange notes with the EU terminating the treaties. Unlikely to happen, but possible. Of course the EU might collapse or throw us out (equally unlikely). Private prosecutions of government ministers, seeking to prove that by signing EU treaties they exceeded their authority and committed treason, might be successful. A petition to the Queen under powers granted to us under Magna Carta, 1215, and confirmed in the Declaration of Rights, 1688...any one of these events would have much the same practical effect.

The best way for the UK to withdraw must be by a decision taken by the Houses of Parliament. Repeal of the European Communities Act, 1972, and the Single European Act, 1985, brings the whole sorry EU edifice crashing down, at least in Britain.

So the real need is to elect a House of Commons with 330 MPs (50 per cent, plus one) vigorously in favour of repealing EU-enabling legislation. However, the brutal fact is that Europe is not currently at the centre of the UK's political agenda, except for an important and vocal minority of voters to whom it matters a great deal. Despite the best efforts of a great many euro-realist groups and the UK Independence Party (UKIP) there is still a long way to go.

Fortunately the British are a bloody-minded lot when the mood takes them. We are capable of total intransigence, especially when we believe the power we granted to others is being abused. The many for whom this battle truly matters will never surrender to Brussels, no matter how long it takes.

As Winston Churchill said: "The British people...bitterly resent being deceived or finding that those responsible for their affairs are themselves dwelling in a fool's paradise."

He, too, felt passionately about the unaccountability of governments, the abomination of courts of justice making laws on the hoof and to suit the political correctness of the day, the threat to free speech, and discrimination between individuals and officials of the state.

In a message to the newly liberated Italian people, on 28th August 1944, he said: "It has been said that the price of freedom is eternal vigilance. The question arises – what is freedom? There are one or two quite simple, practical tests by which it can be known in the modern world...namely:

"Is there the right to free expression of opinion and of opposition and criticism of the government of the day?

Have the people the right to turn out a government of which they disapprove, and are constitutional means provided by which they can make their will apparent?

Are their courts of justice free from violence by the executive and from threats of mob violence, and free of all association with particular political parties?

Will these courts administer open and well-established laws which are associated in the human mind with the broad principles of decency and justice?

Will there be fair play for poor as well as for rich, for private persons as well as government officials?

Will the rights of the individual...be maintained and asserted and exalted?"

When he revisited these words ten years later, Churchill wrote: "This does not seem to require any alteration today."

It is an horrific measure of how far we have travelled away from our roots that no government minister today could or would be heard uttering such plain truths.

Yet today's Labour government is not as incompetent as we might think. Their destruction of the constitution is not mismanagement. It is the result of careful planning to complete the process of changing this country fundamentally and permanently from the independent democratic nation it was 30 years ago to a region of Europe governed by officials. Instead of defending this country's best interests it has flouted them in pursuit of its own agenda.

That agenda has been spelled out in Will Hutton's *The State We're In* and Peter Mandelson's *The Blair Revolution*, which clearly reveal the attraction of Continental Europe's methods. They prefer working in secret. They like not being held accountable.

Contempt for history, obligations, and the legitimate interests of others is visible throughout Tony Blair's administration. For them, the world started on 1st May 1997. Nothing before that was worth a fig. Everything that's good has to be new. "New Labour" says it all.

Today, the UK is being governed by political lightweights with no understanding of history, no respect for our culture and traditions and the arrogance to think that none of it matters.

The EU wants to abolish the British system of justice – so let it. The EU wants to take over foreign affairs and speak for the whole continent – so let it. The EU wants to control defence, usurp the role of NATO, take over defence procurement, and put generals answering to Brussels in command of British military forces – so let it.

The EU wants to take over control of our money and taxes – so let it. The EU wants its own police force operating across all 15 member states, answerable only to a European public prosecutor – so let it.

The EU wants to abolish nations, their borders, their cultures, traditions, and way of life – so let it. The EU wants to replace parliamentary democracy with government by bureaucrats – so let it. The EU wants to convert the UK to 12 regions of Europe and ultimately make Westminster redundant – so let it. The EU wants to take over the running of this country – so let it. The EU wants to create a single country called Europe – so let it.

We, the people, are paying a colossal price for such acquiescence. But what does Tony Blair get out of all this?

Charlemagne ruled Europe. Napoleon ruled Europe. Hitler almost ruled Europe. They all used force of arms. Tony Blair uses stealth. Fortunately his name doesn't have quite the same ring to it. Nor does he instil fear like the others. Contempt, yes. Fear, no.

Within living memory, there has rarely if ever been a time when serious-minded people have questioned the probity of a prime minister. Yet, today, even doubts about Blair's sanity sometimes surface. Here is a man for whom history is bunk. His government, despite its manifesto promises, regards itself as having a clean sheet. It can do anything it likes. And given the huge and distorting parliamentary majority won in 1997 it is probably right. For Blair, nothing matters more than retaining power itself, indefinitely into the future. The unaccountable system of government in Europe is the natural home for such a man. Like many an aspiring pope before him, he will probably end up a failed cardinal.

This is a man to whom words are merely for the moment, to be discarded when no longer appropriate. A man routinely described as a "control freak" who is involved directly in almost every issue of the day, whose government is run almost entirely by spin doctors and appointed cronies. Where opposition exists, he simply removes it as quickly and ruthlessly as possible.

Little wonder the protests are growing more vocal.

When the House of Lords debated its own abolition, the Earl of Burford leapt onto the Woolsack, shouting:

"Before us lies the wasteland, no Queen, no culture, no sovereignty, no freedom. Stand up for your Queen and country – vote this treason down."

His protest did not last long – the serjeant at arms ejected him from the House. Outside, the Earl of Burford then told reporters:

> "This bill was drafted in Brussels. It is treason. What we are witnessing is the abolition of Britain. It concerns the liberty of every individual in Britain. The truth is that Tony Blair is evicting the hereditary peers from parliament in order to remove what he perceives to be the last obstacle to his plans to surrender our nationhood to Brussels.
>
> Blair has been ordered by his world government masters to bring the British constitution into line with the other EU countries in preparation for full political union. And he is doing it in flagrant

contempt of both parliament and the Crown. Indeed the very existence of the monarchy is threatened.

For if the Lords are stripped of their constitutional powers, then Blair will have presented himself with a *prima facie* case for revoking the constitutional powers of the monarchy."

A few weeks later the Earl stood for parliament at the Kensington and Chelsea by-election. He lost. But he had stood up and been counted, like millions of others, who are now fighting the EU tooth and nail.

The EU's key phrase, and the strategy, is "ever closer union". The tactics are insidiously small steps, taken one at a time, and each one introduced as a minor change. Each one is an acorn. What we see is the acorn. What we get is the oak tree.

Lord Denning used another metaphor: "No longer is European Law an incoming tide flowing up the estuaries of England. It is now like a tidal wave bringing down our sea walls and flowing inland over our fields and houses – to the dismay of all."

"The British Parliament in Westminster retains the final right to repeal the Act which took us into the Market on January 1, 1973. Thus our continued membership will depend on the continuing assent of Parliament." These were the government's own words during the 1975 referendum campaign.

Our constitution determines that parliament rules only with consent of the governed, who may remove that consent at any time, and by any means necessary.

It is fundamental to English constitutional law, and it has been repeated by every learned commentator on English law over the centuries, that the people are sovereign and that parliament can make and unmake any law at any time, save only that the freedoms, rights and customs of the people are not prejudiced.

The rule of law depends for its legitimacy on a few crucial factors that are, ironically, not capable of being enforced by law:

> ➤ The law is seen as reasonable, and has the support of the people.
> ➤ It is widely regarded as necessary.

> ➢   It is capable of being upheld and policed.
> ➢   It carries an appropriate punishment for offenders.
> ➢   Breaking that law is unacceptable to the majority.

One of the most vivid and recent examples of the reality of these criteria has been the discovery by the UK government that none of these conditions applies in the case of metrication.

Rodney Atkinson: "If the only way we can trade fairly and freely with some countries in Continental Europe is to destroy our democratic constitution, by-pass our parliament and make our courts redundant, then we are being blackmailed by our enemies, not welcomed by partners."

Mrs Thatcher had a short bill drafted to repeal the European Communities Act, 1972, while renegotiating the UK's contribution to the EU, in Fontainebleau. She did not introduce it to the House.

"...Then they came for the Jews and I didn't speak up because I wasn't a Jew. Then they came for the trade unionists but I didn't speak up because I was not a trade unionist. Then they came for the Catholics and I didn't speak up because I am a Protestant. Then they came for me – but no one was left to speak up" – Rev M Niemoller (1892–1984), Dachau, 1945.

"I no more want to be European than I do an Eskimo. So far as I'm concerned I'm bloody English and proud of the fact" – Ian Botham.

"If ever time should come, when vain and aspiring men shall possess the highest seats in government, our country will stand in need of its experienced patriots to prevent its ruin" – Samuel Adams, 1780.

Winston Churchill, speaking in his victory broadcast on 13th May 1945, expressed similar sentiments when he said:

"Never have the forces of two nations fought side by side and intermingled in the lines of battle with so much unity, comradeship and brotherhood, as in the great Anglo-American Armies. Some people say: well, what would you expect, if both nations speak the same language, have the same laws, have a great deal of their history in common, and have very much the same outlook on life, with all its hope and glory. Isn't it just the sort of thing that would happen? And others may say: it would be an ill day for all the world and for the pair of them if they did not go on working together and marching together and sailing together and flying together, whenever something has to be done for the sake of freedom and fair play all over the world. That is the great hope of the future.

On the continent of Europe we have yet to make sure that the simple and honourable purposes for which we entered the war are not brushed aside or overlooked in the months following our success, and that the words 'freedom', 'democracy' and 'liberation' are not distorted from their true meaning as we have understood them. There would be little use in punishing the Hitlerites for their crimes if law and justice did not rule, or if totalitarian or police governments were to take the place of the German invaders."

Chapter Two

It's the Principle of the Thing...

"By what authority are the people of the EU governed?" – the most important constitutional question of them all, and the one the EU chooses to ignore.

The officials who make up the EU and its institutions lack the political legitimacy, practical competence and international experience to justify any confidence in their integrity, ability or motivation. When we consider the people concerned in this venture, and their actions over the last quarter-century, it is preposterous even to begin thinking about abandoning our independence, self-determination and national sovereignty.

Yet that is precisely what we have done. Already the EU claims direct power over us as individuals and as a country. In their book, we are permitted no powers to refuse their decisions on any matters on which the EU chooses to legislate.

In the UK, the sovereignty of the people and the authorised power of government are totally separate. The government has no power over sovereignty. If anything, it has a responsibility to preserve, protect and respect it. Sovereignty of the people is absolute. It is not something that can be pooled or diluted in some way.

None of that inhibited Tony Blair from saying on television immediately after his 1997 election win that "MPs are not here to represent their constituencies – they are here to support the new government". Not just a Freudian slip, more a statement of contempt for the people who had just elected him to power.

The principal activity of government is not necessarily to do things. Rather it is to maintain the rule of law, the principles of justice, and involve itself in the provision of resources and infrastructure that enable individuals and groups of individuals to achieve things for themselves. Then government should stand well back and allow people to get on with their lives.

Anglo-Saxon culture is basically libertarian and is completely at odds with the prevailing culture on the Continent. This is perhaps most evident in the legal systems. English police are responsible for upholding the law and are accountable for their actions as subjects of the Crown, while French police are not accountable and act under direction of the executive.

As we have seen, in England, with its legal system based on common law, everything is permitted that is not expressly forbidden by law. On the Continent everything is illegal unless expressly permitted by law. That is a fundamental difference between the European system of government and that of the UK. The relationship between the state and the individual is exactly reversed.

In the UK we elect representatives to parliament who, from time to time, agree to change the law. If we, and they or their successors change our minds later, we change the law again. Two crucial benefits flow from this flexibility – respect for the law and confidence in its essential justice. We are not a particularly obedient people, nor do we accept the decisions of a government without question. But we do have a basic belief in the system and those elected to power.

Across Continental western Europe, none of this is true – at least not to the same extent. It has been the norm in the past in most Continental member states for bureaucrats to make the law, which is then administered partially and only when it suits. Choosing to ignore the law because nobody cares is unexceptional. Italian lawlessness is not controlled any better by having more laws than the rest of us. The people of France have no effective democratic control over the state system that rules them, but that does not inhibit their displays of disrespect for it. It should not surprise us unduly that in so many member states of the EU the law is permanently held in contempt.

In the UK, we accepted the proposition that we should join what became the EU. As an essentially law-abiding nation, we therefore accepted its laws. Now things are different. Now we know we have been cheated. On the other hand, for example, the French see nothing new or different. To them, the EU is just more of the same stupid bureaucracy. They ignore the laws they don't like, and ignore the squabbling officials who invent them.

These differences are central to the issue of UK membership. We accept and enforce EU law while other member states simply disregard what is inconvenient. So the problem of unaccountability matters in the UK, passionately, while other member states regard it as normal and unimportant. This incompatibility between the UK and the other member states is fundamental and deep-rooted. It will not go away.

In a free society, in addition to the enabling function of government mentioned earlier, the role of government is to uphold the rule of law, to protect private property, to provide a stable infrastructure and currency for the free exchange of goods and services.

A government which fails to protect private property or attempts to seize it for its own purposes without full compensation, which restricts trade, or which undermines contracts freely entered into by individuals, violates the freedoms and rights of us all.

Many EU leaders have spoken openly of their fundamental objective as a single European superstate – not a federation, as that involves the devolution of powers. The abolition of duty-free was simple, incontrovertible proof that Europe is to become a single country. Yet most British merely shrugged their shoulders, blamed the politicians and grumbled about losing a perk. The underlying truth was almost entirely ignored.

The EU already has the embryos of 130 embassies around the world, and demands a seat at all the most important international gatherings. It will soon be a single country, governed from the centre, over-regulated, anti-democratic and anti-Anglo-Saxon. It will also be composed of regions – just like Germany. Virtually all of this exists already, and the missing elements are now actively under construction.

For the vast majority of British, these ideas are an anathema. They run contrary to everything we stand for, everything we have ever fought for, and everything we aspire to. Given such fundamental differences, it is easy to see why we do not and cannot fit harmoniously into a country called the United States of Europe.

One of the signatories to the Magna Carta Society's pamphlet *Defence of the Realm*, David Bourne, wrote:

"Pursuit by Germany of its historic mission has brought nothing but death, destruction and chaos to the continent of Europe and beyond.

"Many millions, by their supreme sacrifices, ensured the succession of the monarchy in this country, and its liberty and freedom. They also helped to give back to many of the peoples of Europe those same liberties and freedoms which they were in serious danger of losing.

"These freedoms are our precious birthright. Men have died for them. We have no right to ignore them, let alone give them away. It is our clear duty to preserve and protect them, hold them fast for our children and our children's children. We are their caretakers – not their owners."

The concept of the nation state and sovereignty goes back to biblical times; not, as France and Germany like to say, "only" to the 17th and 18th centuries. That has not discouraged Germany from trying still – after centuries – to tie the UK into its own sphere of influence.

The 1997 Amsterdam Treaty says: "Island regions suffer from structural handicaps linked to their island status, the permanence of which impairs their economic and social development. The conference accordingly acknowledges that community legislation must take account of these handicaps and that special measures may be taken, where justified, in favour of these regions in order to integrate them better to the internal market on fair conditions." That any UK government should even consider signing such a text is truly incredible. What other purpose could it have than to seek to legitimise EU interference in UK affairs in general, and UK trade in particular?

All of this points up the stark contrast between what we thought we were joining in 1972 – a free trade area of independent states – and what the EU really is – a customs union and a unitary state intended to tie previously independent countries to an inward-looking economic area.

The later disgraced chancellor of Germany, Helmut Kohl, told a Council of Europe meeting in September 1995: "We want the political unification of Europe. If there is no monetary union there cannot be political union, and vice versa. A European police force and army lie at the end of the road to political union."

The authorisation for those components of the new country of Europe was laid down two years later, in the Treaty of Amsterdam, which included the words "…bringing about the legal termination of the independence, sovereignty and right to self-government for all time…". Again, it beggars belief that a British government could so much as contemplate signing a document containing such treasonous words.

But successive British governments have been rolling over in front of the European juggernaut for more than 25 years. Little wonder that Kohl also said that the future of Europe would be German. Later, the new chancellor, Gerhard Schroeder, said that he wanted to see a federal Europe constructed on German lines. They both know who has been winning the battle of wills.

In 1999, the euro-realist activist Rodney Howlett submitted a petition to parliament:

> "Sheweth, that in 1975 the British people, in a referendum, agreed to remain in a Common Market; a group of equal and free European nations trading together without barriers and tariffs.
>
> By default the British people have, without their consent, become citizens of a European Superstate run by a non elected bureaucratic Commission in Brussels. This foreign power has suborned our legal system and the authority of our parliament.
>
> Wherefore your petitioners pray that your Honourable House do all in its power to re-establish our sovereign right to rule ourselves in accordance with the freedoms, liberties and rights granted to Us and Our Heirs forever by Magna Carta in 1215."

The government's response said:

> "The EU is a body of nation states working together under Treaties freely entered into and approved by the national Parliaments of every nation state. The UK cannot and will not be forced to accept forms of integration against our will. Where the EEC (now the EU) has developed since the 1975 referendum, each Treaty change has of course been ratified by the

democratically elected British Parliament. Without that ratification, the Treaty changes could not have been made.

The primary legislative bodies in the EU are the Council of Ministers and the European Parliament. The Council is made up of Ministers of national governments, each elected by, and accountable to, their own citizens. Members of the European Parliament are directly elected by, and accountable to, their electorates.

As a result of membership of the EU, we have pooled some areas of our national powers with those of our European partners. But no irrevocable transfer of sovereignty has taken place. The UK continues to be governed by its own democratically elected institutions. The majority of decisions affecting British citizens are taken at national, regional or local level.

The Government firmly believes that membership of the EU is in the UK's interest. The success of the EU is key to our current and future prosperity. We will continue to work with our European partners to develop a prosperous and successful EU that responds to the needs of its citizens."

Romano Prodi, shortly after his appointment as the head of the EC, set out his goal for the next five years as the creation of a single European economy and full-blown political union. He also proposed a single passport for all new-born children in Europe and the abolition of national passports for that generation and beyond; and the introduction of a European income tax payable by all citizens to fund the EU.

And this was the man whose candidature for the post was supported by the British prime minister, Tony Blair.

Today, the Westminster parliament has lost great swathes of power. Ministers plead that they cannot influence, let alone change rules generated from Brussels that damage individuals or whole sectors of industry. Our MPs are there only to give the spurious impression that there is some sort of democratic control over the EC. If that is democracy, it is now a truly tender plant. It is in danger of being trodden underfoot. Soon, Brussels will kill it off altogether.

David Hearnshaw, chairman of Business for Sterling's southern area reported a conversation he had with Sir George Young, his local Tory MP. He told him: "We elect our politicians to run the shop, not give away the keys behind our backs and without our permission." He was rewarded with what Mr Hearnshaw later described as a "wan smile, and not much else".

Edward Heath said, during the Common Market referendum, in 1975: "There is no question of any erosion of essential national sovereignty."

When interviewed by the BBC in 1998 he was asked: "Did you know, when you took us into the common market, that it would lead to federalism?" His exact reply was: "Of course I bloody did!" – not the first time he had admitted lying. The recent release of government papers from that time has confirmed the truth of Heath's admission.

Norman Lamont, former chancellor of the exchequer and a member of the team that negotiated Britain's Maastricht opt-outs:

> "We deceive the British people and we deceive ourselves if we claim we are winning the argument in Europe. There is no argument in Europe. There is Britain's point of view, and there is the rest of Europe. The only question at Maastricht was how much Britain could swallow and what special arrangements could be made for us. There is not a shred of evidence at Maastricht or since that anyone accepts our view of Europe. The plain fact acknowledged by every Continental politician – except those on the fringe of power – is that the other members want a European State whether they express it in these precise terms or not."

It has often been claimed that Winston Churchill was, or would have been, a supporter of a united Europe. There have even been suggestions that the EU would have had his support. Nothing is further from the truth. New (well, old, to be precise) evidence puts the lie on both claims.

Speaking in the USA at the end of 1941, Churchill referred to:

> "…comradeship in the common cause of great peoples who speak the same language and, to a very large extent, pursue the same ideals.

...by our sacrifice and daring our children shall not be robbed of their inheritance or denied the right to live in a free and decent world."

Just over a year later, in an inter-departmental note dated 14th February 1943, Winston Churchill wrote:

"We have no right whatever to tie the hands of future Parliaments...I could not as Prime Minister be responsible...for binding my successor." Those words were first published in *The Hinge of Fate*, Appendix F, p862.

The next piece of evidence about Churchill's thinking dates from some three months later. It comes from the notes of a meeting between the allied war leaders in Washington. During a conference to plan the next phase of the war as a whole, and the invasion of Sicily as a stepping-stone to Italy in particular, the group met regularly over several days.

One of these meetings was over lunch at the British embassy on 22nd May 1943. Roosevelt and Churchill were both present. During the luncheon, Churchill was invited to offer his views on a question that had hitherto not attracted much attention. However, it was now becoming clear that, eventually, the allies must win the war. The question was: "What happens afterwards?"

Talking about the organisation of the post-war world, Winston Churchill expressed the wish that the whole of the British Empire (as it then was) and the USA should work together in a way that would confer advantages on both, but without what he called sacrifice or hindrance. A free association of sovereign and like-minded states was what he had in mind.

He thought that the citizens of all these nations, which had Anglo-Saxon roots of one kind or another, should be able to settle and trade in freedom with each other. They should enjoy equal rights, but without losing sovereignty.

He imagined some sort of common passport or visa, a common citizenship perhaps. He envisaged citizens of this large group of nations enjoying voting privileges in each other's countries, subject to residential qualifications. They might also be eligible for public office in their new country of residence, subject of course to the laws and institutions of that country.

He did not offer a fully developed plan – just a few principles and embryonic ideas. But his thinking was crystal clear. He had in mind a close but free association of countries based on culture, traditions and language, rather than one based merely on accidents of geography.

As for Europe, on that occasion at least, Churchill anticipated nothing more than a regional council – to pick up the pieces, ensure that the warring nations could not start a third conflagration, and to act as a single voice for a devastated continent in some sort of world forum.

He also suggested a similar regional council for the Pacific area. The seeds of the United Nations, NATO and the South East Asia Treaty Organisation (SEATO) can be found in this luncheon party.

These ideas and quotations are important today for entirely new and different reasons. They demonstrate beyond reasonable doubt where Winston Churchill's instincts lay, in terms of the sovereignty of nations, the traditions of Anglo-Saxon government, the potential collective strength of the Anglo-Saxon world, regardless of its distribution around the globe, and the desirability of creating some means of maximising that strength for the good of all.

Even allowing for the profound changes that have occurred around the world and over the years, after half a century Churchill's underlying message is undiminished.

Here is a clear and ringing reminder of where the great man stood. His words also set another goal further ahead still, if we have the collective will to strive for its modern equivalent.

But his ideas on a common citizenship even within the Anglo-Saxon world are not likely to be popular today, especially after the extraordinary muddle the British government has got itself into with supposed EU citizenship.

In mid-2000, the operations director of the passport agency was confirming that there was no such concept as "EU citizen". By the autumn he was quoting the Maastricht Treaty, which says the opposite. He was unable to explain the contradiction, nor say which statement was correct.

It was put to him: "Assuming for the moment that it does exist, you say that EU citizenship does not replace British citizenship (as you choose to call it). I never suggested it did. My objection is quite specific – I was born English, I live here, I remain English, and all the scraps of paper in the world cannot change that. I did not apply for, nor do I want, citizenship of any other nation, neither actual nor as the figment of some Eurocrat's imagination. Nor will I have such a ludicrous concept imposed on me. I will come to my rights in a moment.

"I asked about the supposed 'duties' of EU citizens. What are they, precisely? How are they to be enforced? You ignored my question and tell me, instead, that citizenship confers four 'special' rights. Two I have already – the right to vote in elections here, and diplomatic protection abroad. One needs no reinforcement – the right to move abroad. The last is laughable – the right to appeal to the European Ombudsman. What does he know about English common law, pray?

But having answered a question I didn't ask, I note that you have not answered any of the specific questions I did ask – namely:

1   How can the EU (a non-country) claim it can impose citizenship on me without my agreement?

2   Where in law does the state take the right to create the notion that dual-citizenship is somehow compulsory?

3   Where in law does parliament claim sovereignty over my birthrights?

4   Given the terms of the oath sworn by the monarch at her coronation, and the oaths sworn by her ministers and senior civil servants, how do you or they explain or attempt to justify the present inherent and fundamental contradictions involved?

5   At one stage in the EU's metamorphosis, the issuing of an EU passport was merely a 'recommendation' by the EU. In which case, was citizenship merely a recommendation, too? And is it still?

6   What happens to the legal status of supposed citizenship if and when the EU purports to seize 'legal personality' for itself in the forthcoming Nice Treaty, after which it can then claim to be a country?

7   Are you aware that attempting to force EU citizenship on me may well breach articles 15 (2) and 20 (2) of the United Nations Declaration of Human Rights?

8   Recently, we have been faced with two new and highly questionable charters of Human Rights, both of which seek to prohibit discrimination. I am told my 'rights and freedoms [are] secured without discrimination on any grounds such as...association with a national minority...birth or other status'. Since our government has foolishly subscribed to these terms it must abide by them. By attempting to impose an unwanted foreign citizenship on me you are directly breaching my human rights, as defined above. I have a right and freedom to be a subject of the crown, and to be described as English within the UK. By being described as an EU citizen as well I am being discriminated against as a member of the English minority in the EU. On these grounds alone, logic suggests you should now withdraw mine and all other unwanted EU passports.

Which brings us back to the nub of the issue – my rights. These rights are beyond the reach of parliament or its servants. They are enshrined in common law, they were formally recognised in The Magna Carta (which the House of Lords Records Office has recently confirmed stands to this day – not that there was any doubt), these same rights were re-affirmed in The Declaration of Rights, entrenched in statute law in The Bill of Rights (which the Speaker of the House of Commons confirmed in 1993 stands to this day), and they were specifically renewed in the coronation oath sworn in 1953 by the present monarch.

Essentially, common law rights cannot be subverted by ministers and other servants of the crown. They have only the same powers and rights as the people who elected or appointed them. Their forebears were appointed specifically on condition that they would respect and defend the rights, freedoms and customs of the people. Nothing has changed the substance of that commitment since then. Furthermore, parliament has a duty of care to preserve and protect the rights and freedoms of the people who elected it.

In the UK, the people are sovereign. The monarch is the embodiment of that sovereignty. Parliament is elected and answers to the people. Unlike Europeans, we British are free men. Here, the state answers to us – not we to the state, as in Europe. There are a great many things a parliament cannot do, and one of them is diminish or restrict common law. Statutes can 'improve' common law, but even if that statute is later repealed the original common law still stands. Thus it follows that the imposition of a foreign citizenship on a natural-born Englishman is beyond the powers of parliament since it purports to impose a system of law which makes an Englishmen subservient to the state – and that is an attempt to restrict sovereignty.

What's more, present attempts to turn me into a citizen of the EU rely on legislation and treaties passed and signed from the 1950s onwards. So the EU's present actions reduce to this: the imposition of a citizenship on people who do not want it, by an organisation which did not exist when they were born, to subjugate them to an alien system of government in which they have no confidence. Were they real, these would be near-magical properties…alternatively you may think them absurd. Retrospective law is widely held by parliamentarians and lawyers to be unsound and dangerous. In my case, having been born in 1936, am I now to believe that I was born into a country which did not exist and that the second world war was merely a civil war? It didn't seem like it at the time, let me assure you.

So here is my formal renunciation of 'citizenship' of the EU on the grounds that no such thing exists, I do not want it, and the EU is not a country. It has now and can never have any jurisdiction over my status as a subject of the crown, and as a free Englishman I have the absolute right to reject any such sham. I hereby do so.

Since you apparently will not issue the correct passport document to me I have amended the erroneous one you sent earlier this year. You may take the view that this is wilful damage to crown property. In which case I will make the evidence available to you and I invite you to issue proceedings which you can assume will be vigorously defended for as long as it takes and as far as it goes."

There was no reply – nor has the "crime" of defacing Crown property ever been pursued.

❖

The thought-police are coming.

The nightmare forecast in George Orwell's famous book *1984* is about to become a reality – courtesy of Brussels. Anyone who might commit a crime at some time in the future will soon risk being locked up indefinitely without trial. So will every criminal and suspect.

The thought-police are being introduced, and all our rights and freedoms under Magna Carta abolished, under a new legal system about to be forced on the British from Brussels.

These proposals are known as *corpus juris*[1], which simply means "body of law". They permit the arrest of people on suspicion of intending to commit a crime and may, in the future, also mean that we can be arrested for arguing withdrawal from a treaty that does not permit it, since that will be self-evidently against the law! Further, it might be argued that such activities were treasonable or seditious.

The changeover process from English common law to *corpus juris* has already started. The European commissioners who replaced the commissioners who resigned in disgrace after evidence of corruption in 1999 have decided to introduce a new system of justice…would you believe…officially to fight fraud in the EC.

But – like so much from the EU – it is actually intended to achieve something quite different. It is the first step towards what the EU calls in its own words "a future European criminal code. A simpler and more efficient system of repression".

It has already started to create more conflict between London and Brussels. And again Britain is likely to come off worst.

This new EU system of justice will abolish British trial by jury. It will abolish the right to be presumed innocent until proven guilty. It will abolish our famous *habeas corpus*, which was first formally recognised in Magna Carta – signed by King John in 1215. This gave us the right to have the *prima facie* evidence against us considered in public by a court of law within 48 hours of arrest. There will be no requirement for a public appearance, and no early opportunity to refute the *prima facie* evidence. Instead, the suspect will face indefinite detention without trial.

Corpus juris will abolish the right of the accused to see the evidence against him or her before committal. Trial by jury will become trial by so-called "professional" judges, while lay magistrates will disappear from our courts.

For over 400 years in the UK, if a suspect has been acquitted of a crime he or she has been safe from prosecution on the same charge again. Not any more, if the EU has its way. *Corpus juris* would reintroduce "double jeopardy", which allows the prosecution to appeal against a not-guilty verdict, and continue appealing until it gets a conviction. Much to the astonishment and dismay of thinking people, both the UK government and the opposition now support such an oppressive proposal.

And there's more. Risking arrest on mere suspicion that you might commit a crime at some time in the future is already being considered seriously in the fight against football hooliganism. But that is not the least of it. Under *corpus juris*, you can also be arrested and extradited to a foreign country without any evidence being presented to a court, nor shown to you, whether you might have committed a crime or were merely thinking about it!

The police and prosecution become one organisation. And all but the judgment at the end of a trial can be in secret.

Much of this new system of so-called justice is based on the code, also known as *corpus juris*, originated by the Roman emperor Justinian. It was later perfected by the Holy Inquisition and finally modernised and imposed across Continental Europe by the conquering Napoleon 200 years ago. It has been used on the Continent ever since. Today, the introduction of *corpus juris* across the EU is seen by euroland-enthusiasts as one of the last big planks in the construction of a single European state run by bureaucrats.

The Home Office says Britain can veto these proposals, but that is not true. They cannot be vetoed when they are introduced under Article 280 of the Amsterdam Treaty, which allows qualified majority voting in the fight against fraud.

All this is a far cry from the strongly held views of Winston Churchill, who found time in the middle of a world war to concern himself with the plight of one family whom he regarded as enemy sympathisers.

In a minute to the home secretary, dated 21st November 1943, he wrote about the fascist Mosley family, then imprisoned without trial for some three years:

> "...the great principles of *habeas corpus* and trial by jury...are the supreme protection invented by the British people for ordinary individuals against the state. The power of the executive to cast a man into prison without formulating any charge known to the law, and particularly to deny him judgment by his peers for an indefinite period, is in the highest degree odious, and is the foundation of all totalitarian governments.
>
> Nothing can be more abhorrent to democracy. This is really the test of civilisation."

As the British finally recover their sense of outrage and our national sense of what is right and wrong, the howls of protest from Britain will grow louder as more and more people begin to think that Churchill was right then, and right now.

The unique British concept of *habeas corpus* obliges a policeman or prosecutor to place evidence of a crime before a court, normally within 24 hours of a charge being laid against the accused. At that time, the accused can argue that there is no case to answer and that he or she should be discharged, or can apply for bail. If this is allowed, the defendant walks free until the trial. If the defendant is detained, the courts must reconsider bail applications on a regular basis until the case is heard or sent for trial.

On the other hand, the European Court of Human Rights has demonstrated many times that it regards six months as a reasonable time to incarcerate a defendant before he or she appears in court to hear the evidence against. During that time, to help the defendant decide to confess to the crime of which he or she is accused, he or she may be locked up with violent prisoners, cell-mates with the HIV, rapists and all manner of other disagreeable people. This may sound far-fetched, but the evidence is there. The Continental system of justice permits it, and it happens regularly in Italy.

The jury system in the UK is a further safeguard against the corrupt application of the law. We, the people, judge the rightness of a charge. It is not left to professional judges who are dependent on the state for the progression of their careers.

Indeed it might be argued that a British judge who tolerated such changes in our criminal law would be breaching Magna Carta, which says:

> We will appoint as justices, constables, sheriffs, or other officials, only men that know the law of the realm and are minded to keep it well.

> No free man shall be seized or imprisoned, or stripped of his rights or possessions, or outlawed or exiled, or deprived of his standing in any other way, nor will we proceed with force against him, or send others to do so, except by the lawful judgment of his equals or by the law of the land.

> To no one will we sell, to no one deny or delay right or justice."

The final arbiter is the law itself, and for the accused it is the decision of a jury. Magna Carta and the Declaration and Bill of Rights all categorically state in their own ways that anything detrimental to the rights of a subject of the Crown shall be disregarded.

If you know your obligations and rights as a member of a jury, you can help to protect the rights of the individual if you believe the law being applied in the case being tried is unconstitutional or unfair. You simply vote "not guilty". When juries find a defendant not guilty in cases where the defendant did in fact violate the law, the effect is to nullify the law in that particular case.

If regular nullification of a law makes it impossible for the government to enforce it, repeal or amendment follows.

One of the earliest occasions when the power of a jury to nullify the law was first exercised occurred in London over 300 years ago. The circumstances were featured in an article by Godfrey Lehman in the American journal *The Justice Times*.

He was referring to "Bushell's Case" – and the ordeal suffered by 12 jurors in defending the rights of a preacher. "Its 20th century oblivion belies the respect it commanded in the 18th, and conceals its enduring influence." Lehman was right. This was probably one of the most influential single events in the entire history of humanity's attempts to govern itself.

"It was spontaneous, unlike any other great charter of liberty, and it was accomplished without deliberate, conscious planning; without great public agitation, and did not require the signing of a formal document. It did not involve any highly-placed persons. It arose directly from the people."

This is the story of the trial of William Penn, who had committed the then serious offence of preaching Quakerism. The Conventicle Act proscribed all religions except the Church of England.

The jurors suffered nine weeks of psychological pressure and mental torment to stand by the principle that every person has a right to worship according to his or her own conscience. They stood firm, despite the ordeal. And they won.

The Conventicle Act fell before these 12 inconsequential unknowns – "bumbleheads", "simple-witted cockneys" were two of the more polite epithets used to pour scorn on them. They had no standing in society, they had no rank, nor a position in government. But in practical terms they changed the law. There were no further prosecutions.

The repealing legislation passed without difficulty as the government backed down before them. They gained no personal advantages, indeed they suffered for what they believed was right. And afterwards they disappeared into unrecorded history. Today we know almost nothing about them.

"By nullifying a law, the jury corrects governmental abuses and usurpations one at a time, without violence, within the arena of the courtroom, preventing the formation of a long chain, which unchecked, could lead to revolution, as it did in 1776. The jury should be highly respected and honored," Lehman wrote.

A summary of another celebrated case that established the (common law) right of juries to deliver any verdict they chose to, despite the judge's directions or the law, can be read on a large plaque on the first floor of the Old Bailey in London.

A similar case occurred in what was then the colonies. In November 1734, a New York printer, John Peter Zenger, was arrested for seditious libel against His Majesty's government. At that time, the colony of New York forbade any publication without prior government approval. Freedom of the press was not permitted. Zenger defied this censorship and published articles strongly critical of New York colonial rule. When brought to trial nine months later Zenger admitted publishing the offending articles, arguing that the truth justified publication. The judge instructed the jury that truth was no justification.

Indeed, the judge reasoned to the jury that the truth made public unrest more likely. Since the defendant had admitted to the "fact" of publication, only a question of "law" remained.

Then, as now, the judge said the "issue of law" was for the court to determine, and he instructed the jury to find the defendant guilty. It took only ten minutes for the jury to disregard the judge's instructions on the law and find Zenger not guilty. That was – and still is – is the power of the jury.

The jury is the last safeguard against unjust law and tyranny.

The right of juries to judge the justice of laws was argued with great clarity in 1852 by Lysander Spooner in his *Essay in the Trial by Jury*.

He wrote:

> "For more than six hundred years – that is, since Magna Carta, in 1215 – there has been no clearer principle of English or American constitutional law, than that, in criminal cases, it is not only the right and duty of juries to judge what are the facts, what is the law, and what was the moral intent of the accused; but that it is

also their right, and their primary and paramount duty, to judge of the justice of the law, and to hold all laws invalid, that are, in their opinion, unjust or oppressive, and all persons guiltless in violating, or resisting the execution of, such laws.

Unless such be the right and duty of jurors, it is plain that, instead of juries being a 'palladium of liberty' – a barrier against the tyranny and oppression of government – they are really mere tools in its hands, for carrying into execution any injustice and oppression it may desire to have executed.

That the rights and duties of jurors must necessarily be such as are here claimed for them, will be evident when it is considered what the trial by jury is, and what is its object.

The trial by jury, then, is a 'trial by the country' – that is, by the people – as distinguished from a trial by the government. It was anciently called 'trial per pais'. The object of this trial 'by the country,' or by the people, in preference to a trial by the government, is to guard against every species of oppression by the government. In order to effect this end, it is indispensable that the people, or 'the country,' judge of and determine their own liberties against the government; instead of the government's judging of and determining its own powers over the people. How is it possible that juries can do anything to protect the liberties of the people against the government, if they are not allowed to determine what those liberties are?

To secure this right of the people to judge of their own liberties against the government, the jurors are taken from the body of the people, by lot, or by some process that precludes any previous knowledge, choice, or selection of them, on the part of the government. This is done to prevent the government's constituting a jury of its own partisans or friends. In other words, to prevent the government's packing a jury, with a view to maintain its own laws, and accomplish its own purpose."

We have come a long way since 1852. We are now fairly used to judges suggesting to juries that they (the jurors) should take the law as they (the judges) explain it, no matter how the jurors might feel about it. This has regularly given defence teams subsequent grounds for appeal.

On the other hand, jurors might reasonably think that, under the terms of the oath they swear, if the law is repugnant to them, they have a duty to repudiate it in the jury room. Since to insist on the oath being sworn is itself duress, jurors who have sworn might reasonably consider it their duty to serve on the jury to prevent what might otherwise be a miscarriage of justice.

The most valuable lesson to be learned from the ordeal of the Bushell jurors is that we do not need legislation nor any dilution of the powers and standing of juries to preserve this bulwark of liberty. We need only to preserve our knowledge and understanding of our common law rights, and a determination not to submit to any dilution.

According to *Juror's Handbook*, given to potential jury members in the USA, "the jury has more power than all of government. It has the final power of veto over all statutes concerned with criminal law. It is one of the crucial checks and balances in the system.

"The government cannot deprive anyone of their liberty without the consent of a jury. If a juror sincerely believes that a law is unfair, or that it infringes the defendant's God-given, inalienable or constitutional rights, a vote of not guilty declares that the offending statute is really no law at all and that the violation of it is no crime."

No one is bound to obey an unjust command – a key argument at the Nuremberg trials. The other side of that coin is that the jury must be free to say so.

Thus, our liberty depends heavily on the honesty of jurors. None of us can do better than follow the example of the Bushell 12, and act according to our conscience and common sense. It is far easier to stop the enemies of liberty in the jury box than on the streets.

The jury's role is to act as a counter-balance to the statements, views and arguments of case-hardened judges and toughened prosecutors. The idea that juries may judge only on the "facts" is absurd and contrary both to historical fact and law. Juries are not present merely to rubber stamp even reasonable, let alone tyrannical, acts of government. As sovereign in our own land, who can claim a higher right to decide whether our laws conform to the constitution?

One of the justifications claimed for abolishing trial by jury relates to cases of fraud – the fig leaf behind which *corpus juris* presently hides. But it is simply not true that professional judges are more able than juries to decide complicated fraud cases. This concedes a vital principle about juries. We know that, sometimes, evidence is hard for the layman to follow and understand fully. But any criminal trial is ultimately about depriving somebody of their liberty. This is an issue anybody can understand, and about which any reasonable person can have a view, based on the totality of the evidence.

It would be an outrage for professional judges to decide a case against a defendant, and then claim that the evidence – and therefore the verdict – were beyond the comprehension of ordinary people. The Roskill committee concluded by majority vote that juries were unsuited for fraud cases, but the government of the day preferred the view of the dissenting minority report.

One of the proposals under *corpus juris* is to create a "Judge of Freedoms". It has to be assumed that no irony was intended by the humourless bureaucrats who invented that name. The term is a contradiction in itself. And the powers of this judge will allow him to reach a decision in secret, without explanation, and – if he wishes – without reviewing the evidence against the accused. This so-called "Judge of Freedoms" can also commit the accused for trial. So much for freedom.

The whole concept of *corpus juris* was unveiled at a conference in San Sebastian in 1997 as "an embryo of a future EU criminal code". A report by the committee for civil liberties, dated 2nd December 1997, referred to *corpus juris* as "the basis for more general European judicial cooperation". The Amsterdam Treaty confirmed that judicial cooperation between states was required on criminal matters.

A West Country journalist trying to obtain a copy of the EC's explanatory book on *corpus juris* was first told it did not exist, then asked why he wanted it and finally given one when he said he understood it was a super proposal that furthered European integration.

The text refers with breathtaking arrogance to the need to avoid having "simple jurors" hearing trials involving finance or corruption. The long-standing English bastion of being tried by "twelve good men and true" or "twelve of your peers" is simply torn up and thrown away. This is a vivid and undisguised display of EU contempt for the rights and freedom of the individual, and their preference for the supremacy of the state.

Corpus juris includes references to its functioning "within a largely unified European legal space, an attack on crime that is fairer, simpler and more efficient". These phrases demonstrate the true purpose of *corpus juris*. They make no reference to any concept of justice, and appear to ignore totally the legitimate interests of the accused.

The booklet also includes one particularly curious and significant sentence:

"At this stage of European construction, the question is whether...we must resign ourselves to waiting years and years for any slight improvement in the criminal justice system." Note the words "European construction" – yet another open admission of the ultimate goal to build a single state. Consider the phrase "years and years" – a clear signal from one bureaucrat to others of the boredom and frustration of having the politicians getting in their way. The message is, "we know best". Finally, and even more importantly, look at the choice of the words "criminal justice system". No pretence that *corpus juris* was solely to fight fraud in the EU, which is the version used to defend it publicly in Britain and elsewhere.

Don Jose-Maria Gil-Robles, president of the European parliament, described *corpus juris* as constituting "an important model for the realisation of a common European judicial space...against all and any criminal activity".

Mrs Diemut Theato, chairman of the committee on budgetary control, said that *corpus juris* was a step towards drawing up common instruments to deal with common problems in accordance with the collective wishes of Europe's citizens. She did not say when or how they had been asked.

A questionnaire issued to delegates asked the question: "Has the concept of a European judicial area been sufficiently taken on board by the public? How could national parliaments and the European parliament increase the public's acceptance and understanding of this idea, which is so important for civil society?" The assumption in the use of the word "acceptance" will not be lost on British sensitivities.

On the Continent, what counts is not who is right, or what the law is, but simply who has the power to decide, and how they can be influenced. This reality was illustrated by Giolitti, an Italian prime minister before the First World War, who said: "The law is something we apply to our enemies. For our friends we interpret it." That is still the attitude on the Continent today.

Our forefathers long ago figured out ways of redressing the balance in criminal cases. They acknowledged the paramount importance of avoiding the conviction of an innocent person. *Habeas corpus*, the presumption of innocence, the whole burden of proof resting on the prosecution, and trial by jury, are all part of that defensive structure. Added to that, protection against "double jeopardy" ensures that an acquittal is just that. If his or her evidence overwhelmed the accusers, or they failed to produce sufficient evidence to convince a jury, the defendant has won the right to live without fear of repeating the ordeal at the whim of a defeated prosecutor.

Our constitution protects the liberty of the individual without qualification. The Declaration of Rights, 1688, was entrenched in the Bill of Rights, 1689. Both specifically recognised the right to trial by jury (Clause 11) for example. Neither has been repealed. Indeed, the Declaration cannot be repealed, nor can parliament touch it. It is a treaty (some prefer the word "covenant") directly between the sovereign and the people, and was specifically renewed in the coronation oath sworn by the Queen in 1953.

This government – any British government – has no power to overthrow the constitution. Nor may it legislate on matters outside its reach.

None of that has discouraged the present Labour government from making three separate attempts to introduce elements of *corpus juris*. The home secretary has attempted to reduce the use of trial by jury (on the alleged grounds of cost). The government has enacted legislation to stop football hooligans going abroad on the grounds that they might commit an offence when they get there – i.e. merely on suspicion that they *might* commit an offence abroad. The home secretary has also proposed to give the prosecution the power to appeal against a not-guilty verdict, which will abolish our freedom from "double jeopardy". That same proposal will also have the effect of eroding the obligation on the prosecution to provide the burden of proof before the accused stands at risk, contrary to common law. Finally, as a further step towards *corpus juris*, magistrates are now called "district judges", so preparing the way for the eventual line of control from the European public prosecutor and his professional judges in Brussels, to courts in the UK, as *corpus juris* is introduced.

The extent to which these planned changes undermine our constitution and common law is made clear by the relevant legal ruling quoted in the preface to *Stones' Justices Manual*:

"Throughout the web of the English criminal law one golden thread is always to be seen, that it is the duty of the prosecution to prove the prisoners' guilt...no matter what the charge or where the trial, the principle that the prosecution must prove the guilt of the prisoner is part of the common law of England and no attempt to whittle it down can be entertained."

The sheer scale and full implications of these profound changes in our law will probably strike home when an Englishman is deported and held without trial in a European country.

If a prosecutor from countries with whom we share a common legal heritage – most of the English-speaking world – seeks the arrest and extradition of a suspect in the UK, the prosecutor has to make out a *prima facie* case against that suspect, which is heard before a court.

But, in future, under *corpus juris*, a prosecutor from France, Greece, Spain or anywhere else in the EU will not have to face such a test of the evidence collected. The accused will be whisked off without knowing the evidence against, without having a chance to dispute it, or have it tested in a British court under British law.

In much of the Continental EU, there is ample evidence to show how deeply corrupt a professional tribunal consisting of a judge and two assessors can be. That corruption can be financial, legal or political, or some combination of all three. In Europe, judges are bought and sold for political as well as financial favours. They are there to manage the law, not to uphold it.

In 1879, an unknown English lawyer wrote a brief commentary on the profound differences between the system of justice he had found on the Continent, and that enjoyed in Britain. He said:

"All the power of a State is employed against the accused; the Crown is prosecutor, and has unlimited sums of money and resources at its command, to collect evidence, secure the attendance of witnesses and to obtain men of the highest rank at the bar to conduct the case.

Therefore, as the first object of the law is to protect the weak against the strong, it throws every possible shield around the accused against the abuse of power. He is not bound to criminate himself; it is for the prosecution to prove his guilt, not for him to prove his innocence.

He may not be heard upon oath to contradict, or explain, what has been deposed to by his prosecutors; therefore the case against him must be made out beyond any doubt such as would occur to the mind of a reasonable man, or he is entitled to his acquittal.

The direct contrary of these wholesome provisions appears to prevail in many continental States. There, the prosecution starts with the assumption that the prisoner is guilty, and calls upon him to prove his innocence.

He is cross-examined by his judges with a view of getting him to make admissions from which his guilt may be inferred. Poor and ignorant as the great majority of those accused of crime in all countries are, it is an easy task for a practiced mind to wring from the most guiltless person, by this process of mental torture, some contradiction or equivocation that may condemn him.

Every act of his life is raked up against him, and it is sought to prove that he committed the offence for which he is being tried, by showing that at some other time he was found guilty of something that has nothing whatever to do with it.

Worst of all, he may be tried and convicted in his absence upon a charge of which he may be utterly ignorant. The cruelty and bad policy of a system which shuts out reformation to the convict, is apparent.

Our law is more just and logical. It does not seek to find a man guilty of murder because, when he was a boy, he stole apples; but our neighbours across the Channel would gravely state that fact in the indictment. They prove previous convictions against the prisoner at the outset of his trial. We allow them to be mentioned only after it is concluded."

Our legal system has virtually nothing in common with that of the Continent. Nowhere in Europe does genuine trial by jury exist. Even in the few places where juries appear, the jury members are not free to reach their own independent verdict. They have professional judges in the room with them, inevitably influencing the verdict.

A report on *corpus juris* by the House of Lords concluded that it was open to serious objections as it demanded major changes to UK criminal law, and offered uncertain benefits. Their lordships suggested, among other things, that *corpus juris* lacked a proper legal base within the various EU treaties, questioned its feasibility, and pointed out that the European public prosecutor would not be democratically accountable. Its lack of protection of defendant's rights would not be acceptable to the UK. "In our view the scheme does not offer an acceptable way forward…and the single legal area cannot be justified in the present climate of public opinion."

The report appeared to suggest that the UK had a veto, but recognised that others in Europe believed we did not. That in itself caused concern in the Lords. Their report condemned *corpus juris* and the government said it would oppose its introduction.

Yet on pp84–5 of the report two members of the EU's parliament told the members of the Lords' sub-committee that the EU intended to introduce *corpus juris* under Article 280 of the Amsterdam Treaty – which provides for majority voting on "measures against fraud" – the official reason for introducing *corpus juris*. Under Article 280, objections by just one country, the UK, will not be enough to stop its being imposed on all the countries of the EU.

The differences between tyranny and liberty are but tiny changes in the law.

❖

At the EU meeting in Tampere, Finland, in October 1999, the UK proposed and got agreement for the "Mutual Recognition of Judicial Decisions", which permits legal decisions taken in other EU countries to be enforced in the UK without investigation. Continental judges will be allowed to order the imprisonment of British subjects in their own country, and their extradition to Europe.

We are faced with inquisitional judges acting as investigators, operating under laws that have nothing in common with British law, operating above the law itself so that they cannot be held to account for their actions in Britain, able to interrogate British subjects in Britain, and order them to be arrested by British police on British soil and deported to a foreign country to stand trial without so much as a hearing in a British court first. These are truly despotic powers, which represent a profound threat to our rights under English common law.

No evidence will be required by the UK authorities, and no appeal will be possible to a UK court. The accused could be forcibly shipped to Europe at the pleasure of the Continental judiciaries, where there is no *habeas corpus* and no British court will have any right to intervene.

This will mean that, say, under Spanish law, an investigating judge in Cadiz will be empowered to issue an arrest warrant for, say, a British fisherman living in Cornwall, and the Cornish constabulary will be obliged to arrest and transport him abroad immediately. He will have no right to any extradition hearing or any intervention by a British court at all. Once in Spain of course he will have all the "rights" afforded to prisoners by Spanish law. Spanish law will have been presumed (under the terms of the Tampere agreement) by Britain to be just as fair as our own law.

At the time of writing it is not yet clear how "mutual recognition" is to be made binding on British constabularies. Many lawyers believe that a mere document signed by the home secretary and a few other EU "ministers of the interior" will not have the necessary legal force. So will the government introduce a Bill? In that case, will British MPs actually vote for such a draconian measure? Even they might consider these proposals a step too far.

The weasel phrase "mutual recognition", like so much that emanates from the EU, disguised something quite different – in this case an attitude to law enforcement that would be childishly absurd to the British way of thinking were it not so deadly serious.

The Europeans expect us to stick to the letter of their laws. But our courts have always held themselves free to interpret the spirit of the law. We use the law to seek the truth and apply justice. We understand and use the concept of "intent" – what did the legislators intend; what are the circumstances of this particular case? Judges apply common sense. Justinian/Napoleonic law takes the letter of the law as the only basis for a judgment.

A root-and-branch review of the UK's criminal justice system, focusing particularly on the courts, was launched by Derry Irvine, the lord chancellor, and Jack Straw, home secretary, at the end of 1999.

The most contentious element of the review was likely to be an assessment of how far magistrates courts should be professionalised. This could lead to a move away from the centuries-old tradition of justice being delivered by the 30,000 lay magistrates who voluntarily deal with more than 97 per cent of all cases that appear in court.

"We live in the only country in the world where you can be sent to prison for up to a year by a neighbour with little legal training or expertise and where there is basically no chance of appeal," a Labour government spokesman told the media at the time. "It's high time we assessed whether this is really fair or efficient."

This quotation is profoundly flawed in fact and in understanding of the British constitution on almost every count. First, this is not the only country with the equivalent of magistrates dealing with petty crime. Lay magistrates are both trained and guided by professional clerks of the court. And they cannot hand down a prison sentence of more than six months on any one charge.

If a "neighbour" were on the bench, and knew the defendant personally, he or she would have to withdraw from the case. It is incorrect to talk of "a neighbour" in this context, as one lay magistrate cannot sit alone in judgment. There have to be at least three sitting on the bench for each case.

Lack of legal training is not synonymous with a lack of understanding about justice. On that premise, it is possible to argue that only lawyers should be allowed to vote at elections. If it were only experts who had power, whose interests would they serve? This attack on lay magistrates is basically an attack on democracy, as is the attack on trial by jury. In any case, any defendant can appeal against the magistrates' sentence – and this right of appeal will take him or her, if necessary, all the way to the House of Lords.

Towards the end of 2000 the Home Office revealed that many hundreds of lay magistrates had resigned from the bench. They were unable to accept the added burdens imposed by the new Human Rights Act, much of which conflicts directly with long-standing common law, nor the prospect of the EU's *corpus juris* and its new Charter of Fundamental Human Rights and the potential for irreconcilable friction between the components of future British criminal law.

❖

That brings us to the question: who polices the police?

Early English common law found the answer, and it works – "The Rule of Law", applied equally to all. Under common law, all persons are equal before the law, and all persons are accountable under the law.

A simple, elegant, shrewd idea. Perhaps not perfect, but it expressed the supreme wisdom of holding even those in the highest offices in the land at the mercy of the law, just like everyone else.

No one in Britain is above the law, and that includes the prime minister and lord chancellor. No policeman is above the law. No soldier is above the law. It is the law that no one is above it.

Except, in future it seems, the EU's police. Article 8 of the Treaty of Amsterdam says members of Europol are "immune from legal process of any kind for acts performed...in the exercise of their official functions". The exact words! So even if they falsely imprison someone, knowingly or without a shred of evidence, or smash property during a search, they will be beyond the reach of the law. They will answer only to the European public prosecutor.

It is precisely this ultimate and crucial sanction – the application of the rule of law to all persons – that our present government is willing to discard, acting on instructions from Brussels. Their view is akin to that recorded in *The Incredible Bread Machine*:

"The Rule of Law, though clear enough
Has proved itself deficient.

We much prefer the Rule of Men;
It's vastly more efficient."

The EU's plans for law enforcement are chilling. Already they have set up Europol, which is a police force operating throughout Europe as if no borders existed. It is to be developed as the enforcement agency for *corpus juris*. The police will be armed, they will be able to go anywhere in the EU, including Britain, with legal authority. They will have total diplomatic immunity other than for traffic offences, and they will be free to enforce their own Continental law on us.

These plans to create a single police force covering all member states are well advanced. More than 350 Europol offices already occupy a building in the Hague, once the home of the Nazi Gestapo. Eventually there will be 5,000 of them.

According to the author Lindsay Jenkins, these EU police are already issuing instructions to UK policemen. Officially, Europol is required to fight crime, racism and xenophobia. As racism and xenophobia are incapable of precise definition – because they are attitudes of mind – this attempt to extend policing into the realms of mind-control is deeply worrying. It bites deep at the essential freedoms of speech and the expression of opinion. In the UK, it is unquestionably illegal. We have an unassailable right to free speech.

This has not stopped Europol setting up files on people who might – one day – become suspects. The British police and other official sources have already been asked for information about British subjects for the files of Europol. The fact that these individuals may have committed no crime, and Europol has no jurisdiction here at present, is being ignored.

Europol officers' full diplomatic immunity was granted by statutory instrument in 1997. Despite the blatant breach of the British constitution, this matter was never debated in the House of Commons, and three years later had still not been raised. Yet this is the first time in history anyone other than foreign diplomats (who are not normally armed and have no legal authority) have been given such privileges. Even more dangerously, the government has removed the fundamental safeguard of accountability that applies to all British subjects.

Europol's state-of-the-art computer analysis system, which collects data from all EU member states, uses that data for European-wide analyses. But British police have no access to those analyses. The information is available only to Europol, which now has the right to ask the British police to carry out investigations into British nationals in Britain as Europol builds up its database on criminals, suspects, witnesses and other sources of information.

Lindsay Jenkins has made a special study of Europol's methods, and established that the organisation's database includes at least 56 fields of data on each individual, including racial origins, nationality, religion and known political affiliations. It is still far from clear why such personal details are deemed necessary, though the implications and potential use of such data are blisteringly obvious. Nor is it clear whether the British police can refuse Europol orders to collect and supply such information.

As Lindsay Jenkins commented: "We are only one step away from a police state." Europol is likely to be the first experience many people have of the new powers of the EU, with a midnight knock on the door from a politicised police force working to Brussels' orders. They will then encounter the unpleasant realities of *corpus juris*.

Of course in most Continental European countries that is the way things are – and have been for centuries. The problem is that, once again, a fundamentally different British way of doing things is being forced to change to the Continental system. Once again, we lose out. Once again, the price of membership of this club is proving far too high. And once again, the bureaucrats of the EU know that they must fudge the issues in Great Britain so that the people of these islands don't know the truth until it's too late.

Just consider the differences in the enforcement of law and order, and in the administration of justice. In Britain it is the police themselves who take the initiative to investigate a crime. They then arrest a suspect – off their own bat if it's urgent. Otherwise they obtain a warrant from a magistrate – a member of a body that is detached from the police and that exercises a controlling and restraining influence on them (one of our system's famed checks and balances).

On the Continent – and in the planned *corpus juris* system – it is a member of the investigating/prosecuting career judiciary (under *corpus juris* it will be the "European Public Prosecutor") who initiates investigations, and then arrests a suspect after obtaining the agreement of a colleague who is a fellow-member of the career judiciary, and part of the same professional brotherhood as they. In Italy this colleague of the investigator is called "Judge of the Preliminary Investigations". Under *corpus juris* that person will be called "Judge of Freedoms" – a bitter irony mentioned earlier.

Once the machinery of a supranational court is set up and the principle of its supranational jurisdiction has been firmly established, how sure can we be that one day it will not be taken over and used as a vehicle to impose different, or opposite value systems to those originally intended?

Iran's fatwa death sentence against Salman Rushdie was a clear attempt to assert trans-national jurisdiction and impose illiberal principles.

How do we make it impossible for the ECJ or the recently proposed international criminal court to be taken over by madmen or tyrants? If "religious freedom" is already recognised as a basic "human right", then for religious fanatics of whatever persuasion – and the world is full of them – this can extend quite easily to a "right not to have one's basic religious sensitivities offended". From there to the crime of blasphemy is a very short step. And for some religions blasphemy is and can be only a capital offence – and you may well offend their religious sensitivities if you try to say otherwise.

National sovereignty does not give us a perfect world. But it makes possible having and holding enclaves of sanity in a world still full of extremists and violent fanatics. Abolishing the safeguards of national sovereignty makes it easier for the mad and the bad to impose their will across borders.

The more powerful the instruments of control, whether legal or military, the greater the need for vigilance.

That leads us to a curious fact. The UK has the only unarmed police force in the EU. Nonetheless, in 1998 a high-priority order was placed by the Home Office on behalf of the police force for 30,000 sub-machine guns, over 100,000 rounds of ammunition, 8 sniper rifles, and 12,000 12-bore riot-control shotguns. They were all delivered to the army camp at Catterick, Yorkshire.

As a result of the tragedy at Dunblane, and successive moves by various governments over the last few decades, hardly a gun still exists in the hands of people who enjoyed shooting for pleasure or sport. Today, in the UK, there are more guns held illegally than ever, almost entirely in the criminal fraternity. Buying one on the black market is easier than ever. But they are almost entirely in the hands of the irresponsible.

Meanwhile, the honest, the enthusiastic and the knowledgeable have been deprived of their weapons as the police have become more heavily armed than ever. Why? The question has to be asked: is this overwhelming imbalance in favour of state control part of a bigger plan to prevent insurrection at some later date?

❖

Becoming part of the EU's economic and monetary union means abandoning the pound sterling and joining the euro. It is not, and cannot be, a purely economic question, as Tony Blair and others would have us believe. It is a constitutional issue of the most fundamental kind.

"I have never understood why public opinion about European ideas should be taken into account" – Raymond Barre, former French prime minister.

"Give me control of a nation's currency and I care not who makes the laws" – Mayer Rothschild.

"'The single currency is the greatest abandonment of sovereignty since the foundation of the European Community.... It is a decision of an essentially political nature. We need this United Europe...we must never forget that the euro is an instrument for this project" – Filipe Gonzales, former Spanish prime minister, May 1998.

"Monetary union is a path of no return. No subsequent revision or withdrawal of any kind is either legally or politically provided for" – Hans Tietmeyer, then president of the Bundesbank.

"The process of monetary union goes hand in hand, must go hand in hand, with political integration and ultimately political union. EMU [Economic Monetary Union] is, and always was meant to be, a stepping stone on the way to a united Europe" – Wim Duisenberg, president, ECB.

"The euro is a conquest of sovereignty. It gives us a margin of manoeuvre. It's a tool to help us master globalisation and help us resist irrational shifts in the market" – Dominique Strauss-Kahn, French finance minister, January 1999.

"The euro raises no constitutional issues at all" – Geoff Hoon, Blairite defence secretary, Radio 4, October 1999.

"[Scrapping the pound] is fundamentally a political rather than an economic issue. It would involve ceding control over important aspects of public policy" – Eddie George, governor of the Bank of England, April 2000.

The Europeans and the realists know the truth. Those who seek to drag a protesting British people into the euro still use deceit and stealth. They know the truth will destroy them.

There are good reasons to believe that the government's plans to take the UK into the euro are illegal. Our constitution clearly states that we, the people, have an absolute right to enjoy our freedoms and customs – one of which is the pound sterling. An attack upon our freedom to print and mint our own currency is an attack upon our country, its independence and sovereignty. No government has the power to limit or remove these freedoms and customs. Common law says they can be "improved" only – in the sense of strengthened.

Those who advocate a referendum forget that our freedoms belong not to the government or parliament, nor even to the passing parade of electors who put them temporarily in power. They belong to the generations still to come, who – like us – will hold them in trust for those who follow. That is the great strength of the British constitution, and we forget it at our peril.

These rights, liberties and customs are most certainly not in the gift of a few politicians. They do not own them. They cannot be given away.

So the government is acting unconstitutionally on five counts – it has no mandate, it has a duty of care not to waste public funds, it is attempting to exceed its powers, the ministers concerned have broken their oaths of allegiance to the Crown that specifically exclude such actions, and – above all – they are seeking to overthrow our freedoms and customs...the constitution itself.

The British people have not given permission for the pound sterling to be replaced by the euro. Even if they were asked, the answer would be a resounding "No".

A series of polls has conclusively demonstrated that the British do not want the euro. Three-quarters of businesses oppose the euro. Two-thirds of trade union members oppose the euro. Over two-thirds of the general public oppose the euro. The public believes that business does not want the euro.

None of that has diverted the present government from its long-promised referendum on joining the euro. In spring 2000 it announced plans to spend some £3.5 billion of taxpayers' money to fund the changeover from sterling to the euro in the public sector.

The ultimate cost of converting the whole country to the euro has been estimated at £36 billion – or 4.2 per cent of our GDP. That is roughly equal to £650 for every man, woman and child in the UK. It is also roughly equal to the annual running costs of the NHS, double the amount spent on education and employment together, one and a half times the defence budget, double the value of agricultural production from our farms, and double the sum spent by British industry on research and development. And all for a change few outside government want.

The EC has warned that Britain's long-term membership of the EU could be in question if it remains outside the single currency. Pedro Solbes was quoted in the British media as saying that "part-time membership of the EU is not good enough. In the longer term it's not possible to be in the EU and outside EMU".

Britain and Denmark ratified the Maastricht Treaty on the basis that they had a permanent legally guaranteed opt-out on the single currency. Bernard Connolly, a former EU official who wrote a damning book on the EU in general and the euro in particular, commented: "Mr. Solbes is basically saying that the Danish opt-out isn't real. He is suggesting that the treaty can be overridden in the general interest of the Community, and if it can be done with Denmark, it can be done with Britain."

Of course one of the most alarming aspects of the UK's joining the euro is the immediate seizure of our gold and currency assets by the ECB.

The Maastricht Treaty lays title claim to the UK's $48 billion-worth of gold and dollar reserves. The transfer to Brussels has already started by slyness – the EU's normal technique when it knows a proposal or directive does not have popular support. The chancellor, Gordon Brown, started selling the UK's gold and buying euros with the proceeds in 1999, years before any such handover became obligatory. He lied when he claimed it was a purely commercial decision. It was intended to show support for the euro, and it started to meet our treaty obligation to transfer our national assets to the ECB if the UK were ever to join the euro. It also assumed that the result of the promised referendum would be in the government's favour and completely ignored the known views of the public. It is highly unlikely that the Labour government would have won the 1997 election at all, let alone in a landslide, if they had said that they intended to sell a significant proportion of the UK's gold reserves – whatever the reason.

Gordon Brown is actually trying to drag Britain into the euro by deceit. He sold 415 tons of gold bars (at about $290 per ounce, or £4 billion-worth). This is more than half the UK's total holdings of gold. There are now 300 tons remaining of the original stock. Gold reserves now represent a mere 7 per cent of total reserves, instead of the previous 17. The cash used to buy the euro propped it up for a while, failed to stop the slide, but effectively met the demand that all the UK's gold and dollar reserves be passed to Frankfurt. And all without anyone being asked, agreeing or voicing a view. By mid-2000, the chancellor was sitting on a loss of some £26 million.

This procedure has neatly avoided the need to make physical transfers of gold to Frankfurt, as required under the Maastricht Treaty. The potential flashpoint that would have started a revolution has been smartly sidestepped.

Even our politicians wouldn't be so stupid as to load up a fleet of Brinks-Mat vans and drive them to Dover. Even they realise that would bring people onto the streets, blockading motorways, storming the dockside or the shuttle. Such a blatant transfer of our assets would have triggered rebellion and anarchy.

It was much easier to sell the gold here, buy the euros, and let the ECB buy gold at their end. Alternatively, sending a letter signed by the chancellor and the governor of the Bank of England, transferring ownership, but keeping the physical gold in London, would have achieved much the same result.

All much easier, much less controversial, and perhaps no one would notice. That's the insidious nature of the EU. Consider the response to one letter of enquiry to the Foreign Office's "EU department" in May 1999. It said: "If the UK joined the single currency, it would be necessary under the EU Treaty to transfer part of our foreign exchange reserves to the ECB. We would receive an equivalent claim on the ECB. This would amount to an exchange of assets, not their surrender." More weasel words, which beg numerous questions.

If that is the case, then why do it? How do we recover our assets when we leave later? If the spurious "assets" we have apparently acquired – essentially printed paper – fall in value, can we sue for restitution and damages? As it will hold title to the UK's assets, will the ECB subsequently be able to dispose of them without our permission?

And the most important questions of them all: By what right does the EU claim our national assets? And by what right does the UK government claim to be able to dispose of them?

But having got their hands on our assets, what will we ever know about the decisions the ECB takes over their use and disposal? The pro-EU *Financial Times* said: "The ECB intends to make decisions in secret, using forecasts it will not reveal, to achieve objectives it does not need to justify."

Its own chief economist, Otmar Issing, said of the ECB: "Making individual members' voting behaviour public would encourage undesirable scrutiny of members' voting patterns. This, in turn, would encourage external pressures on the Council members, arising from local interests."

So, as usual, no accountability. Are we surprised? Our gold and currency assets will simply disappear into a black hole and be gone forever.

Ambitions and greed in Brussels and Frankfurt know no limits. They may want control of our gold and other reserves, but they also want our oil as a common resource. And here's another curiosity about the sale of our assets and their movement to the EU. Our constant trade deficit with the EU is about £2.5 billion every month. We sell them 40 per cent of our gas, crude and finished products. Crude rose 200 per cent after mid-1999, although it later fell back. Yet we were still running a monthly trade deficit. It did not add up, unless the UK government was accepting euros instead of US dollars in payment.

North Sea oil sells at a premium, it has a low sulphur content, doesn't require expensive desalination, and could be sold anywhere. So why do we export so much to Europe? Is there a treaty obligation – have the Continentals got their sticky fingers on this asset without the rest of us knowing? Or, put another way, how can they ever hope to have a stable euro when the Continental EU countries are 11,000,000 barrels a day oil-negative in a commodity priced in a hard currency?

The UK's oil reserves are estimated to be worth over $400 billion, and that's before any future discoveries. Yet the Maastricht Treaty, Preamble 8, Title 2, describes our oil as a "shared resource".

This is the law of contract gone mad. Contracts are normally agreements to exchange assets or benefits. Usually, money from one party is exchanged for goods or services from the other. But on this occasion, just signing a piece of paper magically converted a national asset of the UK into someone else's property, without any counter-balancing transfer of benefits to us. We did not sell this asset – we simply gave it away, just as our fish were given away by the Heath government in 1972.

But there is more, and it gets worse. In October 1997 Jacques Delors claimed that the EU would share all the assets of member states – and all the liabilities! So, take our fish, our gold and our oil...and then saddle the UK with part of the EU pension debt of over £1,200 billion (yes, billion!). But we will deal with that later.

❖

The Amsterdam Treaty, which claimed to give the EU and the ECJ precedence over national law and the constitutions of member states, also included a "Subsidiarity Protocol". This refers to the "principles developed by the ECJ". But courts of law exist to interpret and administer the law – not to make it. Except, apparently, in the EU. In this case, the phrase reflects what actually happens.

During the 1960s and 1970s the ECJ gave a series of highly questionable judgments that sought to establish the supremacy of European law over national law. Such power was never agreed or laid down in any of the original treaties. Nor was it made law until the 1997 Treaty of Amsterdam. Previously, the judges had literally taken the law into their own hands, inventing it as they went along. The Amsterdam Treaty of 1997 for the first time authorised such methods of law-making, and gave European law status over national laws. It also, retrospectively, authorised law made by the ECJ over the previous 20 or so years.

It is all the more surprising that such fundamental and retrospective authorisation should appear under a "subsidiarity" clause, because a year earlier nobody knew what the word actually meant. As we have seen, many words used by the EU and its institutions mean what officials want them to mean. EU bureaucrats, Europol and the ECJ can interpret them in any way they wish. Even in the UK we have already seen such laws being used to prevent free speech. During the European elections of June 1999, George Staunton, a 78-year-old Liverpool pensioner, was arrested and hauled before a magistrates court charged with causing "racially aggravated criminal damage". He had fly-posted a UKIP poster and written on it "Free speech for England" and "Don't forget the 1945 war". The charge he faced carried a maximum sentence of 14 years' imprisonment. After a deluge of protest and a sudden bout of common sense by the police and judiciary, he was "let off" with a police caution.

His case was clear evidence of a serious erosion of our fundamental rights as free people. Instead, we now have the beginnings of the "thought police", long forecast by George Orwell in his book *1984* (only Orwell's timing was wrong). Mr Staunton made two statements that anyone can make. Provocative perhaps, but he had an absolute right to make them. English common law says so. Whether we might agree with them or deplore them is irrelevant. What matters is his right to speak out without fear of arrest.

Sadly, the day is coming when these issues will need to be tested in court. There is now a serious need to re-establish the common-law rights of the people of Britain in the minds of the judiciary and the police, especially since the EU is already planning to introduce criminal offences for what it calls "xenophobia" and "racism". These will be offences that allow arrest for expressing opinions. Then, it will be entirely possible for the EU to ban public meetings, letters to newspapers, books and magazine articles opposed to the EU. It is entirely within the bounds of EU logic that, eventually, "racism" will be used to ban the flying of the Union Flag in the UK and national flags throughout the EU.

Yet Britain was the first country in the world to enshrine the concept of freedom of expression in its constitution. Britain is the home of free speech. Unless opposed now, this trend will soon reach the point where it will become a criminal offence even to speak of opposition to the EU. Books like the one you're currently reading will be prohibited.

How ironic, then, that this same pseudo-government of Europe introduced in the Amsterdam Treaty the idea that member states who transgress human rights will be liable to lose their voting rights, while still retaining all the other obligations of membership. There was no mention of the EU's own transgressions of human rights. Nor did its apparent concerns for human rights prevent it from inventing these new crimes of racism and xenophobia, despite their obvious conflict with the human right to free speech. No wonder the EU cannot define them in the context of criminal activity.

It is plain to lawyers and others who have attempted to explain to Europeans the concepts of freedom enshrined in the British constitution that almost nobody in Europe has any idea about the differences between the Anglo-Saxon and Continental systems of justice. Nor do they appear to understand the damage that the proposed introduction of *corpus juris* will have on the British system. Most Europeans simply assume our system is like their system. The enormity of the change proposed is lost on them.

The French have a system of law devised by Napoleon, based on Justinian principles, and intended to counter Jesuit domination in France 200 years ago. France is run by career bureaucrats who have little experience of the outside world. Young students complete the equivalent of a university course in national administration, called the ENA, after which they go directly into the service of the state for a minimum of ten years. Being so highly trained, many have now worked their way up to the highest levels of bureaucracy in the EU. Most of the various EU treaties were the work of such people, who have little time for the input of mere elected politicians with no training. The very idea that such career bureaucrats might care about the sensitivities of the British is bordering on the comic.

Equally bizarre is the structure of judicial systems elsewhere in Europe. For example, Turkish criminal law is an exact copy of Italian criminal law as drafted by Mussolini in the 1930s, in turn based on France's Napoleonic code. In the EU, and even among prospective members, the systems of justice are similar. The odd one out is the Anglo-Saxon model.

Our strong sense of being an independent nation is also unmatched in

Continental Europe. Perhaps it stems from our living on a small group of islands. Europeans are much more relaxed about federalism. In the main, they are glad to see the borders go.

Germany is the extreme example. Germany was never a state. It has always been more of a grouping of peoples with shared culture, language and ethnic origins. It used war, and now economics, to establish its borders. The hard-core euro-zone (Germany, France, Benelux, Austria) gives Germany the power to control the economics of Europe while remaining free of constraints that don't suit it. The driving-force is economic, not political. Yet the UK (and France, as it happens) are nations first and economic areas second.

Germany already consists of 16 provincial governments under the supposed control of the federal government. However, the federal government cannot act in certain circumstances without unanimity from the provinces. And here the EU's relationship with Germany becomes significant. If the German provinces don't give their consent to a measure introduced by the EU, the EU itself could take legal action against only the federal government of Germany. The provincial governments didn't sign any treaties with the EU. The federal government can put pressure on the provincial governments only to cooperate. One day, perhaps over the weak euro, this omission of a formal relationship between the provincial governments of Germany and the EU may become a serious problem for the bureaucrats.

Europhiles sometimes point to the USA as a shining example of successful federalism. Leaving aside the loathing for the USA among many Continental Europeans, they conveniently forget that the USA has a number of ingredients crucial to successful federalism that are spectacularly absent in Europe. Europe does not have a common language, nor a common economic structure, nor – genuinely – a common currency. It does not have free movement of labour, nor a common lifestyle. The EU superstate offers none of these things. Neither does a federation of states like the USA deprive its citizens of a vote that directly influences legislative decisions at all levels of government.

Language, lifestyle, electoral accountability and the free movement of labour, are all positively discriminated against by the EU. As for the other key components of a successful federal structure, the EU has no prospect whatsoever of achieving them in the foreseeable future. Even its ill-conceived and over-hyped euro has become an embarrassment.

Federal states like the USA, Canada and Australia delegate as much to the individual states as possible – at least in theory. The federal government in these countries essentially deals with the big issues – defence, international relations, monetary policy, shipping, the law, and the like. The EU works in reverse. The more trivial the issue, the more they interfere and try to standardise. The bigger the issue, the less influence the EU has, although the bureaucrats are now trying to change that too.

Pan-European idealism is a heady drink and a dangerous one. The Organisation for Security and Cooperation in Europe (OSCE) grew out of the Helsinki conference of 1975. On the face of it, this might have been regarded as a worthy cause.

But...instead of being a defensive alliance concerned with upholding human rights, its more recent pronouncements show that it aspires to achieve a powerful level of pan-European control. Its chairman has said: "Comprehensive security means more than mere military security." In attempting to interfere and legislate on human rights – for workers, minorities and women – it is becoming a trans-continental military police force.

The Russians are members – and used the OSCE protocols to justify the invasion of Chechnya. As one (French) writer put it: "Russia is able to use the OSCE to flout the principle of self-determination with utter impunity."

Even though Russia is not part of the EU, it has a judge appointed to the European Court of Human Rights in Strasbourg. This gives its parliamentary delegates and judges the right to determine policies of the Council of Europe and to influence the rulings of the court. But Russia has categorically stated that it will not abide by any such rulings affecting Russia, all of which it will regard as interference in its internal affairs.

Of course Russia itself is a basket case. Its continuing "administration" of pre-1989 USSR satellite states – Ukraine, Byelorussia, Azerbaijan, Georgia, and others – by Moscow's puppet regimes is blatant. Even the same men are involved – Shevardnadze in Georgia, for example – and they show all the same signs of exchanging newly won liberty, statehood and democratic free choice for central planning by a single-party state.

Under communism, the government of the people ultimately became the administration of things — a world in which the independence, objectivity, rigour and clarity of the law was replaced by bureaucratic convenience. Is it any wonder, then, that Jacques Delors was horrified at the breakdown of the USSR. He saw it as the newly freed states of eastern Europe going in the opposite direction to the EU. Likewise he saw the abandonment of the rouble clearing system as going in the opposite direction when he was trying to invent and launch the euro.

Such centralist bureaucracy is everywhere in the EU. It wants to limit or stop the Channel Islands and the Isle of Man from lawfully trading with the rest of the world and providing banking and financial services. It seeks to stop the use of these independent sovereign states for offshore banking.

Under the chairmanship of Labour minister Dawn Primarolo, who is not exactly noted for her experience of trade, industry or wealth-creation, EU ministers and officials have been meeting in Brussels to consider ways of "harmonising" tax. They also want to do away with what they call "harmful tax competition". Harmful to whom? They do not say. We can assume only they were referring to those member states already over-taxed.

At the time of writing, some 187 measures were under consideration, 7 directly concerned with Guernsey tax legislation, and 4 with Jersey. If such plans are adopted in due course, they could be the last straw for both islands, who will then almost certainly declare full independence. And who could blame them? The EU — and the UK — has no right to interfere with their internal affairs or their international trade, especially as none of these islands has ever signed the Treaty of Rome.

Meanwhile, travellers to the Channel Islands from Gatwick now go through a new departure routine, which means they pass a video camera and a bar code is added to their tickets. The Home Office says a new system is on trial — but what system, for what purpose and why? Will the EU eventually have closed borders? Will no one be allowed to leave without permission, let alone take their own assets with them? Are we watching the laying of the first bricks in a new iron curtain?

❖

The totality of these attitudes can be summed up in a single word — contempt. The bureaucrats who run the EU have nothing but contempt for the people they claim to govern. It is an attitude with a history that goes back at least half a century.

"Liberalism denied the state in the name of the individual; fascism reasserts the rights of the state as expressing the real essence of the individual." – *Fascism: Doctrine and Institutions*, by the Italian dictator, Benito Mussolini.

Joachim Fest said in his book *The Face of the Third Reich*:

> "Hitler's path to absolute power...remains...the classic model for the totalitarian capture of democratic institutions.
>
> Linking the processes of the revolutionary assault with legal actions that a screen of legality, dubious in individual cases and yet convincing as a whole, hid the illegality of the system from view. The concealed manner of the conquest of power, which took place behind the facade of the old institutions deliberately preserved for that purpose, was the crucial feature. It was part of the plan that certain areas of public life were provisionally spared. Islands on which the rule of law prevailed were left amid an ocean of lawlessness [that made it] harder to assess the legality or illegality of the regime.
>
> Each step was a consequence of the one before, and created the factual, technical or legal pre-conditions for the next."

Hitler defined politics as being "the attainment of a goal by all conceivable means; persuasion, cunning, astuteness, persistence, kindness, slyness, but also brutality".

Peter Thorneycroft, then a Tory MP and later chancellor of the exchequer, wrote a book with others just after the Second World War. It was entitled *Design for Freedom*. The authors applauded the "good" Hitler had done by preserving Europe as one economic unit. They praised central socialist economic planning such as the Monet plan in France and they wanted to abolish tariffs. From Tories of the time, this was perhaps surprising but understandable.

But then they went on: "No government dependent upon a democratic vote could possibly agree in advance to the sacrifices which any adequate plan would involve. The people must be led slowly and unconsciously into the abandonment of their traditional economic defences, not asked in advance of having received any of the benefits which will accrue to them from the plan to make changes of which they may not recognise the advantages to themselves." An astounding statement to make, and exactly what has followed in the development of the EU.

In May 1994, Claude Cheysson, former French foreign minister, told *Le Figaro* that the Europe of Maastricht could not have been constructed without bypassing democracy. He went on to complain that the (then) problems that had arisen in France were caused by a democratic debate that had been "allowed" during the run-up to a referendum.

In truth, European institutions are not intended to be democratic. They are intended to make decision-making easy. Executive and technical power has replaced legislative power.

The whole edifice was built back-to-front. It started with coal and steel, then agriculture, atomic power, the Common Market, and now economic planning, taxation and centralised bureaucratic government. By using a series of technical institutions as building blocks a federal state has been created.

Had the proposition been clear at the start, had the politicians been honest, had the whole structure been shown and established in reverse...it would never have been acceptable. Hence the stealth...the piecemeal process.

The treaties which created the EU – those of Rome, Maastricht, Amsterdam – are like the Bible. There is always a clause or a form of words that means what you want it to mean. So even if you think you have signed up to one thing, in time your opponents will find a clause somewhere else that proves the opposite.

A typical example was the decision to force the social chapter on the UK after John Major's government had negotiated an opt-out. The 48-hour week was subsequently introduced as a health-and-safety measure because health and safety was subject only to majority voting. Thus the British veto could be neatly sidestepped. In any case, the Amsterdam Treaty included a catch-all clause that enables the EU to do and impose almost anything without further consultations or agreements with member states.

Discovering the truth about the meaning of words in EU treaties is particularly difficult. There is no equivalent of prime minister's questions at which MPs can raise, for example, the apparent curious contradictions in the Amsterdam Treaty. Article 6 deals with fundamental human rights. But, as so often with the EU, what is given with one hand is more than taken away immediately by the other.

Of course, we have a small problem with this particular treaty because no official English translation has ever been published, presumably so that EU bureaucrats can claim that we have the wrong meaning when it suits them.

The first four clauses of this article read:

1 The Union is founded on the principles of liberty, democracy, respect for human rights and fundamental freedoms, and the rule of law, principles which are common to the Member States.

2 The Union shall respect fundamental rights, as guaranteed by the European Convention for the Protection of Human Rights and Fundamental Freedoms signed in Rome on 4th November 1950 and as they result from the constitutional traditions common to the Member States, as general principles of Community law.

3 The Union shall respect the national identities of its Member States.

4 The Union shall provide itself with the means necessary to attain its objectives and carry through its policies.

So there it is. Clause 4 removes all the apparent safeguards previously offered. It is a straight contradiction of Clauses 1 to 3. And under pressure, can there be any doubt which of the four clauses would prevail to preserve the EU's power? The same device was used again later, when the EU's so-called Charter of Fundamental Human Rights was unveiled. The last clause allows all the others to be overturned or ignored if the EU thinks itself threatened – thus rendering the whole thing worthless.

Articles 2 and 3 of the Amsterdam Treaty make it clear that a single country is the ultimate destination of the EU. Article 7 says our vetoes – and even qualified majority voting – may be suspended at any time by the European parliament and the Council of Ministers acting together. So much for even the fig leaf of democracy. Articles 98 and 99 lay the groundwork for forcing us into the euro whether we like it or not, and as we have seen the Nice Treaty produced the enabling powers. And if we were ever to join the euro, we would quickly become again a region of Europe – just as we were in Roman times.

The EU already treats countries simply as regions. In fact, even now, the UK is being carved up into 12 regions by the Blair government to meet the demands of Brussels. Of course he never says so – he dare not admit it. The regional assemblies for Northern Ireland, Wales, Scotland and London exist already. The other regions of England are now in the pipeline, and the regional assemblies exist in embryo. On top of them, an unelected Committee of the Regions will ensure that EU law is enforced at local level.

The regional assemblies openly claim that they represent the first step towards regional government in the UK. Almost all of them, particularly in England, cover areas so large that they do not naturally form economic or social areas that would instantly recognise themselves. What, for example, has Kent got in common with the north of Oxfordshire? But they are both part of the EU's idea of the Southeast of England. Eventually, these regional authorities will compete with each other in Brussels, begging bowls held aloft, asking for their share of the UK taxpayers' money that EU officials choose to allocate back to us – just as our County Councils do already.

Each of these regions came to life briefly for ordinary people during the European elections of 1999, when they returned between 4 and 11 MEPs each. But the way the elections were organised in the UK, and the electoral system used, was an insult to democracy and to the people. Blair claimed that the use of party-list voting aligned the UK with European systems, but that was not true. At least one of the EU treaties refers to constituency voting.

Despite that, the European elections held in June 1999 used the closed-list system of proportional representation for the first time in the UK. So the party bosses decided who went to the European parliament, not the people. And the MEPs now answer to those party bosses if they wish to be at the top of the list next time.

Thus the fundamental accountability of the elected to the electors was irreparably broken. Members were insulated from local issues or responsibilities. They become one among several supposedly representing a region – so every issue that arises is always going to be someone else's problem, or belong in someone else's bailiwick.

Curiously, the explanatory leaflet about the new voting system showed no anti-European parties on the list, and presupposed that everybody wanted to vote for a party that favoured staying in the EU. That was an error of judgment that confused voters and angered countless electors.

The Labour Party manifesto for those euro-elections had "Made in Europe" stamped on it. Among its 21 pledges, it referred to a "co-ordinated economic policy" – not "policies" – across Europe. And it claimed that the euro would "provide growth, jobs, and stability". One was revealing, the other a demonstrable lie.

All three major political parties were pro-EU – so there was actually no choice on the great question of the EU itself, except by voting for UKIP. Even euro-realist Tories had pro-EU candidates at the top of their lists, thus minimising the number of sceptics elected. A few managed it, and UKIP had three MEPs elected. But by-elections were abolished, and vacancies theoretically were to be filled by previous losers. However, when the UKIP leader resigned from the party he chose to retain his seat and no effective means of replacing him with the next candidate on that party's list could be found in the inadequate legislation that had set up such an electoral system in the first place.

So the UK has 87 MEPs out of 626 in the European parliament. They are in a permanent and tiny minority. Before the June 1999 elections, not one of the UK's MEPs represented the majority view in the UK over the euro or the EU itself. Now, at least, there are three.

Of course, genuine democracy is about the people controlling the levers of power. The EU denies that. The real power lies with the commissioners, who are nominated by governments, not elected by the people. Remove the government at the next election – and the commission remains!

❖

Magna Carta began the process of formalising English common law, but it was based on custom and practice that went back into the mists of recorded history. Even by the time of King Alfred, what we now know as common law was well established. There are many recorded instances of Saxon trials in Mercia that used the concept of trial by jury, for example. And early in the 12th century, Henry I introduced jury trials to replace the primitive ordeals that were plainly irrational to any reasonable person.

So the barons who wrote Magna Carta did not invent common law. Their two great achievements were to have common law recognised formally as the law of the land, and they established that nobody, including the sovereign, is above the law.

The law consists of common law, statute law (primary legislation) and regulations authorised by statute (secondary legislation). The word "common" conveniently identifies two principles as one – what has been the common custom has become the law, and the law applies in common to all.

This is in complete contrast to the Continental system, where rights derive from the permission of the state, and can be taken away by the state. The state may therefore dispose of the lives and property of its citizens as the ruling clique chooses.

When the French riot police clear a rioting crowd of students or football hooligans they are immune from individual responsibility for their actions. In contrast, the British police are a civil force, not a military force. They are under the control of locally elected authorities. They are servants of the local community, not servants of the state under military discipline. Constables are accountable under the law as individuals.

The British constitution is a written constitution, contrary to popular belief. Those in government who suggest otherwise seek to muddy the waters and claim that they can – more or less – do what they like. Our constitution is quite clear on all the fundamentals and not half as obscure as is sometimes suggested.

It gives each one of us as individuals simple, clear, specific and unambiguous rights, and some responsibilities. These rights, liberties and freedoms are peculiarly Anglo-Saxon and are not found in most other countries – certainly not in Europe.

Despite their responsibility to uphold the law, over the years the judiciary has allowed common law to be set aside. The judges have given up legislative supremacy to parliament. And they have done this because no one has gone before a court and claimed his or her common law rights. Those rights of the subject are written down in Magna Carta and in the Declaration and Bill of Rights. Magna Carta and the Declaration of Rights are constitutional treaties (some prefer the descriptions "covenants" or "contracts") made directly between the monarch and the people. They are the cornerstones of the British constitution. Over the years they have become covered in dust and forgotten. But they are still there, and apply "in all time to come".

They are the last line of defence against the present greatest danger to us all. If government believes that it can do as it wishes without the restraint of a constitution that is enforceable through the courts, then no one and nothing is safe from the whims and prejudices of the legislators.

Lord Mackay of Clashfern told David Bourne, one of the signatories to the Magna Carta Society's pamphlet *Defence of the Realm*, that parliament can "completely do away with a common law principle". This statement is untrue, and can readily be proven wrong. The full horror and enormity of such a fundamental error lies in its source. That a senior law officer could make such a statement at all beggars belief. It is a truly dreadful indictment of the highest levels of government and the judiciary.

Lord Mackay also told Mr Bourne that parliament could do as it wishes, "subject to its obligations [to the EU]". This itself implies a transfer of sovereignty. But again he is wrong. UK sovereignty is absolute, and no parliament can bind its successors.

John Locke, the philosopher, was a major influence on the generation that debated what became the English Declaration of Rights in 1688. When attempting to protect the rights and liberties of the people, they devised the phrase "in all time to come". They understood the underlying issues much more readily and a great deal better than we do today.

John Locke wrote:

> "Man is a maker of things, and a property owning animal.... .
> From the right to self-defence and protection of property comes
> the right to the rule of law, and a multitude of like rights, such as
> the right to privacy expressed as 'An Englishman's home is his
> castle'. A ruler is legitimate only in so far as he upholds the law.
> A ruler that violates the law is illegitimate. He has no right to be

obeyed; his commands are mere force and coercion. Rulers who act lawlessly, whose laws are unlawful, are mere criminals.

The right of self-defence is the first law of nature; in most governments it has been the study of rulers to confine this right within the narrowest limits possible. Wherever standing armies are kept up, and when the right of the people to keep and bear arms is, under any colour or pretext whatsoever, prohibited, liberty, if not already annihilated, is on the brink of destruction."

The Declaration of Rights is not an Act of Parliament, but a declaration of the common law. It is not statute law. Therefore it cannot be repealed. It is a job specification for Crown servants, MPs and the judiciary, and forms the basis of the contract between them and the Crown. They swear allegiance to a sovereign whose ancestors were appointed on condition that they would respect the rights and liberties of the subject, including the right to arms. Each sovereign, including the present one, has sworn to rule "according to our laws" in all time to come. Those laws include the common law.

Crown servants cannot subvert the subject's common law rights because they have only the same powers and privileges as the people. Any attempt to do so would be beyond their power and constitutes the common law crime of "misconduct in office". Parliament itself is made by the law and is not above it.

The only method by which the constitution and the rights that it protects could be changed would be by revolution. And for such a revolution to take effect, all Crown servants would have to be persuaded to take a new oath of allegiance. Even a revolution by stealth, led by a renegade government such as the one now in power, would ultimately have to face the issue of the oaths of allegiance. And that is exactly what is now happening. The oaths sworn by the police in Northern Ireland, and by commissioned officers in the forces, are already under review.

Civil servants swear an oath of loyalty to the government of the day. In April 1999 this was changed to allow regional civil servants to swear an oath of allegiance to EU-inspired regional assemblies. They will become responsible for transport, environment, land use, planning, housing, waste management and economic development, all under the direction of Brussels, while the Westminster parliament will be increasingly sidelined. Such is the nature of revolution by stealth. "Whom God would destroy, He first sends mad."

Shortly before he died in 1999, Max Beloff wrote an article for *The Times*. He said:

> "Sovereignty is more than just a constitutional abstraction. It is the right of a people to order their affairs as they wish. To talk of pooling sovereignty is to forsake it.
>
> At the heart of the argument is a basic intellectual flaw. To suggest that the economic arguments are one thing and the constitutional issues are another is to misunderstand both. Sovereignty is not an optional extra, something to be taken or left. It is the essential power to make decisions. To suggest, as Blair does, that sovereignty pooled is sovereignty enhanced defies both history and logic.
>
> None of which stops States from acting together in their common interest. But retaining sovereignty means retaining the right to change your mind or to take a different course of action if it is needed.
>
> There is no equivocation on the continent that the EU is all about forming a United States of Europe. But this objective is a solution to what can only be described as the German problem. The French are using Europe as a means of reining in the Germans. They supply the brains while the Germans supply the muscle within a single institutional structure – or that was the plan."

Beloff also wrote: "Blair talked of Europe-bashing when the British press criticised the corrupt commission which was forced to resign *en masse* and then stayed in office. But if you are prepared to sacrifice British sovereignty why worry about filching a few million pounds on cronyism."

He concluded: "We cannot abandon centuries of self-government for a minority voice amongst foreigners." Indeed not. Especially as we are and always have been so totally out of step with what has become the EU. Why should this change in the future?

Beloff was right to be fearful. Only a few months earlier, Professor Manfred Dammeyer, president of the EU's Committee of the Regions, speaking in Austria, said: "The nation state is increasingly losing its ability to stimulate growth, safeguard employment and allocate tax revenue, making it increasingly difficult for it to guarantee the foundations of its own legitimacy."

While such extraordinary statements might well apply to some Continental countries, it is solely because of the enforcement of profoundly misguided policies of bureaucratic socialism, which the EU now seeks to impose on all member states, that the nations of Continental Europe have been reduced to such a sorry condition.

Some of our great statesmen of past generations understood only too well the crucial link between money and sovereignty.

William Pitt the younger said to the House of Commons, on 31st May 1781: "[You] hold the strings of the national purse and are entrusted with the great important power, first of granting the money, and then of correcting the expenditure. To delegate this right, then, is a violation of what gives you your consequence in the legislature and what, above all other privileges, you cannot surrender or delegate without a violent breach of the constitution."

William Gladstone, who was speaking at Hastings, on 17th May 1891, said: "The finance of the country is ultimately associated with the liberties of the country. It is a powerful leverage by which English liberty has been gradually acquired.... If the House of Commons by any possibility lose the power of the control of the grants of public money, depend upon it, your very liberty will be worth very little in comparison. That powerful leverage has been what is commonly known as the power of the purse – the control of the House of Commons over expenditure."

A century later, there was a famous exchange in the House of Commons between Nigel Spearing MP and the then prime minister, Margaret Thatcher.

Prime minister: "The president of the commission, Mr Delors said at a press conference the other day that he wanted the European Parliament to be the democratic body of the community, he wanted the commission to be the executive and the council of ministers to be the senate. No. No. No."

Spearing: "Despite what the prime minister has just said is it not clear that it is the wish of our partners that there should be a loss of national identity on currency? Is it not true that even the hard ecu, coupled with fixed exchange rates, would lead inexorably to economic and monetary union and to government either of bankers for bankers by bankers, or to a strong political central government that would usher in a new euro state? If the Prime minister is to save Britain as a self-governing nation, had she not better make that clear and galvanise the people of this country and all parties in parliament to say a very polite no to economic and monetary union?"

Prime minister: "If I believed that I would do just as the honourable gentleman says, but I do not believe that his interpretation is correct."

By ratification of the Amsterdam Treaty of 1997 the British parliament brought all that into being. The EC became the EU's cabinet, the Court of Justice its supreme court, and the Council of Ministers became a form of upper house.

The treaty was approved by the British parliament on 17th December 1997, at 23.25 hours. At that moment, British sovereignty illegally and ostensibly passed away.

The government also chose to ignore a centuries-old principle that constitutional matters before parliament are never subjected to restrictions on the time available for debate. Despite their huge majority, the Labour government used a guillotine motion to restrict criticism.

No UK government has ever been elected on a mandate to sign away the supremacy of its law-making powers, nor does it have the power to do so. Furthermore, Germany's government has never conceded such powers to Brussels. They have retained the right to enforce the supremacy of their own laws in their own country. Even their membership of the euro was conditional and has never been ratified.

In theory, of course, there is no exit from the euro. In practice, it may well self-destruct. Or, possibly, one of the countries involved may reach such a point of economic strain that it has to leave, come what may.

Constitutional principles are not add-on extras to be discarded "when the economic circumstances are right", but are fundamental to our right to govern ourselves. Those suggesting such moves would do well to reflect that attempting to overthrow, let alone succeeding in subverting our constitution, is treason. This point is argued at some length and in detail in the Appendix (p233), first published in pamphlet form in April 2000 under the title *Defence of the Realm*.

To swear an oath is a matter of integrity and honour. Oaths carry sanctions to make them meaningful. A witness in a court of law is liable to the criminal charge of perjury if caught lying. Every commissioned officer in all three services, all privy councillors, the judiciary, the prime minister and ministers of the Crown all swear oaths of loyalty to the monarch. The law lords swear an oath to uphold the supremacy of the laws of England.

On appointment, magistrates are required to swear or affirm that they "will be faithful and bear true allegiance to Her Majesty Queen Elizabeth the Second, her heirs and successors, according to law", and that they "will well and truly serve our Sovereign Lady Queen Elizabeth the Second in the office of Justice of the Peace, and will do right to all manner of people, after the laws and usages of this realm without fear or favour, affection or ill will".

All policemen make a declaration – a form of oath – that says: "I do solemnly and sincerely declare and affirm that I will well and truly serve Our Sovereign Lady the Queen in the office of constable, without favour or affection, malice or ill-will; and that I will to the best of my power cause the peace to be kept and preserved, and prevent all offences against the persons and properties of Her Majesty's subjects; and that while I continue to hold the said office I will to the best of my skill and knowledge discharge all the duties thereof faithfully according to law." The Police Federation strongly opposes any change to this declaration.

A serviceman's oath is liable to enforcement by courts martial. Policemen are discharged. Magistrates are asked to retire. Why have privy councillors and ministers never been called to account over the erosion of sovereignty by their collaboration with the EU? There is a clear *prima facie* case against many of them, from Edward Heath onwards.

Then we come to the vexed question of the EU commissioners – currently Kinnock and Patten, previously Jenkins, Brittan and others. They have all been sworn in as privy councillors, but have later sworn oaths of loyalty to the EU, which purports to take supremacy. The EU also claims superiority over the sovereign in her own land, and undemocratically makes laws that it claims take precedence in the UK.

The office of the Privy Council was asked in 1986 by a Mr Wolfenden, writing on behalf of the Citizens' Forum, about the apparent conflict between the oath of allegiance sworn by a privy councillor and the oath subsequently sworn if and when that privy councillor became a European commissioner.

The reply was extraordinary. It suggested that if a member of a subversive organisation became a privy councillor that person was no longer subversive on account of the position he or she had attained. It went on: "No question of conflict of interest can therefore arise."

By such convoluted, officially approved, Alice-in-Wonderland logic, then, the holders of these high offices appear to face no sanctions and equally appear free to break their oaths of loyalty with impunity. Today we are faced with the terrible responsibility of looking to the sovereign to uphold her coronation oath as a matter of integrity and honour and for the protection of her people from foreign rule and the loss of their rights and freedoms.

Shortly after Maastricht was ratified, these same law lords who had sworn to uphold the supremacy of English law decreed that EU law was superior to UK law. That same treaty – claimed Prime Minister John Major – meant that Her Majesty was now the subject of a foreign government in her own sovereign land. This was, and is, absurd. The claim that foreign law takes precedence is equally unconstitutional.

Acceptance of government and law from a foreign source *ipso facto* abolishes sovereignty and independence, and makes the sovereign a subject. Effectively the British nation has been placed, arbitrarily and without our being asked, in a political prison. This is the equivalent of the whole nation being subjected to wrongful and unlawful arrest.

How is it that we can be held to be subject to EU law when the same government that says so then goes on to claim that we are still a sovereign nation? How can we be subject to EU law without our having been stripped of our rights and freedoms? These are logical and legal impossibilities. Yet they have never been put fully to the test.

Magna Carta says that no treaty can be enjoined nor Act of Parliament passed that is to the detriment of the people, to their rights and freedoms. So why was Maastricht signed by ministers of the Crown who had sworn oaths of loyalty to the sovereign and why did MPs – who have also sworn oaths of loyalty – then ratify it?

"...here is a law which is above the King and which even he must not break. This reaffirmation of a supreme law and its expression in a general charter is the great work of Magna Carta; and this alone justifies the respect in which men have held it" – Winston Churchill, 1956.

The area around the shuttle terminal in Kent is now governed under French law. A short time ago, a French-born Englishman was arrested there and taken to France for court martial for having failed to report for national service in France, even though he speaks no French, lived there for only three months as a baby, and has an English father. The implications of this case were truly horrific. In theory, if not in practice, it meant that, under EU law, the Queen as a citizen could now be arrested in her own kingdom and taken to another country for trial. She would have no redress.

In 1960, Lord Kilmuir told Edward Heath (minister of state at the Foreign Office) that Britain would risk losing some sovereignty under the Treaty of Rome. It would have three effects –

1 Parliament would surrender some of its functions.
2 The Crown would transfer some of its treaty-making powers.
3 The British courts would sacrifice some degree of independence.

In 1972, Lord Wilberforce briefed Edward Heath (by then prime minister) over the supremacy of the ECJ, saying it would involve a total loss of sovereignty. All these men had sworn oaths of loyalty to the monarch, and none of them appears to have sought to stop the process. Some 20 years later Heath finally admitted lying to the British public.

Such a response suggests that officials are actually terrified of admitting that the underlying issues exist, and dread the implications if they address them.

The discredited Peter Mandelson, when minister without portfolio, said that the Labour government was "prepared to cede more of our national sovereignty to the EU". This demonstrated that he did not understand the meaning of the word sovereignty, and it also showed that – even in his terms – some sovereignty had already been ceded. By implication, his statement also admitted an unconstitutional policy that exceeded the government's powers, and that there had been a clear infringement of the oath of loyalty sworn by ministers.

If advice from ministers breaks either their oath of loyalty to the sovereign or endangers the contract the sovereign has with the people, the sovereign is duty bound by the coronation oath to act according to that oath. Again, the details are in the appendix below, *Defence of the Realm*.

Said King George III:

> "Where is the power on earth to absolve me from the observance of every sentence of that oath [the coronation oath], particularly the one requiring me to maintain the protestant reformed religion? Was not my family seated on the throne for that express purpose, and shall I be the first to suffer it to be undermined, perhaps overturned? No, no, I had rather beg my bread from door to door throughout Europe, than consent to any such measure.
>
> I can give up my crown and retire from power. I can quit my palace and live in a cottage. I can lay my head on a block and lose my life, but I cannot break my oath. If I violate that oath, I am no longer legal sovereign in this country."

Yet another letter to David Bourne, this time from the speaker's office at the House of Commons:

> "The Speaker has asked me to explain that the UK is a constitutional monarchy under which the Sovereign is required to act on the advice of Ministers who are themselves accountable to Parliament. Under long-standing legislation Members of Parliament are required to swear an Oath of Allegiance or to make the solemn Affirmation before taking their seats.
>
> The Oath does not have a time limit attached to it, and does not expire once a general election is called. The legal concept of allegiance is that every natural-born subject owes allegiance from birth, and that allegiance cannot be cast off. The allegiance, therefore, already exists – the Oath is simply a public expression

of it. All Members returned to Parliament are required to swear the Oath or make the Affirmation, whether or not they served in a previous Parliament.

The Oath: I swear by Almighty God that I will be faithful and bear true Allegiance to Her Majesty Queen Elizabeth, her heirs and successors, according to Law. So help me God."

So parliament has not only sworn loyalty, but by doing so it has acknowledged that its own powers are limited by that collective oath. Thus, parliament cannot pass a law undermining the constitution. Indeed, no parliament has even attempted to take such powers. They have just gone ahead and changed the constitution anyway. Today, we have virtually no politicians or lawyers with the "intestinal fortitude" to stand up and call a halt to the constitutional mayhem which has been going on since 1972.

The last few words of Lord Wilberforce's speech in the House of Lords in 1997 provide the key. Our sovereignty is "firmly secured already by the common law of this country, and not intended to be superseded or modified by new inter-state obligations".

The US Supreme Court once ruled: "All laws which are repugnant to the constitution are null and void."

A person who becomes aware of a treasonable act that threatens to overthrow the laws and constitution of the UK is obliged to bring that to the notice of a magistrate or constable. Failure to do so puts that person in danger of committing the common law offence of misprision of treason ("when a person knows of treason, though no party or consenter to it, yet conceals it, and doth not reveal it in convenient time" – R V Thistlewood, 1820). In other words, misprision means "criminal neglect".

Unfortunately when individuals have attempted to take direct action through the courts their efforts have been circumscribed in recent years by the pretended power that the judiciary have awarded themselves to declare individuals to be "vexatious litigants".

Ultimately, of course, the remedy should lie with parliament itself, or with the Crown. But, today, there another problem arises. Petitions to the House of Commons should be debated. In recent times, however, the House of Commons has routinely passed petitions to the department which is the subject of a complaint for them to answer. This is manifestly wrong both in law and logic. It breaches the common-law prohibition of sitting in judgment in one's own cause.

Finally, there is the option of a petition to the monarch. But, again, these are usually intercepted and – again – passed to the department that caused the grievance, thus closing the loop and leaving no remedy.

This disgraceful and underhand interception of petitions to the Queen is a relatively recent phenomenon. It has evolved only in the last few decades as the power of the throne has been further diminished by successive governments. Rarely has this been by agreement or statute. It has been by a succession of relatively minor changes in custom and practice. John Major accelerated and tightened the procedure significantly, and he did so specifically to prevent petitions about the EU from reaching Her Majesty. Tony Blair has since turned this new – and illegal – practice into an art form.

Contrast such behaviour with the words of great statesmen who understood these issues and the responsibilities they bore somewhat better than the present clutch of politicians in Britain.

The American president John F Kennedy said, in 1961: "We are proud of our ancient heritage and unwilling to permit the slow undoing of those human rights to which this nation has always been committed.

"Let every nation know…that we shall pay any price, bear any burden, meet any hardship, support any friend, oppose any foe…to assure the survival and the success of liberty."

Some 40 years earlier, another president of the United States, Woodrow Wilson, said: "Liberty has never come from the government. Liberty has always come from the subjects of government. The history of liberty is the history of resistance. The history of liberty is a history of the limitation of governmental power, not the increase of it."

The great Austrian economist, Friedrich Hayek, once remarked that "you can't plan the world". A free, advanced society does not need planning. Left to its own devices it is rational, not anarchic as the planners would have us believe.

The Chinese communist revolutionary Mao Tse-tung once said: "A fish rots from the head down."

Do we, the British, want to control our own affairs in our own way, or have others do it for us by bureaucratic directive and majority voting behind closed doors? There are no lifeboats on the EU Titanic. If we stay on we drown.

The treaties of the EU do not address the question of withdrawal. Even during the Amsterdam Treaty negotiations EU officials were claiming that it was essentially a voluntary association of states. It also seems possible that the EU wishes to ignore, or one day dispute, the British parliamentary freedom to repeal any Acts passed by its predecessors.

Yet the government's campaign for the "Yes" vote in the 1975 referendum issued a leaflet that included the words: "The British Parliament in Westminster retains the final right to repeal the Act which took us into the Market on January 1, 1973."

The right to self-determination and the election of our government belongs to us – the people. We delegate it to our representatives at Westminster for a maximum of five years at a time. In effect we "lend" it to them, and it is always subject to our continued consent, which may be withdrawn by us at any time.

Therefore, it follows that no government of the day has the right to give away those powers to a third party.

These rights were inherited by us, and we are custodians of them. We inherited this earth, and are custodians of that too, for generations yet unborn. No generation has the right to give away these rights – for they belong to our children and to their children just as much as they belong to us. No passing parade of electors may deprive future generations of their rights and freedoms. We are merely trustees.

Some argue that any referendum – however the question is posed – and any treaty offering or purporting to sign away those rights must be – by definition – inherently unconstitutional, and therefore invalid.

A letter from Sir John Hoskyns appeared in *The Times* on 3rd March 1999. He wrote:

> "I have more confidence in Britain's imperfect arrangements than I do in euroland's out-of-touch politicians, undemocratic institutions, dubious electoral system and legal processes, financial corruption, creative accounting, secrecy, administrative incompetence, mercantilist instincts, foreign-policy confusion,

institutionalised animosity towards the United States and Charlemagne-flavoured delusions of empire."

He spoke for millions.

---

1 *Corpus juris* grew out of the "European Legal Area Project", started in 1995 at the request of the EC. Proposals were published and launched to European jurists in San Sebastian, Spain in 1997. The programme preamble to that meeting used the words "which has been conceived as the embryo of a future European criminal code".

Corpus juris was approved by the European Parliament on 13 April 1999. Almost all UK MEPs voted for it, but the Tories later said they had made a mistake!

The wise-men committee, set up to combat fraud in the EU, announced on 10 September 1999 that *corpus juris* should be introduced and the first pan-European public prosecutor appointed.

Home affairs ministers of the EU met on 16–17 September 1999 in Tampere, Finland, to discuss practicalities of introduction, and on 29 September the EC proposed using Article 280(a) of the Amsterdam Treaty to effect its introduction.

Corpus juris document, published by the EU: the phrase "a simpler and more efficient system of repression" appears on p40, Paragraph 3. The full quotation reads: "…designed to ensure, in a largely unified European legal area, a fairer, simpler and more efficient system of repression."

Single legal area   Article 18
Indefinite detention   20, iii
Indefinite detention on suspicion of a future crime   20, iii
Police/prosecution one organisation   20/21/22
Extradition   21, i, b
Professional judges   26
Double jeopardy (loss of presumption of innocence)   27, ii
Accused told charges, but NOT evidence   29, iii
Secret trials   34
– except for judgment   34, iii

Chapter Three

Don't Look Back

The EU's Museum of Europe will open in 2003, next to the parliament in Brussels. It will omit all references to the cultural origins of Europe to be found in pre-Christian Britain, ancient Greece and Byzantium. Official EU "history" will start with Charlemagne's first federalist attempts at unification in the eighth century. King Alfred's pioneering that set in train the development of Anglo-Saxon England will be ignored.

So will many of the other genuinely formative events and periods in the development of the continent of Europe. There will be nothing, for instance, about the German reaction, after the 15th-century Renaissance, when England opened its sea-trade route via the Cape of Good Hope to India. England's subsequent mastery of international sea trade ruined the German economy. The Rhine and Baltic never recovered their previous dominance as trade routes between Europe and the East.

Ever since, Germany has sought to frustrate the UK's global trade and tried several times over the centuries to tie us into a Europe that they dominate – and it's still going on today. Over time, Germany has tried to control Europe by trade or war alternately. As Napoleon said: "Each country pursues the politics of its geography."

The EU museum is also unlikely to reveal the importance of the English group that came to be known as the Levellers. They emerged as political activists during the rule of Oliver Cromwell, when a great debate raged about the nature of liberty and freedom. They believed that the ancient rights of Englishmen lay in the notion of "self-ownership". These self-evident "natural rights" permitted the individual, for example, to worship as he chose. Their leader, Richard Overton, in a pamphlet called *An Arrow Against All Tyrants* argued that everyone owned themselves, and had an absolute right to life, liberty and property. "No man hath power over my rights and liberties, and I over no man's."

The Bill of Rights, of 1689 (exactly 100 years before the French got round to a more violent version of the same idea), is equally unlikely to feature in the EU museum. This was a seminal moment in English constitutional law, when the new King William and Queen Mary agreed to recognise and respect the "true, ancient and indubitable rights" of Englishmen.

A year later, 1690, John Locke's great work *The Second Treatise of Government* asked: what is the point of government? His answer was witheringly simple. People, he argued, have always had rights. They existed before governments. They are natural rights because they are to be found in the very nature of humanity.

They are rights we are born with, rights that we inherited from our earliest ancestors, rights that are ours to preserve and protect, rights that we own absolutely and squander at our peril. They will exist even when they have been abused or lost or cast aside. The next generation will always inherit them, though they might have to fight to re-establish them in all their glory.

Groups of people form governments to protect those rights. They could do so without creating a government, but the very idea of government offers – theoretically at least – an effective means of codifying and managing that protection.

But if that government oversteps the mark, if it takes powers beyond those granted by the people, if it attempts to restrict or deny the very rights it was elected to protect, then the people have the (natural) right to dismiss that government and to elect another. That is the essence of a democratically accountable system of government. It serves the people and preserves their rights.

As John Locke said: "A government is not free to do as it pleases. The law of nature stands as an eternal rule to all men, legislators as well as others." It is, he wrote, the role of government to protect the lives, liberties and estates of the people.

It was 100 years later that the great thinker Adam Smith held the same view. These great truths, the underlying principles of government, had not changed.

Indeed, a series of newspaper articles at that time, which came to be known as "Cato's Letters", were again denouncing the government of the day for eroding the natural-born rights of Englishmen to enjoy the liberty to trade freely with each other. John Trenchard and Thomas Gordon argued for a return to a commercial environment that was unhindered by monopolies, guilds (trade unions in today's parlance) and high taxes. The government should remove the constraints on commerce, they argued, and wealth would surely follow.

David Hume took the argument further by pointing out that everyone benefited from the prosperity of others. The role of government was to protect those rights that enabled that prosperity to be achieved through trade. One of the most important was the law relating to contracts. If two parties entered into an agreement binding on them both, that contract demanded the force of law behind it. Furthermore, provided it did not impinge on the rights of others, the government should not interfere in it beyond providing the mechanism for upholding it in the event of a subsequent dispute.

So, individual freedom, limited representative government and free markets became the three great cornerstones of the transformation achieved during the latter part of the last millennium, which we know today as the developed world.

Thomas Paine, in *Common Sense,* pointed out that "society is produced by our wants and government by our wickedness". Society, he suggested, is a blessing, and government – at best – a necessary evil. At worst, it was intolerable.

Most succinctly of all, Thomas Jefferson, drafting the Declaration of Independence in 1776, wrote: "We hold these truths to be self-evident, that all men are created equal, that they are endowed by their creator with certain inalienable rights, that among these are life, liberty and the pursuit of happiness. That to secure these rights, governments are instituted among men, deriving their just powers from the consent of the governed. That whenever any form of government becomes destructive of those ends, it is the right of the people to alter or abolish it."

In a nutshell, the people delegate powers to government, and take them back as and when they choose. People had rights before government existed, they retain those rights not expressly delegated to government, and the government of the day has no authority from the people to take more powers than it has been granted.

At the federal convention in Philadelphia in 1787, what became known as the Virginia Resolutions were used as the working-paper from which the Constitution of the United States was drafted. They originated in a letter of 8th April from James Madison to Governor Randolph, which was regarded as "the earliest [sketch] of a constitutional government for the Union to be sanctioned by the people of the States, acting in their original and sovereign character".

During the convention George Mason, James Wilson and James Madison spoke in favour of the fourth resolution – that what became the House of Representatives should be elected by the people, not by state legislatures. And, in the face of other members' preference that the constitution should be ratified by the state legislatures, Madison insisted that "the new constitution should be ratified in the most unexceptionable form, and by the supreme authority of the people themselves".

Two years later, in 1789, the French promulgated the Declaration of the Rights of Man and of the Citizen, among which rights were: "The law is an expression of the will of the community. All citizens have a right to play a role, either personally, or by their representatives, in its formation."

All of that contrasts sharply with the mindset to be found in other parts of Europe. The Zollverein (Customs Union) of 1817 was originally created as a device to achieve a unified central Europe, exclusive of others and dominated by Germany. As recently as the Amsterdam Treaty of 1997 the Germans were still pursuing the same aims.

In the middle of the 19th century – 1867 to be precise – a proposal for the establishment of a European monetary union germinated in Italy. At the time it was taken quite seriously. Indeed, the great English constitutional commentator, Walter Bagehot, wrote of the danger of Britain being left out in the cold. "Before long, all Europe, save England, will have one money." So – we have been here before. We did not join then, the idea withered on the vine, and we came to no harm. In fact the next 50 years saw phenomenal growth and wealth-creation in Great Britain. There was nothing inevitable about being part of Europe then!

Later, of course, the Irish established the punt as their currency, independent of the pound sterling, and that served them well enough. At least, it did so until they joined the euro in 1999 and discovered the problems that flow from having an interest rate that is not appropriate for their economy.

In 1914, the then German chancellor wrote what he called the "September Economic Programme". It was a proposal for a European customs union including France, Germany, Belgium, Holland, Denmark, Poland, Austria-Hungary – and possibly Italy, Sweden and Norway. Sound familiar?

Twenty years later, in 1934, a pro-Nazi German magazine denounced what it called "the liberal Anglo-Saxon order".

The Third Reich was the first state to outlaw the private ownership and use of firearms, starting with rifles in 1933, then moving on to handguns by 1935. It was the first state to establish the link between smoking and lung cancer, and make anti-smoking rules a matter of public policy. It was the first to recommend dietary practices to its people. It was the first to regulate by statute private hunting in "forest lands" (although Goering did what he liked).

In the USA in the 1930s, under Roosevelt's New Deal, the US Congress started passing laws that left the fine details, and the subsequent administration of those laws, up to administrative agencies. This was the first step on the slippery slope towards rule by bureaucratic diktat.

In 1935, Roosevelt wrote to the chairman of Ways and Means: "I hope your committee will not permit doubts as to the constitutionality, however reasonable, to block the suggested legislation." Decades later those same first steps away from full legislative accountability drew the comment that they were "tortured interpretations of a document [the Constitution of the United States] intended to prevent them".

Today, there is talk in the USA of specifically prohibiting by law the delegation of law-making powers to any administrative agency of government. The ninth amendment of the US Constitution establishes that all rights, other than those given temporarily to the elected congress, are retained by the people.

As we have seen, this deplorable trend is now well entrenched at Westminster, and has been taken to extremes in Brussels.

By 1937, according to *The House That Hitler Built* by Stephen Roberts, professor of modern history at the University of Sydney, Hitler developed the idea of establishing regions of Europe as a means of destroying national identities. Hitler's concept of "divide and rule" was intended to smash each defeated nation into several little regions to be ruled from Berlin. It has since served as the model for the EU's regional policy, which aims to turn the UK into 12 regions, all ruled from Brussels.

By 1938, Henri Spaak, one of the founding fathers of the EU, was openly calling himself a "national socialist" (Nazi). He talked of Hitler's "magnificent achievements". He was one of the activists who encouraged Belgian rail workers to strike when Germany invaded in 1940, and he helped ensure that the British and French troops failed to establish a defensive line against the invaders.

On 22nd June 1940, Hermann Goering made the first reference to what he called "the European Economic Community". At a conference held in Germany at that time, it was suggested that "England has to be evicted from the continent once and for all, and the new Europe keep its distance from the United States".

That same year, the former Kaiser Wilhelm wrote: "We are becoming a United States of Europe under German leadership, a united Europe."

The German ideal was growing fast. They now dominated Europe militarily. By 1941 von Ribbentrop was confident enough to claim that "integration is inevitable...it is impossible to stop the trend". Where have we heard that before?

In sharp contrast, despite the awesome tasks still ahead of them, Winston Churchill and President Roosevelt met in August 1941 to discuss much more than their war strategy and tactics. They sought to define their true purpose, beyond the (mere) defeat of tyranny.

They conceived what became known as the Atlantic Charter, which they both signed before they parted. It affirmed that their underlying aim was to "respect the right of all peoples to choose the form of government under which they will live".

Back in Europe, the blueprint for the Treaty of Rome, on which the EU is based today, was being developed by Herr Heydricht. He called it "The Reich Plan for the Domination of Europe". Heydricht's proposals were finally published in 1942 and widely circulated at the time. But they have now mysteriously disappeared from library shelves all over the world. A few still exist. The text bears remarkable comparison with what is now the Treaty of Rome.

Heydricht's plan coincided with a conference organised by the University of Berlin in 1942, entitled "Europaische Wirtschaftgemeinschaft" – the European Economic Community (or EEC). Some of the papers had particularly chilling titles, which still resonate today: "The Economic Face of New Europe", "Development of the EEC", "European Agriculture", "European Transport", "A European Currency", "European Trade and Economic Treaties", "Is Europe a Geographical Concept or a Political Fact?"

The introductory comments to the conference included the observation, "The age-old English doctrine of the balance of power has been militarily smashed". There were references to "the political union of Europe".

A year later, in March 1943, von Ribbentrop "invited" 13 countries to join a European federation under German leadership. But, of course, Holland, Belgium, Luxembourg, Italy, France, Denmark, Norway, Finland, Greece, Portugal and Spain were all then either under the German military yoke, or known sympathisers.

Robert Schuman – another of the founding fathers of the EU – was a Vichy minister during the 1939–45 war. He was also a member of the National Assembly that voted the French parliament out of existence. He was apparently quite happy to ignore the fact that the elected representatives were – and are – the custodians of national sovereignty and democracy – not the owners of it. The assembly had grossly exceeded its powers.

In August 1944, when the Germans knew the war was lost, a secret conference took place between the heads of the German Nazi government and top German industrialists at the Hotel Rotes Haus in Strasbourg. They laid plans to salt away finance to continue the fight for control of Europe by stealth. It was a plan on the grand scale, set in the context of decades. It was a plan to be implemented so slowly that no one would realise what was happening. Today we may be perilously close to the end-game of that same plan.

The theme of the meeting was this: "How will Germany dominate the peace when it loses the war?" The agenda included the exporting of large sums of capital, and the establishment of German industrial concerns in countries that were not overly antagonistic to the Nazi aims. Massive funds left Germany shortly afterwards, much of them via Madrid.

This was a careful attempt to hide and put on ice the Nazis' dreams of world domination, perhaps for generations. The price demanded was that these industrialists would then support the Nazi Party when it came out of hiding, which it was estimated would be at least 40 years after the eventual defeat of the Third Reich. Elan Steinberg, of the World Jewish Congress, has recently asked: "The central question is whether it has been carried out."

Elsewhere, similar discussions were going on at precisely the same time. A meeting took place at Dumbarton Oaks between the USA, Great Britain, the USSR and China to discuss what eventually became the formation of the UN after the war. Broadly agreed about the principle of a UN, the four countries were unable to resolve the question of what to do about Germany.

Afterwards, Winston Churchill's staunchest supporter during the Second World War, Field Marshall Smuts, told him: "Europe's 2,000 year problem of Germany will remain as great as ever."

In his broadcast to the nation on Victory in Europe Day – V-E Day – 8th May 1945, Winston Churchill said: "I must warn you...that you must be prepared for further efforts of mind and body and further sacrifices to great causes if you are not to fall back into the rut of inertia, the confusion of aim, and the craven fear of being great."

In 1948, the Universal Declaration of Human Rights was proclaimed by the UN General Assembly. Article 21 states:

(1) Everyone has the right to take part in the government of his country, directly or through freely chosen representatives.... .

(3) The will of the people shall be the basis of the authority of government...

None of that discouraged the European federalists from trying to breathe life into the German wartime plan again. German planners in Madrid re-created the framework of Hitler's "United State of Europe" (he had been the first to use the phrase), which then became the basis for German Chancellor Adenauer's strategy in Europe over the next decade or so, and which eventually evolved into the EU.

Germany's long-term strategy included carving up eastern Europe again, gaining control over the vast food-producing areas of eastern Europe, sharing the spoils with Russia and creating a European trading bloc to cut out or rival the USA.

By 1948, a new organisation, the European Union of Federalists (EUF), produced a document setting out their policies, which were all confirmed by the Hague Congress on European Union held later the same year. Of their seven "Resolutions on Political Union", the last said that "the creation of a United Europe must be regarded as an essential step towards the creation of a United World".

Official UK government booklets dated 1947 and 1948 confirm our involvement even then in discussions clearly intended to lead to a single European state.

The EUF was disbanded within a few years, but the ideas lived on, initially with the active encouragement of Prince Bernhard of the Netherlands. He had been a Nazi sympathiser (there are claims that he was a senior party official and Waffen Schutzstaffel (SS) officer). In 1954 he called a conference at the Bilderberg Hotel in Osterbeek, near the Hague.

The three leaders of the Bilderbergers were Prince Bernhard (who was elected chairman), Paul van Zeeland (former Belgian prime minister and communist) and Dr Josef Retinger (Comintern agent, communist and Fabian). The Bilderberg meeting of 1954 included Unilever chairman Paul Rykens and the American banker David Rockefeller. Bilderberger meetings are annual events to this day. No one is elected, everyone has access by invitation only. The Bilderberg Group is – and always has been – one of the most secretive groups of the rich and powerful in the world. It largely consists of royalty, presidents, prime ministers, top industrialists and financiers.

Shortly after that first meeting the European Iron and Coal Federation was set up. It was the first brick in the wall that now rings western Europe – the EU.

Tony Blair, Gordon Brown, Edward Heath and Kenneth Clarke have all attended Bilderberg meetings and the two latter have lied about doing so. This secretive group of powerful politicians and industrialists seeks to make decisions and influence events to meet their own, undeclared purposes. They conduct their affairs in a profoundly undemocratic fashion, which would not matter but for the fact that they seek to influence and take decisions that affect us all. They actively subvert the right of free peoples to determine openly their own futures, to exercise their sovereign independence, and to sustain their right to self-government.

This group is never reported in the press, nor pestered by them, perhaps because too many media tycoons have been involved over the years. The few journalists who have tried to infiltrate Bilderberger meetings have met with little success and much aggravation.

Questions about the Bilderbergers are always evaded or fobbed off. In answer to a question in the House of Commons about the attendance at meetings of the Bilderberger Group by EU commissioners, a minister said:

"The Bilderberg meetings are an international forum in which political leaders and economists express their personal views on topics of general interest, particularly in the spheres of foreign policy and world economics.

"The participants attend meetings in a private capacity and the statements which they make are not binding on the Commission; no resolutions are passed, no votes are taken and no political communiqués are issued."

With the reunification of Germany after the fall of the Berlin Wall in 1989, the Germans were once again able to pick up their historic long-term goal to expand their sphere of influence over eastern Europe. The first step was in the former Yugoslavia. Germany's unilateral recognition of Bosnia started the destruction of the Yugoslavian federation. In 1990, despite strong opposition from the rest of Europe, and from the UN, the USA and Great Britain, formal diplomatic recognition was given by Germany (and by the Vatican) to Slovenia and Croatia, both keen supporters of the Third Reich some 50 years before. The immediate result – civil war in both "countries".

Elsewhere in the region, Austria was annexed by the Third Reich in 1938, uses German as its principal language, and looks to Germany for much of its heritage and culture. The Czech and Slovak republics split apart within a few years of gaining their freedom from the USSR. Both have significant indigenous German populations.

Albania also has a long association with Germany. The deep-water ports on the Adriatic are of huge strategic importance, especially to a large and powerful nation that is landlocked to the south. Albania's location is perfect for an aggressive maritime nation. But, to get there, the Germans need a route, and the best land-route to Albania and the Mediterranean is via Montenegro. How fortunate, then, that Montenegro uses the German Deutschmark as its currency and wants to leave the Serbian-dominated Yugoslav Federation.

Germans make no bones about these issues and their goals. Since the fall of the Berlin Wall, Germany is now well on its way to restoring its historic spheres of influence in the Balkans and other parts of eastern Europe. That is why it is so keen to expand the EU to the east.

Herr Immo Stabreit, former German ambassador to Paris, writing in *The International Herald Tribune* in September 1999, said: "It is only natural that the eastern part of the continent will become our preoccupation for years to come because Germans see this as a matter of historical destiny. The most fundamental priority we have is trying to integrate all of Europe. But for France the underlying issue is all about coming to terms with its loss of influence in the world."

❖

Some anti-EU campaigners argue that the EU has its roots in Catholicism. They argue that, when the EU has its own army, it will eventually find an opportunity to confront Islam. They see Catholicism as a proselytising, unforgiving, guilt-dispensing governance masquerading as a religion, and intolerant of opposition. They suggest that the Vatican supported Mussolini and Hitler's attempts at ethnic cleansing because it was coincidentally the cleansing of the enemies of Catholicism.

Whether or not there is any underlying truth here, it is certainly true that Rome has opposed the UK at many crucial moments in its history, ever since the signing of the Magna Carta. This great charter was denounced by the Vatican within weeks. Magna Carta was signed on 15th June 1215. By the end of August letters had arrived from Rome in which the pope, Innocent III, wrote bluntly to the English abbots and bishops who had signed the document, saying they had done something "abominable" and "illicit". The pope also assumed powers to annul Magna Carta. Given the speed of a horse, this timetable is remarkable and clearly indicates the importance given to it by Rome. In under ten weeks, not only had the text of Magna Carta arrived in Rome, and been carefully considered. A response had been drafted and it had arrived back in London.

Three centuries later, of course, Henry VIII finally threw the Roman Catholic Church out – even if for entirely deplorable reasons. His act of rebellion is still talked about in Rome to this day. The British have not, and never will be, forgiven for such heresy. It was no surprise, a few decades later, when the pope offered a papal blessing and a great deal of money to Philip of Spain as he launched his armada to attempt an invasion of England. The pope at the time, Sixtus V, supported it and promised Philip 1,000,000 gold ducats if his invasion were to succeed.

King James' authorised translation of the Bible into English was scorned by Rome. At the time, the murder of some of the translators was attributed to agents of the pope. The revolt of 1745 was primarily to place a Catholic monarch on the British throne once more.

When Napoleon sought the crown as emperor of the Holy Roman Empire the deed was to be done by the elected president of the papal states. Then, 100 years later another pope was strengthening ties with the belligerent Kaiser Wilhelm, with the assistance of a future pope, Eugelio Pacelli. Twenty years later still the pope concluded a treaty of friendship and mutual support (a concordat) with both Continental dictators – Hitler in Nazi Germany, and Mussolini in Italy. The Vatican had no such concordats with the allies. Eugelio Pacelli was enthroned just before the Second World War, throughout which those concordats remained in full force. The agreement with Nazi Germany was finally revoked at the end of 1947, two years after the end of the war, when the Vatican had finished helping Nazis to escape to South America.

In more recent times, Britain has been in a Catholic nutcracker, squeezed between pressure from the EU on the one side, and from the Irish Republican Army, or IRA, on the other. When the IRA terrorists were bombing London in 1996, the pope positively refused to condemn them. The Vatican was loudly condemning the Hamas bombings in Israel at the time, but the Vatican press office refused three times to condemn the bombings in London, when asked by the *Wall Street Journal Europe*.

Instinctively, the Vatican thinks and works in the long-term, and has many times over the centuries revealed ambitions of global power. It had its hand in Charlemagne's glove. It has consistently backed the aggressive players on the world stage who offered to spread Catholicism. The very word itself means "universal".

Catholicism is not comfortable with Protestantism, despite its lip-service to the ecumenical movement. It seeks and encourages weakness in its competitors as it fights for the hearts, minds, loyalty and financial support of the people.

The Vatican signed a "concordat" with the Lutheran Church in Germany in late 1999. The Lutheran Church in Sweden is being disestablished. As a result, the only positively non-Catholic nation left in the EU is Britain, and there are now moves to destroy the Protestant hold on Britain. The Vatican has every reason to support the EU's plans to "unite" Europe. It will be a big beneficiary.

So the proposal to lift the ban on Catholics on or next to the throne of England has more to it than meets the eye. It is yet another step on the constitutional slippery slope. It is yet another step towards losing our sovereignty. It is yet another step towards losing our identity and becoming submerged in the Catholic Europe of the EU. British – and Protestant – rights and freedoms are as much at risk from this source as from others.

It is hardly surprising that until the coronation of King Edward VII the coronation oath contained a clause to keep this land free from "Catholic superstition".

The reason for not having a Catholic monarch is clearly spelled out in the Declaration of Rights and also in the Bill of Rights. It is inconsistent with the safety and well-being of this Protestant kingdom.

This proposition was entrenched in the Act of Settlement, 1701, and in Article 11 of the Treaty of Union, 1707, which embodied the substance of the Act of Settlement. And since this treaty was not incorporated into statute law it cannot be repealed by an Act of Parliament.

Nor can it be altered. Like the Bill of Rights, it offered no method of repeal. Repeal of the Act of Settlement would have no effect, either. The Act specifically calls for non-allegiance if the event were to occur.

"And whereas it hath beene found by Experience that it is inconsistent with the Safety and Welfaire of this Protestant Kingdome to be governed by a Popish Prince or by any King or Queene marrying a Papist the said Lords Spirituall and Temporall and Commons doe further pray that it may be enacted That all and every person and persons that is are or shall be reconciled to or shall hold Communion with the See or Church of Rome or shall professe the Popish Religion or shall marry a Papist shall be excluded and be for ever uncapeable to inherit possesse or enjoy the Crowne and Government of this Realme and Ireland and the

Dominions thereunto belonging or any part of the same or to have use or exercise any Regall Power Authoritie or Jurisdiction within the same.... And in all and every such Case or Cases the People of these Realmes shall be and are hereby absolved of their Allegiance."

Why should the constitution be changed to allow a Roman Catholic to be the consort of the monarch, or the monarch to be a Roman Catholic? The people who propose this change see the present situation as discrimination against Catholics. But there is much more at stake.

Whatever well-meaning British Roman Catholics may think, it is a cold, hard fact that the head of the organisation, whom they are obliged to believe to be infallible, is positively sympathetic to the EU and seeks to limit British independence. He is also actively and demonstrably anti-American. He endlessly campaigns against the death penalty in the USA, but not in Iraq, Iran, or China. He vigorously opposed the Americans and British when they went to war against Saddam Hussein in 1991.

The Vatican is not beyond whipping up anti-American popular fervour as part of a blatant "hate America" campaign, which is more open in France, but profound in Italy. Over the years it has been remarkably successful, even in the face of endless Anglo-Saxon entertainment on film, television and disc.

The issue of religion is entirely a matter of private belief. But when a religious allegiance translates into supporting or opposing a particular political stance, and a specific foreign policy, it is impossible to ignore. It is no longer just a matter of private belief.

When asked, as many Englishmen since Thomas More have been asked, over the last 500 years, "Who, sir, do you hold for? The Queen of England, or the Bishop of Rome?", all Catholics have to say "Bishop of Rome" or be excommunicated. Of course the pope and the curia are no fools, and usually play their flock on a long(ish) leash. But in times of crisis and emergency, the collar and lead are always there, and can be yanked violently at will by the men in red.

Precisely because the Roman Catholic Church is a hierarchical organisation that takes an active and continuous interest in politics, and pursues a foreign policy that is often diametrically opposed to Britain, no

Roman Catholic should ever hold a position of great constitutional power in British affairs of state. The law banning them from the throne may be intolerant and "politically incorrect", but it is absolutely essential to British long-term sovereignty and independence.

Broadly speaking, even though the Church of England is part of the state, it does not involve itself much in political issues. But many religions take a very different view. They demand a say and want the state to be run according to their principles. When they are in a minority, as in Britain, they keep quiet. But when they are in a majority, as in Italy, they make their weight felt continually. They even have their own political parties, which argue for Roman Catholic doctrine to be made the law of the land.

In a united Europe they will be in a permanent majority capable of forming a euro-government, as they have done already in Spain, Germany, and Italy. By becoming a part of a federal superstate, the British would also be drawn back into long-term domination by Roman Catholics and papal dogma.

The symbolism is already there for those willing to look. It is subtle but important. No eurozone country will be allowed to put its head of state on euro coins when they are issued on 1st January 2002. The British government has already enquired about putting the Queen's head on euro coins if we were ever to join the euro. The answer was a categoric "no".

In early 2000, the Vatican City was officially declared part of the eurozone. It has since been given special permission by the EC to mint its own euro coins with the pope's head on one side. These coins will circulate throughout euroland, including the UK if we are forced to join.

A series of written parliamentary questions in the European parliament about this decision – including "When was this decision made, by whom, and why?" – have never been given meaningful answers.

And so we return to that profound distinction between the liberal free-thinking of the Anglo-Saxon world and the *dirigisme* of the Continental mindset. It was no accident that the Industrial Revolution occurred in Britain. But the Protestant Reformation had to happen first. Otherwise, the conditions for such an outburst of free enterprise would never have existed.

Over time, a curious irony has become deeply embedded in Anglo-Saxon attitudes towards church and state. While it is still broadly accepted that the church is part of the state, the popular view is that it should keep out of politics. That is why the proposal to include in the 2001 UK census questions about religious beliefs is so insidious. Of what relevance might that be to the government? It is a private matter.

Given that the UK is the only country in the EU that has a Protestant majority this question about religion may have been inspired from elsewhere in Europe and have another motive behind it.

As we have seen, the Roman Catholic church dominates Europe. For it, the UK is unfinished business stretching back 500 years.

❖

Taking the longer, historical view of our relationship with Europeans, and our involvement with them over the centuries, much of Continental Europe has good reason to envy and seek to settle old scores with the people who live in the British Isles.

The Germans, French, Spanish and Dutch have all at one time or another sought to dominate international affairs and trade, only to find themselves opposed by Britain.

Millions still alive today have first-hand knowledge of Germany's defeat in 1945, and vivid family memories of its effective defeat in 1918. That resentment is still, understandably, very close to the surface and is quickly exposed at a personal level. The French in particular, and most of the other western European countries in general, have twice in the last century had to bear the embarrassment of having the British come to their rescue in times of war. They also have to live with the embarrassment that we were resolute when they buckled, that they were occupied and we were not, and that we won back their freedom for them as well as preserving our own. Winning is not always popular with those who didn't win, or who suffered more during the campaign.

After centuries of success both militarily and commercially, and after leading the Industrial Revolution and the explosive growth in standards of living, we then ran into the sand after the Second World War. We lost an empire and couldn't find a new role for ourselves. Political mismanagement and a loss of direction combined to see us floundering.

We saw the Common Market as a solution. But it was a trap. Like a beached whale, we accepted whatever help was at hand because we believed at the time that there was no other option available. We made a profound mistake.

It was not a "common market". It was a European state in embryo. And we had offered ourselves up to people with old scores to settle. Why else have we consistently failed to win the major arguments in the EU? Why do the French and Germans consistently set the agenda with the tacit agreement of the other Continentals? Why does the ECJ in particular almost always vote or find against the British?

We are no longer masters in our own house. We are now cast in the role of willing slave. We still live in our own house, but others now control it, and one day they will own it. Unless we throw them out.

Chapter Four

Political Muddy Waters

In his 1982 election leaflet Tony Blair advocated leaving the EEC, as it then was. The leaflet said that it "takes away Britain's freedom to follow the economic policies we need". A year later, he committed himself in a speech: "We'll negotiate withdrawal from the EEC."

Former Prime Minister Margaret Thatcher said, after she no longer had the chance to make a difference: "Europe is always blind, cowardly, ungrateful and incorrigible – a continent without hope... ."

Vaclav Havel, the Czech president, has said: "Politicians should seek office to do what they deem to be right, and not to keep hold of power for its own sake."

A German member of the Maastricht negotiating team said: "There is no alternative to European integration. Any other choice could encourage other countries on the continent to unite against us one day."

The Single European Act and Final Act, 1985, were steered through parliament by a subterfuge worthy of the EU itself. The words "Final Act" did not appear. Its passage was via a tiny sub-clause in a minor Foreign Office Bill debated by a handful of MPs. The clause itself was never discussed.

To get the Bill through the House of Lords, the government issued two order papers for the same debate. The order paper with the correct date went to peers known to be sympathetic. The other, with an incorrect date, went to all the rest. The Bill passed.

Corruption in the EU is one is its most disgraceful features. It is utterly beyond control, and one of the most powerful arguments for its abolition.

Of course the French have these black arts of political mendacity off to a tee. They have generations of experience. They bury their countrymen in bureaucracy.

The Italians go much further, and don't even bother with the niceties of apparently legal procedures. It is beyond doubt that former convicted criminals are supervising law and order in the EU. They are elected representatives of the infamous Forza Italia Party.

Antonio Di Pietro is well known in Italy for his fight against corruption between politicians and businessmen. He is a former public prosecutor in Milan. Several members of the Forza Italia Party, owned by media boss Silvio Berlusconi, faced bribery and other charges thanks to Di Pietro. Today, Di Pietro is an MEP, as are several members of the Forza Italia Party with criminal records for corruption. They sit with Di Pietro on the European parliament's interior committee, which is responsible for supervising law and order in the EU. Signore Di Pietro is known to be horrified, but can do nothing.

Indeed, under the EU's curious logic, these villains can now claim to have some kind of parliamentary immunity. In utter contradiction to the law in the UK, the EU purports to set its bureaucrats, appointees and representatives above the law.

In reality, of course, the committee has virtually no powers. Like all EU parliamentary committees, it exists to offer an illusion of accountability to the people who elected it. The seat of power is the EC, and the commissioner responsible for law and order in the EU is not even a member of the parliament.

It is, nevertheless, discussing – and doubtless has some influence on – anything and everything relating to law and order within the EU – including the proposed new and extensive powers for Europol (the European-wide police force), and international money laundering. Both these topics must be of enormous interest to the Mafia, which operates internationally, and which moves money about with great cunning.

Party leader "Cavalier" Berlusconi MEP is one of the interior committee members. In October 1999, a Milanese court of appeal declared the charges against the media tycoon for illegal party financing to have lapsed. But the court also confirmed massive corruption – to the tune of some 10,000,000 German marks – paid by his companies to a secret Swiss bank account for the benefit of the former Italian Socialist Party leader, Bettino Craxi.

The former Sicilian governor, Marcello Dell'Utri MEP, co-founder of Forza Italia, is also on the interior committee. A lawyer and former manager of Berlusconi's advertising company Publitalia, he was convicted in Italy of falsified accounting and sentenced to 27 months' imprisonment. Other charges relating to falsifying balance sheets and cooperation with the Mafia still lie on the files.

According to Italian law, as a convicted criminal, Dell'Utri should not hold any publicly elected office. Yet he is a member of the Italian parliament as well.

Meanwhile, a Spanish judge, Baltasa Garzon, wants the European parliament to lift the immunity on both Dell'Utri and Berlusconi following accusations that both are involved in embezzlement at the Spanish television company, Tele 5, in which Berlusconi has a major shareholding.

Four other Forza Italia MEPs sit on the culture committee, which deals with the control of the media, among other things.

Di Pietro told the German magazine *Der Spiegel*: "The system of lobbyists and ways to exert influence now operates on a European scale. That is the Berlusconi way." Committee colleague, Martin Schulz, is even more direct in his condemnation: "The Mafia is making the laws here."

All of this is well known in Brussels. None of it attracts any serious attention.

❖

The accumulated cynicism in Britain about the EU has spread rapidly in recent years.

Groups of British schoolchildren were invited to hold mock elections before the June 1999 euro-elections. They were sponsored by the Hansard Society and "an independent think-tank" – code for an EU-funded research group that is, by remarkable coincidence, housed in the same building in London as the European Movement.

The preamble to these mock elections included the observation: "It is no longer possible for any nation state on its own to find solutions to the economic, social and ecological problems of our time." It also claimed that the single currency will "lead to increased financial and economic stability" and attract "world-wide confidence".

How shrewd of the children who took part that the UKIP candidates topped the polls in the first two schools to declare. The results of these elections were never published.

None of that discouraged Keith Vaz, the subsequently discredited and so-called "Minister for Europe", going on a tour of the country, funded by the British taxpayer, between 29th November and 3rd December 1999, as part of the first stage of a campaign entitled "Your Britain, Your Europe" (YBYE). This was organised under the auspices of the Foreign Office.

Several civil servants accompanied Vaz on his campaign bus. They distributed literature at the various campaign stops and wore YBYE stickers.

His tour raised several important questions of legality.

First, is it appropriate that civil servants should behave as though they are political activists? There were never fewer than five civil servants with Vaz at any one time. Was this a proper use of their time at our expense? Was the cost of their salaries for the time they spent out of Whitehall, engaging in political activism, calculated in the overall cost – given as £60,000 – of the first stage of this campaign?

Second, the campaign was coordinated with Britain in Europe and the European Movement. At most campaign stops Vaz was met by activists from these groups – particularly at Waterloo station – who then distributed YBYE literature, in addition to their own materials. Some were seen at times on the campaign bus. At Hull University, Vaz invited students and Labour Party supporters who were pro-EU to join him on his bus and "help spread the word".

This was plainly a piece of political campaigning, funded by the taxpayer, who also picked up the cost of the comedian Eddie Izzard's involvement in the campaign. He travelled first class on EuroStar with Vaz and the rest of the entourage.

And here lies a contradiction. Mr Izzard is quite open in his support of a pan-European superstate. But Mr Vaz claimed repeatedly during the week that the government was opposed to the creation of an EU superstate. So why was Izzard invited to help promote YBYE?

Third, the tour included visits to schools. This almost certainly contravened the Education Act, 1996. Article 406 1b of that Act states that the "local education authority, governing body and head teacher shall forbid the promotion of partisan political activities in the teaching of any subject in the school". Article 407.1 says that headteachers must ensure that "where political issues are brought to the attention of pupils they are offered a balanced presentation of opposing views".

On 3rd December Vaz took assembly at St John's Primary School, Ladywood, Birmingham. A Foreign Office press officer who was handling the PR for the campaign tour, said there was no record of what was said. Presumably, the minister must at some point have mentioned the EU and the alleged benefits of membership. Otherwise, why had he made the visit, given the purpose of his tour? And if he did so, by referring to an institution that is, by definition, a public body with law-making powers, he was making a political statement. And if the EU was mentioned with no counter-balancing comments, then Vaz's comments must have been against the law.

Vaz also spoke at St Joseph's School, Newcastle, to 13- to 15-year-olds, and to 12- to 13-year-olds at Rushey Mead School, Leicester, who were taken by a bus paid for by the local education authority to the *Leicester Mercury* newspaper building. There they were pictured with the minister in a carefully choreographed photo-opportunity.

Finally, why was the tour so blatantly childish, particularly given that it was using public funds? Leaflets and short hustings-type speeches are one thing. Giving away T-shirts, multi-coloured balloons, lapel stickers and carrier bags is something else again. To millions of taxpayers, particularly those on low incomes and still waiting for hospital treatment, such extravagance must have been deeply offensive.

This tour was not the sober public-information-drive of the kind normally staged by government departments.

Worse, the claims in the handouts were highly questionable. Special so-called "fact" sheets were prepared for each area of the country the minister visited. These referred to generous grants and subsidies received from Brussels. No mention was made of the fact that all this money was ours in the first place, and that it represented less than half the total we had paid into the EU. Neither did these "fact" sheets mention that we are actually net contributors, and have been every year since we joined.

Among many other things, they claimed that: "Over 50% of our trade in goods and services is in the EU." This is deliberately misleading. Such a statement would be true only if our huge imports deficit with the EU were included. The impression, however, is that we are talking about exports.

The leaflets also claimed that: "3.5 million British jobs, and one seventh of all UK income and production depends on sales to European countries." This is patently untrue. It could be true only if Mr Vaz was also claiming that – if Britain were not in the EU – there would be no trade between, or economic ties with, EU countries whatsoever, and that all the jobs currently dependent on such trade would disappear. This is a patently absurd proposition.

Mr Vaz's leaflets pointed out that "100,000 Britons work in other EU countries; another 350,000 live there". True, perhaps – but not the whole truth. Those numbers represent 0.15 per cent and 0.58 per cent of the UK's total population respectively. A minuscule percentage, so small as to be almost meaningless. Are we to believe that our membership of the EU is for their benefit, or that they would be thrown out if we left? And what about the percentages of UK subjects who live and work in the USA, Australia, New Zealand and South Africa? There was no mention of them.

According to a report in the *Sunday Express* a couple of months before Mr Vaz's tour, the government was planning to encourage teachers to talk to children as young as five about the EU and its supposed benefits. The previous year, when the UK took over the presidency of the EU for six months, trucks were sent all over the UK distributing videos and glossy brochures about the EU to schools.

Like Mr Vaz's activities, all this was and is in direct contravention of the Education Act, which specifically forbids teaching which is not objective, impartial and balanced.

Of course the EU long ago recognised the importance of infiltrating the education system, and it has been hugely successful in the UK. Today, over 100 university chairs have professors funded directly by the EU. These "Jean Monet" chairs were set up specifically to teach undergraduates about European integration. They cost the EU some £600 million a year in the UK alone – all paid for by British taxpayers.

And for the graduates who want to go on into public administration, the EU now has an Institute for Public Administration (in Maastricht, would you believe) waiting for them, and a European College of Diplomacy in the pipeline.

Universities receive huge cash grants from the EU for "suitable" research projects, and both they and British schools also receive limitless quantities of teaching aids, all aimed at increasing awareness and acceptance of what the EU persists in calling "European integration", even though it is no such thing. The EU does not speak for the continent of Europe. But that did not discourage Brussels from announcing in August 2000 a new initiative which listed 109 areas of education and training where the EU wanted research carried out prior to further investment in the "development" of the curricula in our schools and universities. History and economics were two of the subjects particularly targeted, for obvious reasons.

Little wonder the EU is quite open about its having a propaganda unit. It boasts its own e-mail address: propaganda.unit@cec.org.uk. But not even the employees in that department could bring themselves to launch the EU telephone hotline in the UK in 1997, when it was launched across the rest of the EU at a cost of £13 million. They knew what would happen, and they were right.

Some six months after his ill-fated schools tour, the minister for Europe, Keith Vaz, accepted a challenge to speak at a meeting arranged by the Democracy Movement in London. The former Labour minister Lord Shore was also among the speakers, but spoke on the opposite side of the debate.

An audience of hardened anti-euro and anti-EU activists listened with increasing astonishment to Mr Vaz. He displayed a seriously limited understanding of English heritage and culture, attached no importance to the fact that they have developed over centuries and more than once been defended to the death. He appeared to believe that less than a lifetime's exposure to them allowed him to discard as much of them as he and his government thought fit.

More than once he attempted to trivialise the debate. He was patronising, evaded the important issues, failed to give direct answers to the many questions from the floor, and completely ignored specific challenges from Lord Shore. Instead, he affected "friendship" towards Peter Shore, which was not an adequate response to the verbal roasting Lord Shore had given him.

Here was a government minister, in public, denigrating his own country. As so often on these occasions, he made few specific references, presumably to avoid dispute from a knowledgeable audience. Nevertheless he was regularly interrupted from the floor. His remarks about our being a small country on the edge of Europe, about needing to be part of something much bigger, isolated and left behind if we didn't join the euro, were as well received as a rat sandwich.

But it was his selective and deliberately mendacious use of the few statistics he did mention that lost him any lingering respect. He appeared to have a highly selective memory-loss that day. He claimed that Britain languished at 12th place out of 15 in the EU league table of GDP per head – which sounds terrible. We were fourth from last, he claimed.

But he somehow forgot to mention that Britain has the fourth largest economy in the world and that it has been more successful in terms of growth and employment than all the rest of the EU over the last 20 years.

He omitted to mention that measurement of GDP on a "per head" basis inevitably throws up legitimate distortions. For example, Luxembourg has a tiny population the size of Croydon, Surrey, but it has a huge banking industry. Its GDP is tiny, but its GDP *per head* is massive. He omitted to mention that – Luxembourg and the two basket cases on the Iberian peninsula excepted – the spread of GDP per head among all the other members of the EU is also tiny. The difference is barely 15 per cent, with 9 of the 15 (Britain included) clustered within 10 per cent of each other. He omitted to mention that the British figure is barely two per cent from the average, Luxembourg included. He omitted to mention that, if fractionalised figures are rounded off, Britain is not 12th at all, but joint 9th. He omitted to mention that differences of this minuscule magnitude matter not at all, except perhaps to academic economists.

And all this came from a man claiming the knowledge and ability to argue the case for essential British interests in the forums of the EU.

❖

The villagers of Hawkhurst in Kent have successfully fought a miniature version of the battle over Europe in their village hall.

The local council planned to twin with various towns on the Continent. First it was proposed to twin with the French village of Audricq. Later the council announced a plan to twin with the Italian town of Oriolo Romano. Angry local people believed it was actually about a secret plan to forge a closer union with Europe and making the whole idea of a single European country more acceptable.

A survey conducted in 1998 by the council showed that 65 per cent of the village wanted nothing to do with twinning. When French delegates arrived in Hawkhurst in June 1999 they were greeted with a picket-line protest. They were later given letters in both English and French explaining why anti-EU campaigners wanted nothing to do with them, and a bunch of flowers to let them know it was nothing personal.

Despite such strong local opposition, the council has since told the Local Government International Bureau, an EU quango that funds exchange visits between twinned towns, that it wants twinning with Oriolo Romano to go ahead in 2002.

It was not a unanimous decision. Abstentions at the council meeting allowed a minority vote to win the day, which promptly started another round of lobbying and argument in the village, which was expected to reach a climax at the next local elections.

"It is a total disgrace," Max Axten, who has lived in the village for almost 40 years, told his local paper. "These twinning arrangements have nothing to do with cultural exchanges or being good neighbours. They are political decisions outside the remit of the parish council, designed to pave the way for a united Europe. Hopefully, we will be able to have a vote to un-twin ourselves."

The people of Hawkhurst have good reason to be concerned. The EU's booklet *A Europe of Towns & Villages,* sets out the twinning oath taken by participating places. The mayor or civic leader swears:

> "We the mayors of…freely elected by vote of our fellow citizens, confident that we are responding to the deeply-felt aspirations and real needs of our townspeople, aware that our age-old urban communities were the cradle of western civilization and that the spirit of freedom first took root in the freedoms they contrived to win, believing that the work of history must be carried forward in a larger world, but that this world can only be on a truly human scale if its people live their lives freely in free towns and cities, on this day give a solemn pledge to maintain permanent ties between the town councils of our two communities, to foster exchanges between their inhabitants in every area of life so as to develop a living sense of European kinship through a better mutual understanding and to join forces to help secure, to the utmost of our abilities, a successful outcome to this vital venture of peace and prosperity: the EU."

It was little surprise, then, that the villagers of Emberton in Buckinghamshire rejected a twining proposal in November 2000, and a number of towns and villages around the country had begun to consider holding parish polls to gauge the level of support for untwinning themselves.

❖

Of course we all know that politics is a dirty business. The appointment of Chris Patten as new UK commissioner on the retirement of Leon Brittan met three objectives for Tony Blair all at once. It removed a potentially more dangerous and effective leader of the Tories, it put a europhile in Brussels, and it put a good administrator and an effective British politician at the heart of the EU.

This bureaucratic drive for order and self-justification is everywhere. Bureaucrats hate disorder…the unpredictable maverick…the original…the inspired…the brilliant…and the plain, downright wrong. Yet it is precisely from these sources – and from no others – that life moves on, develops, expands its horizons, and thrives.

The bureaucratic version of politics is not politics at all. It is about only the administration of the economy and society. Essentially the EU is about the unelected elite seizing and retaining power – the power to organise and control and thus dilute the risk of losing power. They make the awesome assumption that they – and only they – know best and always will.

Ironically, the EU's much vaunted bureaucrats are actually not very good at administration. What have they achieved when we peer behind the façade of grandeur? We discover that the emperor has no clothes. Their nakedness is the declining competitiveness of economies on the continent of Europe, low growth, mass unemployment, corruption and the inefficient political processes we see everywhere in the EU. These are some of the problems which drew the Continentals into "ever closer union" in the first place. Instead of reforming them at home, they are now trying to replicate these same problems at a supranational level.

True political freedom implies risk, uncertainty, unpredictability, the real potential for change – all dangerous and destabilising to the bureaucratic mind, which believes they must be minimised or, better still, eliminated if possible.

We all know we live in a single world. We need order, stability and peace. All nations need accountable government, the rule of law and sound money. But we thrive only on choice, the freedom to make decisions for ourselves, the freedom to react to issues as we think best. And we readily acknowledge the rights of others to the same freedoms.

By and large we accept that it is impossible to know the consequences of state intervention. Too many interactive events are beyond the scope of one mind. We need the subtlety of law to enable individuals and society as a whole to make their own decisions in their own best interests.

Law and politics live in and via language – and in the public domain. Politics is the free association of individuals who think of themselves as a people, tied together by a common language, traditions, culture and customs. Law is not a rulebook for an enterprise – it is the framework that enables individuals to develop an enterprise.

British politics establishes opposition at the heart of the law-making process. Where there is no conflict there is no politics – only management. We have been swept up in an elaborate and expensive charade of seriously doubtful legitimacy. Parliamentary scrutiny of EU regulations has been reduced to an embarrassing farce. New directives from Brussels are routinely being passed into UK law with wholly inadequate scrutiny. Yet British law-making is essentially about providing redress when power is abused. It is about representation and debate, it is about understanding the issues of the day and finding equitable solutions. It is not merely about the headlong generation of new laws.

Here, the torrent of paper and decisions and new laws has overwhelmed not only the people but our elected legislature – parliament – which is supposed to protect our best interests. Parliament's European Select Committee is under pressure to process about 1,000 documents a year. Because the committee meets for only half an hour every week each document gets an average of about one minute's scrutiny. As a result, there is minimal discussion and regulations go through on the nod. Inevitably, the government uses the system to get potentially controversial items passed by burying them in a mountain of others – in other words, surreptitiously.

Example: the European Working Time Directive, which costs British business £2 billion a year, was put to parliament the day before the summer recess, thus enabling the government to slip the measure through with the absolute minimum of scrutiny. Keith Vaz, tackled on this issue, could reply only: "No honourable members can say that they are lacking for debate as far as EU scrutiny is concerned."

This deluge of new red tape, most of it not even discussed, is in sorry contrast with the true role of parliament. It fails, too, when compared to procedures in other member states such as Denmark and Finland, where ministers have to account fully for their negotiating positions.

The evidence is all around us. This book is crammed full of it. Lord Tebbit described how the process works, when he spoke to a meeting of the Bruges Group. He talked about his experiences when he was trade minister, and the EU wanted him to bring in a working-time directive. He told them that they could do so in the rest of the EU if they wanted, but he was not introducing it in the UK. They replied: "But that would leave you with a competitive advantage." He then pointed out that they had spent all morning telling him it was necessary for efficiency and competitiveness. All they really wanted to do was shackle the UK with rules and regulations while they then went off and ignored them.

That is one of the many reasons why the Europeans will never push us out of the EU. They need our trade, our fish, our revenue, and our thoroughness. They also know – perhaps better than we do – that we would prosper still further if we were free to develop our markets and opportunities with unfettered innovation and effectiveness outside the control or constraints of the EU.

The former speaker of the House of Commons, Lord (Bernard) Weatherill, has publicly joined the ranks of the eurosceptics, sadly long after he was in a position to do anything about the headlong dash for European integration.

Like his predecessor, George Thomes, later Lord Tonypandy, Lord Weatherill declared his outrage at the loss of British sovereignty to Europe in an interview for *The Sunday Times*. He warned of "seeds of dissension in days to come" on a scale comparable with the break-up of Yugoslavia.

He forecast that future speakers of the House of Commons would become "about as relevant as the former chairman of the Greater London Council. Nobody has ever asked the British public whether they wanted to join the EU. Our freedoms were signed away by Mrs Thatcher in the Single European Act, 1985, which allowed for qualified majority voting. After she lost the Tory leadership she suddenly realised what she had done and railed against it all".

The Roman senator, Cicero, had something to say about that, in 42 BC:

> "A nation can survive its fools and even the ambitious. But it cannot survive treason from within. An enemy at the gates is less formidable, for he is known and carries his banners openly. But the traitor moves among those within the gate freely, his sly whispers rustling through the alleys, heard in the very halls of government itself. For the traitor appears not a traitor – he speaks in accents familiar to his victims, and he wears their face and garments, and he appeals to the baseness that lies deep in the hearts of all men. He rots the soul of a nation – he works secretly and alone in the night to undermine the pillars of a city – he infects the body politic so that it can no longer resist. A murderer is less to be feared."

Britain today is governed by a party with no respect for our past, our traditions, or our way of life. For them, 1997 was year zero. Nothing good happened before that. Like Lenin, they have consigned it all to what they regard as the rubbish bin of history.

Chapter Five

Economic Realities

The UK has flexible employment laws, funded pensions, and an economy that is fundamentally different from those on the Continent. We have a global pattern of trade, the biggest financial services sector in Europe, a small farming industry, a traditional manufacturing base that is diminishing, a services sector that is growing and high technology that is booming.

On the other hand, the EU is an inward-looking command economy with high taxation and centralised state intervention.

The anarchic individualism of traditional (free trade) liberalism and the unpredictability of capitalism is hated by the state planners in Brussels. Lord Stoddart has rightly pointed out that the true goal of the bureaucrats is not even a federal EU but a unitary state with centralised powers.

Instead of an economy driven by the free movement of money, the EU seeks to intensify its control, which started out as social engineering, and is something more akin to authoritarianism and totalitarianism.

Central planners are not discouraged by the facts. For them, political theory is much more important. They cheerfully ignore the fact that the EU's share of world trade has fallen by 25 per cent in the last decade, almost entirely because labour costs, and therefore prices, are too high.

In the autumn of 1998 a policy document issued by the EU set out plans for centralist planning of the economy. It was full of talk about setting wages, imposing taxes and cutting working hours. It assumed a right to interfere in, and manage, every aspect of economic life. It referred to "the co-ordination of monetary, wage, fiscal and tax policy" across the EU to "firmly re-establish the goal of full employment". Incredibly, it was prepared under the supervision of the leader of the Labour MEPs, Pauline Green. The *Daily Mail* said it read like an "old" Labour tract.

Eighteen months later, wiser words emerged from Dr Otmar Issing, German chief economist to the ECB. He published an extraordinarily frank and controversial report in March 2000 in which he warned that the "deep-rooted" hostility to a market economy and free enterprise, the rigidity of its labour markets and the lack of reform in the eurozone posed an "almost lethal threat to monetary union".

His report continued: "An EU which enchains its huge innovative potential through all sorts of regulations, suppresses economic incentives through high taxes, seeks to protect its prosperity from the outside behind all sorts of trade barriers, and strives to redistribute wealth internally, based on an ideology of equality portrayed as justice, renounces not only an important role on the world stage, but also its own future." These phrases distilled the very essence of the EU's political and economic philosophy. They may well have forecast the ultimate outcome with equal precision.

Dr Issing continued: "At the end of the first decade after the fall of the Berlin Wall one cannot but conclude that the chance to use unification as a spur to modernise firmly entrenched structures has been missed. One can make out signs of mystification which glosses over the catastrophic legacy of socialist mismanagement."

He was convinced that the best way to introduce reform was at a national level. At a European level everyone was free to blame everyone else. Any further attempts to harmonise would result in "rising unemployment and mounting tensions between countries and regions".

As we all know, that tension has been strongest in Britain.

The UK's economic cycle has almost always been out of synchronisation with Europe. There is good reason for our economy being much closer to that of the USA. Like them, and unlike other EU countries, we are global players. So our economies and our currencies tend to respond in the same way to the same economic pressures.

Is it any wonder that our economic cycles synchronise with the USA in particular and the Anglo-Saxon world in general, rather than with Europe? We share the view that, broadly speaking, monetary policy should be rigid, but fiscal policy flexible, adaptable to local needs and based on democratic decisions.

The UK is also like the USA in terms of patterns of spending. We use credit cards and store cards much as Americans do. In Continental Europe, cash is still king because so many people do not use banks or declare earnings.

Of course, manufacturing industry is not the great economic force it once was in the UK. Over the last 30 years it has fallen from more than a third of GDP to less than a fifth. Today, our earnings from foreign investment are greater than all our exports put together. Only the USA earns more from its foreign investments.

We earn far more abroad than inward investors earn here. In 1999 alone, UK investment in other countries more than doubled from £55 billion to well over £115 billion, even more than the US invested overseas. This leap made Britain the biggest global investor in the world, and accounted for a quarter of the global total. Some 63 per cent of our overseas investments went to the USA, more than double the sum invested in the rest of the EU.

Four-fifths (79 per cent) of UK overseas investment and sales are outside the EU. Almost 90 per cent of our overseas income comes from outside the EU countries. So this huge and positive balance in income generated by foreign investment comes from a truly global portfolio. The EU hardly features. The figures speak for themselves. Over the last ten years more than a third of our foreign investment has gone into the USA. Another 30 per cent went to Commonwealth countries. A mere 18 per cent went to EU countries.

Today, 32 per cent of our foreign income comes from the 29 per cent of our assets that are located in the USA, while 19 per cent of that income comes from the 22 per cent of our assets in euroland.

In the opposite direction, by mid-2000 Britain was attracting record foreign investments and had become Europe's most popular investment location by far, despite its known reluctance to join the eurozone. The UK had also overtaken China to become the second most popular destination for inward investment in the world. The Americans remain top.

According to a briefing note published by Global Britain, neither "UK membership of the EU", nor "access to the single market" has ever featured in the top ten reasons for foreign investors deciding to invest in the UK – and that finding is based on research conducted by the government's own DTI!

International business people have much better reasons for creating the tidal wave of inward investment, which has seen a massive £147.6 billion in

1996 rise to an even more astonishing £252.4 billion in 1999. At the time of writing it is averaging over £2 billion pounds every month. Britain's inward foreign investment is now the highest in the EU, double that of Germany and France, and four times that of Italy.

In 1997, US investment in the UK was 40 per cent of the total invested in the EU altogether, and double what was invested in any other single EU country. The UK enjoys the second largest inward investment in the world, and brings in more than a third of the total inward investment by the rest of the world in the EU as a whole.

Foreign investors launched 757 projects worth over £250 billion in the UK during the year to March 2000. The USA generated six times as many new projects here as any other nation, and more than half the total, and four times the investment from other EU countries. The total represented an increase of 75 per cent in five years, with a 16 per cent rise since the start of the euro.

For the first time, in the year to March 2000, the UK's service sector attracted half the total new foreign investment. Only five years previously it had been attracting barely a third. This trend reflects increasing interest in our knowledge-based economic activity.

These new investments created a total of 123,000 new jobs in the UK, with almost two-thirds of them coming from the USA and Canada combined. New employment in the UK generated by other EU countries, primarily Germany and France, accounted for less than 20 per cent of the total.

This torrent of trade statistics may be bewildering, but the sum of the parts is inescapably impressive. It shows beyond doubt that our economy, our trade, and new jobs are not dependent on our membership of the EU.

The reasons are obvious. We enjoy economic stability, a positive, flexible and entrepreneurial business environment, high-calibre staff and facilities, outstanding university-based research, an international attitude to trade, easy access to foreign exchange markets, and the English language.

The British have become rich in the last 20 years. The sick man of Europe is now Germany, with France a close second. But do we yet fully understand how important that is? We live in one of the world's strongest and fastest growing economies. We should not take seriously the preposterous propaganda about our vulnerability outside the euro. As a nation that is thriving, we have the freedom to choose, and must soon find the confidence and conviction to say "no thank you".

The UK has one of the most liberated economies in the world, following the changes between 1980 and 1997. In 1980, the UK ranked 16th but by 1997 had moved up to 5th. The main reasons for this improvement are greater monetary and price stability, the removal of exchange controls, privatisation of previously government-run businesses, personal taxes down from 83 per cent in 1980 to 40 per cent, and the total tax burden down to just over 35 per cent.

An "Index of Economic Freedom" rated the UK at 5.9 in 1975 and 8.9 in 1997. The compilers of the analysis use seven criteria – size of government, the structure of the economy and use of markets, monetary policy and price stability, the freedom to use alternative currencies, legal structures and property rights, international exchange, and freedom of exchange in financial markets.

And while we were moving up to 5th place, the Italians languished at 31st, the French and Swedes enjoyed 25th spot, the Germans were at 22nd and none of the other member states of the EU could manage better than the Netherlands at 9th.

Unlike the rest of the EU, government expenditures in the UK as a proportion of GDP have remained comparatively low, but under the Labour government they are now on the increase. For the time being at least, Britain's rate of corporation tax remains the lowest in the industrialised world.

But, although growth continues at a healthy rate, businesses have been burdened with substantially greater regulation and costs over the three years since the Labour government came to power, and this trend is set to get worse.

Is it any wonder that, today, more than half of the UK's managers would not start another business in the UK because of the added bureaucracy and threat of ever more interference? Meanwhile, nothing has been done to improve the mobility of labour that industry and commerce needs but is positively discouraged by subsidised public sector housing and other disincentives.

But the mood in France is worse. In 1998 one in three Britons was pessimistic about the economic future, while the figure in France was almost two in three. And in the first few months after the change of government in Germany, the economic situation went from bad to worse. Output dropped and unemployment rose.

Today, the City of London alone has a GDP greater than that of Switzerland. It contributes over £25 billion to the balance of payments and more from ancillary services – more than North Sea oil. The City of London is the biggest single contributor to UK export earnings. It is the world's premier financial centre. And it transacts the bulk of its business in dollars.

Most UK high-tech exports – aerospace, pharmaceuticals, microchips – are transacted in US dollars. So are oil and gas, and as an oil-producing country like the USA, the UK is a petro-currency influenced uniquely by price movements in that globally vital commodity, which is one of the key reasons for the stability that has existed between the US dollar and sterling over many years.

Crucially, the UK has no such currency relationship with other EU countries, and no naturally occurring reason to devise one. Indeed, the naturally occurring relationship between European currencies ought to be one of modest volatility as their widely differing economies thrive and recess. The very idea that they can all be crammed into one currency is economic illiteracy of the first order.

We need economic cycles out of kilter. When one goes up another goes down – but the one doing well will help sustain and improve the one having a hard time. Harmonising the economic cycles of too many countries has the potential for real disaster if they nose-dive together. The USA and Japan found that out the hard way, albeit briefly, only a few years ago.

Sterling is a major international currency, and one of the most stable. The US dollar, as the dominant world currency, is the benchmark against which the movement of other currencies is measured. It tends to be more volatile when major economies around the world are in an upheaval.

For example, if Japan started to suffer from the inflation forecast by some economic gurus for the next few years, and the USA is forced to adjust, the impact on euroland – and Germany in particular – could be severe. The so-called fixed exchange rate could be tested to destruction. Germany could be forced to devalue, and the Franco-German euro would collapse.

The evidence is already there. Since 1993, both the German Deutschmark and the Japanese yen have fluctuated widely against the dollar. The spread has been as great as 68 per cent in the case of the yen, and 33 per cent with the Deutschmark. These are colossal moves. During the same time, however, sterling has been relatively stable against the dollar. And because it is the UK's major trading partner, it is the dollar/sterling rate that matters most to the British economy.

There is not a shred of evidence that such a situation would be damaged by our staying out of the eurozone, as the europhiles try to suggest. If anything, the evidence is actually against them – we are doing, and will continue to do rather well by being outside the eurozone. It could also be argued that there are positive benefits from being outside the eurozone, not the least of which is the avoidance of financial damage from a fixed and inappropriate exchange rate.

None of these facts has discouraged the euro-enthusiasts from arguing that black is white.

❖

Now let's have a brief look at the cost of UK membership of the EU. Here, too, the facts speak for themselves.

The government's 1999 "Pink Book" shows that the contribution by UK taxpayers in 1998 was £10.3 billion. Some £5 billion came back in the form of grants, with costs and strings attached, and are not what they seem. Also, they are based on the astonishing proposition that the EU knows better than we do how to spend our own money – but we shall consider that issue later.

Looked at in another way, that £10.3 billion was an export tariff on the £96 billion of goods and services we exported to the EU. In that case, at 10.4 per cent, it was nearly three times the GATT world average of 3.6 per cent paid by the USA, Norway and Switzerland as non-members. Even discounting the grants we receive still leaves a tariff of over 5.5 per cent.

A cost/benefit analysis prepared by the Institute of Directors (IOD) in early 2000 calculated the actual cost of UK membership of the EU at some £15 billion a year, which is higher than the official figures because it took into account other costs the government chooses to ignore. However, it also took account of the net benefit of inward investment from EU countries, which the government also ignores in its own calculations.

The IOD report claimed that these figures were on the low side, but they established with solid facts that the costs far outweigh the benefits of membership of the EU. The logical conclusion was that we would be much better off outside the EU, which is why many hundreds of IOD members were bewildered by the report's Alice-in-Wonderland conclusion that the UK should stay in "for the [unspecified] trading benefits"!

Even more seriously, however, the report raised several important questions. Why did it take a quarter of a century to calculate a cost/benefit analysis of our involvement? Why was it necessary for a private organisation to complete the analysis, rather than for the government? Why are we constantly told we must stay in because of the supposed benefits, while no politician or government department has ever produced a shred of verifiable evidence to demonstrate what specific benefits there are? Indeed, they have consistently refused to do so, despite countless requests.

Perhaps the answer to at least some of these questions lies in the fact that when the Treasury started to run a cost/benefit analysis under the last Tory government, Kenneth Clarke, then chancellor of the exchequer, put a stop to it when it became obvious what the conclusions were.

One of the problems for europhiles is the realities of our foreign trade, as Mr Clarke doubtless found. Total exports to the EU, including the Rotterdam/Antwerp effect (the value of goods shipped to Rotterdam or Antwerp for containerisation prior to onward shipping to other parts of the globe – estimated currently at over £2 billion a year) were some £25 billion in 1998. Exports to Asia (excluding Japan) were over £36 billion. None of that discouraged the British foreign secretary, Robin Cook, from claiming that the UK exported more to the Netherlands than to the whole of Southeast Asia. Why let the facts get in the way?

The latest figures for UK trade relate to 1999, when we exported some 13.5 per cent of our total GDP. Of that, some 49 per cent of the goods and services we exported went to the EU. However, after removing the Rotterdam/Antwerp effect, the actual figure was barely 40 per cent, according to calculations by the co-chairman of the Bruges Group, Dr Martin Holmes.

Over the last seven years, the total share of world trade enjoyed by the Continental members of the EU has dropped by 11 per cent. The UK's has increased by nine per cent – mostly to other English-speaking countries, particularly in North America.

In 1999 our ongoing trade gap with the EU continued unabated. The EU is the only area of the world where we have such a deficit. That year it reached almost £9 billion. Meanwhile, we imported less from the rest of the world, and stand in credit by over £100 billion over the same period.

Added to that, UK exports to English-speaking areas are growing twice as fast as they are to EU countries. And UK exports to the EU have been falling in real terms. The other EU countries now buy less from us than they did before we joined the single market!

Even within the rest of the EU there is a trading problem. The idea that this is a single market, and that businesses and consumers all benefit, is nothing more than a monstrous fiction. Even trade between the core countries – Germany and France – has grown more slowly in recent years than the trade each does with the rest of the world.

According to the IFO research institute in Munich, German exports were expected to improve by at least six per cent in the year 2000. The institute also expected the German economy as a whole to improve on the back of this boost to exports, yielding a much-needed reduction in unemployment. By late 2000 there was little sign of either, partly because the cost of crude oil had risen dramatically while the euro had fallen against the US dollar.

In recent years, the German economy has been in serious trouble. Unemployment was an unacceptable 4,000,000 people, imports were growing faster than exports, growth was stagnant, regulations were being piled on by the EU, and the German government was itself in a political mess of sleaze and dissent.

But the weak euro has at least helped to improve all that, especially as the demand for German exports – cars and equipment in particular – has improved.

The euro has brought another benefit to the Germans, too. They are no longer faced with competitive devaluations by other eurozone countries. The French franc may have entered the euro at a particularly favourable rate of exchange, but at least that rate is now fixed. Neither the French nor the Italians can again undercut German prices by allowing their own currencies to fall against the Deutschmark. They must face the German export drive on what the euro-enthusiasts call a "level playing-field".

But with exchange rates no longer able to absorb the pressures, and interest rates equally fixed between those countries, there are only two other ways for the economic pressures between those countries to express themselves – inflation and unemployment. The German boom in exports is likely to generate even more pain in the rest of the eurozone because the other countries can no longer respond effectively.

❖

Pensions are a sore point between the UK and the rest of the EU, not least because Britain has more money invested in pensions – well over £600 billion – than the rest of the EU put together. Such a massive provision for the future is eyed with envy and greed from Brussels.

As a result of our thriving pensions industry, the UK's unfunded pension liabilities amount to a mere £4,000 per head. But if the UK joined the single currency that level of debt would rise to £30,000 for each and every one of us, according to the *Financial Times* in October 1996.

To meet their pension needs France would have to raise income tax by 64 per cent, Austria by 55 per cent, Spain by 45 per cent, Germany by 29 per cent and Italy by 28 per cent. In Britain, we need a 9.5% rise, while the Danes need one of 6.7. On the other hand, Eire could cut income tax by five per cent.

These figures are horrific. Even in Britain, such an increase would be politically disastrous. In most Continental countries, where the situation is worst in the public sector, it is simply unthinkable. According to the International Monetary Fund (IMF), in 1998 the net liability of public-sector pensions, as a percentage of GDP, was 10 per cent in Britain, 75 per cent in Italy, 110 per cent in Germany, 115 per cent in France and over 200 per cent in Belgium.

Worse, the gross debt of these countries, especially when we include their self-inflicted social security obligations, just carries on growing. The irresponsible fiscal fudging required to meet the Maastricht criteria merely hid the problem.

Even now the EU is talking about "harmonising" pensions. Can we seriously believe that the European bureaucrats wouldn't raid our store if they needed to? Where's the evidence that they would back off? There is none. Quite the reverse is true. All the evidence supports the probability that they wouldn't hesitate.

The president of the ECB put it very well: "Monetary union must go hand in hand with political integration and ultimately political union."

In this context, what else can that mean? It can mean only that he intends to get his hands on our assets. There is no doubt that joining euroland means picking up the tab for their non-funded pensions and social security costs. The liability will be ours.

As long ago as 1995, EU President Jacques Delors made the situation and his attitude crystal clear: "EMU means, for instance, that the EU recognises the debts of all countries in EMU." Two years later, Jacques Delors claimed that the EU would share all assets and liabilities. Thus, pension liabilities throughout the EU of over £1,200 billion, and growing, will be treated as a common liability.

In the UK our public pensions costs are about seven per cent of output. In Germany and France they are about 17 per cent. Our private pension funds have accumulated assets equal to over 75 per cent of national output. In Germany it is only 15 per cent, France 6. Added to that the governments of those countries already take via taxation a higher percentage of GDP.

So there is nowhere else for this additional money to come from. The UK is at serious risk of being bludgeoned into paying the lion's share of these pension liabilities across the rest of the EU simply because we will be the only country which has the money.

The EU relies mainly on paying the pensions of an increasingly aging population from income earned by a diminishing labour force. The Tory minister Peter Lilley confirmed in July 1996 that if we joined the EMU then some of the UK's pension funds could be "put at the disposal of the EU" – code for "given away".

As the population ages, and fewer people work, the books simply won't balance. That means higher taxes, financial instability, higher public debt, and – unless something is done to stop the trend – ultimately a collapse of the system.

The OECD has projected the costs of pensions in 40 years' time as a percentage of national income (GDP) for all EU countries and compared them with the costs in 2000. This paints a potentially catastrophic picture.

With the exception of the UK and Eire only, every other country in the EU is facing a doubling or more of its already gigantic pension liabilities in the next 40 years, unless it immediately takes radical and effective remedial action.

That is why the long and sticky fingers from Brussels have already been quietly dipping in the UK honey pot. On the EU's instructions, the UK government mandated local councils to transfer a portion of their pension funds into euros, when it was launched on 1st January 1999. According to the *Mail on Sunday* a year later, "millions of pounds have been wiped from the value of council workers' pension funds because of Gordon Brown's support for the ill-fated Euro".

The newspaper reported that the biggest losses had been sustained by the London boroughs of Brent (loss of £1.8 million) and Enfield (loss of £1 million).

Nobody asked the pensioners in those boroughs if they agreed, the decision was not made on investment merit, and nobody is likely to volunteer the consequences to those pensioners either. But, like it or not, they will ultimately carry the burden because their pension payments will be that much smaller.

Can there be any doubt that the UK's pension funds will move offshore at the first serious threat of sequestration?

In much the same way, British mortgage holders are likely to carry the burden of EU-wide interest rates if we were ever to become members of the eurozone.

Monetary union means control of interest rates passes to Frankfurt. For most of Europe that may not matter too much. But it matters here. Changes in interest rates in the UK have four times the impact on home owners and businesses, according to the Bank of England and the Centre for Economic Policy Research.

We have a much higher proportion of mortgages, and a much higher level of debt on variable interest rates, than any other country in the EU.

Across much of Europe, the attitude to home ownership is entirely different from that found in Britain. Here, owning your own home is regarded as near to essential as makes no difference. It is the ambition of all young couples to buy their own home as soon as possible. For many, their home is their biggest asset by far, and paying for it is their biggest single monthly expense. None of these factors and attitudes applies to anything like the same extent on the Continent. For most, living in rented accommodation is the norm.

That is why the housing mortgage market is highly developed in the UK, but it is not in the rest of the EU. In the UK, mortgage debt is 60 per cent of GDP. In Germany it is 40 per cent, in France 25 per cent and in Italy 10 per cent.

Over ten per cent of UK incomes goes on mortgages, and they are directly exposed to changes in interest rates. Only in Ireland is there a mortgage situation even remotely similar to that in Britain.

Of course, the ECB has kept interest rates low since the launch of the euro, but it was eventually forced to raise them significantly to help stabilise the currency itself. The benefit to euroland exports has been heavily offset by increased costs of crucial imports – principally of fuel and raw materials – but the impact on mortgages has had a significant effect only in Eire, where the price of housing has gone through its own roof and doubled in four years.

There is no realistic prospect of the ECB ever fully recognising the critical importance of interest-rate movements in Britain, or their impact on the economy, on personal income and expenditure, or on UK inflation. Virtually every mortgage-holder in Britain would be directly disadvantaged by our adopting the euro and passing control of interest rates to Frankfurt.

Euroland lenders are less flexible and less competitive. They have only a small number of mortgage packages available. At the time of writing, the average cost of a home loan was almost the same as in Britain, despite a two per cent disadvantage in interest rates. At one time, when British interest rates were three per cent higher than in the rest of the EU, mortgage interest rates were two per cent lower.

When bank interest rates are lower in euroland than in Britain, the mortgage rates in those countries can still be higher than in Britain because the premium on loans is set so much higher. What is worse, European mortgages are usually set at a fixed rate for the life of the contract, which means they are almost always more expensive than a similar deal would be in Britain. European lenders are also less willing to offer the full valuation of the property. In Italy they rarely provide more than half, while French and German lenders will go to 80 per cent at most. First-time buyers in these countries find the acquisition of a house comes later in life, if it comes at all.

"It is a myth that entry into the eurozone will bring cheaper mortgages." This is according to Mike Lazenby, a director of Britain's biggest building society, the Nationwide. "Our economy is fundamentally different from other European countries. There is nothing to say that joining EMU will push mortgages down to European levels – we could see them rise slightly in the short term."

And in the same way that we do not want the UK's mortgage market damaged by the restrictions euroland would impose on us, so it is equally vital to stop the EU's powerful drive towards tax harmonisation, which is certain to be just as destructive.

Tax harmonisation is demonstrably unnecessary, for one supremely important reason. It stops competition between governments, which are congenitally inefficient institutions and which need competition more than anything or anybody else.

In the USA, there is no tax harmonisation between states. They are entirely free to set their own rates locally. As a result, taxation is always being pressed downwards, and pressure for the efficient use of what is collected is continual. Competitive redistribution of money and competitive economic activity also reduces the risk of any localised potential for boom and bust, and helps establish stability – which is, ironically, the very objective sought by harmonisation. Yet harmonisation will produce the exact opposite of what is required.

The evidence is there, staring them in the face, but EU bureaucrats and politicians refuse to admit it. The simple truth is that they find harmonisation attractive because it reduces competition between governments and makes their bureaucratic lives easier. The notion of tax harmonisation also sits well with socialist ideas of equality.

While the chancellor of the exchequer, Gordon Brown, was trumpeting tax breaks in his 1999 budget, his own financial secretary, Dawn Primarolo, was chairing an EU committee dealing with tax harmonisation, which had at least eight recent UK tax breaks under review for abolition.

The seriousness with which the bureaucrats take the goal of tax harmonisation is vividly demonstrated by the ECJ, which can "override direct tax legislation of member states whenever it considers that the objectives of the single market are not being attained". Of course no one has defined these objectives, so the ECJ is once again free to decide EU "law" as it chooses. It is no surprise that the court now regularly sets aside national tax provisions that conflict with its view of the objectives of the single market.

Not that tax harmonisation is the only area in which the differences are currently unbridgeable, certainly for mere political reasons. The cost of labour is another. To an employer in the UK, and in the USA, the on-costs of employing labour are just over 30 per cent. In other words, if you employ someone at £10,000 a year, the real cost to you is £13,000. In France and Germany, the real cost is £15,000.

An employee pays income tax at a basic rate of 21 per cent in the UK. In France, Germany and Italy that figure is over 35 per cent, while in Denmark that same employee pays double – 42 per cent. Those on higher rates of tax are equally worse off. In France and Germany, top rates of personal tax are still well over 50 per cent.

None of this applies in the USA, where the economy has been enjoying the biggest and longest boom in its history. Its tax take is low as a percentage of GDP, but growing fast in absolute terms as the economy itself grows. Meanwhile, most economies in the EU – with the distinguished exceptions of the UK and Eire – have been sclerotic in recent years, and their problems date almost precisely from the boom in EU interference following the signing of the Maastricht Treaty. Ever since then, businesses in the EU have been struggling with tens of thousands of regulations that US companies don't have to bother with, as well as a mountainous tax burden.

All of that is in sharp contrast to the situation when the UK, as the sick man of Europe, decided to join the booming Common Market all those years ago, as a means of reversing its decline. Since then, for totally different reasons, the economic and attitudinal cycle has turned through 180 degrees. Today, the EU is causing us serious damage, and it doesn't take an Einstein to decide the best way forward.

Take VAT, for example – a hefty 17.5 per cent tax at the point of sale. A tax paid by the rich and poor alike, at the same rate. A tax from which a small percentage goes directly to Brussels as part of our membership fee. A tax that the EU regards peculiarly as "theirs". Indeed, the EC has wanted to "harmonise" VAT ever since 1977. QMV may yet achieve it.

At present, the UK "enjoys" – if that's the right word – relief from VAT on essentials – housing, food, medicines, children's clothes, public transport, and knowledge in the written form of books and magazines. It also has a lower rate of VAT on certain other necessities of life, most notably heating fuels.

But all this will change if Brussels has its way with us. VAT is to become a eurotax – and the power to control it has already passed to Brussels. The EU's sixth VAT directive, signed by the Labour government in 1997, imposes VAT on houses, books, food, public transport, children's clothes and a host of other items. Once implemented, it will not be possible for a future British government to remove these taxes, short of our leaving the EU altogether.

Since the beginning of 2000, the EU has also taken the power to set VAT rates, and the target list now includes postal services, internet transactions (without saying how they might be policed), mortgage-interest payments, and other financial transactions.

The EU even talks of adding VAT to credit-card transactions, on top of the sale price itself. It also wants VAT on profits. This would effectively offer two tax bites at the same cherry as profits arise only from a previous transaction on which VAT would already have been incurred. Such an outrageous proposal, were it to be implemented, would also be directly inflationary, as it would increase the pressure on trading margins and force up prices.

All these proposed additional VAT burdens have yet to be enforced in Britain, but as we have seen recently with metrication, the EU is running out of patience with the British and is increasingly pressing the UK government to get in line. The pussy-footing is over.

Various UK governments have already started to pave the way for at least some of these changes. They claim that VAT on houses would protect the countryside, despite wanting to build millions of new homes on green-field sites at the same time. They suggest that VAT on food would help pay for the new Food Safety Authority, which is itself the lapdog of the European Food Safety Agency. They talk of a full rate of VAT on heating fuel as a way of reducing pollution and improving house insulation. It is quite remarkable how, when a government wants to raise taxes, it suddenly finds benefits and good social reasons that were never mentioned before.

❖

That brings us to the euro. Earlier, we looked at the constitutional issues. But other factors are at play.

The threat that the UK could be forced into the euro, regardless of the UK government's view and a possible "no" vote in a referendum, was established several years ago. It stems from a protocol added to Maastricht in 1997, despite the fact that the same treaty appeared to give the UK an opt-out on the euro. The protocol said that no member state could prevent entry [of all members] to the third stage [the euro] of economic and monetary union. The UK has had no choice since 1997.

The notion of a referendum is spurious. It was offered to placate the fears of the British people, and on the assumption that it could be won. Today, neither British fears have been placated, nor is there any prospect of a referendum being won.

The British people know perfectly well that if sterling disappears we will be suffocated in the swamp known as the EU. Our strength and influence as global players and as the mother country of the Anglo-Saxon world will be seriously undermined.

The City is an open, internationally-minded, outward-looking, thriving, dynamic engine for wealth-creation. What possible benefit can it gain by becoming part of an inward-looking, parochial, highly regulated, inflexible alternative? Being cemented into such a structure would rapidly stifle it. Within months, the UK would lose jobs, opportunities, standing in the global financial markets and status in the world as a whole.

The idea of a referendum on joining the euro is a practical nonsense as well as constitutionally illegal. How can we be asked to say "yes" to joining when the economic conditions are right, when the result of a "yes" vote would eliminate the chance to vote "no" later when the economic conditions were wrong again! It would be like walking a one-way plank. Once we had fallen off there would be no way back.

Any referendum question would have to be based on a profound, perhaps deliberate, misunderstanding of the nature of economic activity. If two economies are converging, and they finally meet (that is, appear to be in step) what is to stop them diverging later?

Of course the government has invented five preconditions for euro-membership, of which sustainable convergence is one. But on this particular one – true convergence – we can never know if it has been achieved until long after the event. Mervyn King, deputy governor of the Bank of England, suggested we might have to wait 300 years.

Imagine two people meeting at a cross-roads. They have come from different directions. Suddenly they're in the same place. But who can say they will not go straight on and soon be as far apart as ever? The same is true with national economies. There is no rational basis for assuming that being together today means being together tomorrow.

Today, there is a real possibility that a referendum will never be held – because the government would lose.

Under a single currency all the important decisions about our economy would be taken by politically motivated bankers meeting in total secrecy. This structure undermines the first principle of taxation – no taxation without representation.

They would have the power to make decisions that could put people out of jobs, increase taxes, introduce new taxes, increase manufacturers' costs that in turn would put up prices in the shops, raise interest rates and increase the cost of mortgages. And none of us, including our own elected MPs, could change anything.

The most dangerous risk of all – one interest rate for the whole of Europe – is already demonstrating its effect, its inability to provide the right economic environment for local circumstances. Today, raging inflationary growth in Eire and growing unemployment in Germany are both being aggravated by an inappropriate interest rate. One needs a higher rate, the other a lower rate, and neither is being helped.

Richard Cobden wrote: "I hold the idea of regulating currency to be an absurdity. The currency should regulate itself – by trade and commerce. It should be left to the discretion of individuals…they know best what is in their best interests."

Sound money is essential to both parties to a contract. Otherwise one or the other is defrauded. Government's only proper role is to ensure sound money, not to interfere with it or its value, nor to try to regulate it.

A planned economy destroys the link between supply and demand and thus undermines sound money. On the other hand, a free market provides open competition between producers and the fullest choice for consumers. And both parties to a contract – even the simple process of buying and selling goods – must be free to determine for themselves the unit of value they wish to use. Normally this takes the form of money and in the UK that money is normally the pound sterling. But neither of these statements is always true, nor should they be.

People use currencies for other purposes, too. It is a store and measurement of wealth, as well as a means of transacting business. It is a commodity. It can be used to establish the value or worth of something else. It can influence supply and demand. It can provide an honest valuation of a contract.

But all of these things are true only if the currency itself is sound, and the government responsible for it understands and values these critical functions. Ultimately, nowadays, the stability of a currency is a measure of confidence in the government and country that issues it. If the economy is growing, inflation is under control, interest rates reflect the current situation and future prospects, the tax burden is not onerous, capital investment is strong and wealth is being created by enterprise, then confidence in that currency will be high.

But the reverse is also true. The less those factors apply, the weaker the currency will be. A currency's value fluctuates whenever there are either more buyers or sellers of it. This is not speculation, it is capital seeking safety. Exchange rates – or the difference between the value of currencies – move directly as confidence moves between them. They also move to maintain equilibrium between economies. Currency movements are a pressure release-mechanism, and clamping such a valve shut will always result in an explosion.

Exchange rates are not an aspect of the economy that can be treated in isolation. Interest rates, in particular, directly influence exchange rates, and are just as directly influenced by them. Every country, particularly those with distinctive economies, need interest rates to meet their individual and particular needs.

The differences between economies must be capable of reconciliation by other means if exchange rates have been fixed artificially so that they can no longer reflect these differences accurately and quickly. There are no other economic solutions possible except disruptive movements in unemployment, growth and inflation, or catastrophic migration.

As euroland has found out the hard way already, exchange rates cannot be abolished. Neither can they be managed in defiance of economic realities. They are the shock-absorber of international trade. They take the pressure created by inept monetary and fiscal policies, and they reflect the success of good management. They are not the plaything of speculators, as inefficient governments love to claim.

Speculators aren't even speculating. They are selling the currency that is not worth its present value, and buying the currency that is worth more than the present price. Speculators are the means by which economic facts of life are expressed. They provide an essential service to importers and exporters. They are in the business of reflecting monetary reality, however much governments might like to argue otherwise.

If movements in exchange rates did not take the pressure and reflect economic trends between trading nations, those pressures would have to be taken by much bigger movements in inflation, unemployment and interest rates. The free movement of exchange rates is essential. It is an asset to a healthy economy, and encourages good management. It is not a liability.

Deutsche Asset Management's chief investment manager has forecast that the euro will cease to exist within ten years on the grounds that the economies of the EU are "too diverse for a one-size-fits-all interest rate policy to be sustainable".

That, of course, is only one of its flaws. There are several more, and every one of them is so critical it would be reason alone to avoid becoming part of the single currency. Setting interest rates for the average need, when there is no average majority, is as absurd as sitting with one foot in a freezer and the other in a hot tub. It is ludicrous then to claim that, on average, you are comfortably warm.

Bigger budget deficits and higher unemployment in other countries should not be the responsibility of those who have pursued wiser economic policies for decades. And by what right do others demand and then enforce an endless transfer of wealth from the rich who created it through their own hard work and sound judgment to the poor who have had much the same opportunities and failed to take them?

Much the same question can be asked of the proposal to harmonise taxation, which is simply code for increasing it to the level of the highest. Again, the real motivation is not to create a level playing-field but to bail out the inefficient. Governments are always inclined to tax their way out of any problems. Either that, or they devalue their currency.

The governor of the Bank of England, Eddie George, became increasingly more vocal in his scepticism about the UK's joining the euro in the months after its launch. On one occasion, he likened it to an elephant getting into the EMU rowing boat. "It would have made it difficult to avoid an inflationary boom." He admitted that the British economy remained divergent from the Continent. He blamed the "persistent weakness" of the euro and criticised EU governments for being slow to improve the flexibility of their economies.

Subsequently, Sir Eddie George (as he now is) warned the president of the ECB, Wim Duisenberg, that there "must be sustainable convergence between the UK economy and eurozone *for the euro to succeed*" (my emphasis). He did not say "...for the UK to join", which is the Labour government's position. Mr Duisenberg had claimed that the UK had a window of opportunity to join the euro.

Meanwhile, research by the Bank of England at the end of 1999 showed that joining the euro would cost the UK up to £9 billion a year. Pension-fund managers Phillips and Drew have calculated that British pension funds alone could lose up to £5 billion if the UK scraps the pound and joins the euro. The company estimated that the total loss faced by the entire UK institutional investor community could be as high as £10 billion.

Not all of euroland is happy about the currency it has already joined. A group of German economists predicted in June 2000 that the euro will fall apart and plunge Europe into a financial catastrophe. The four German experts claimed the launch of the EU's single currency would eventually be seen as a failed experiment. "It is possible that European politicians and their scientific aides see and fear this catastrophe coming and are, therefore, trying to talk the euro up," they said in a joint statement. "But it can't and won't help."

The economists, former Bundesbank director Professor Wilhelm Noelling, Professor Wilhelm Hankel, Karl Albrecht Schacht-Schneider and Professor Joachim Starbatty, said they were wary of the euro from the start. They warned that the EU's economic recovery and job-market improvements were temporary as they were caused by the weak euro. "Mistakes that have already been made will be compounded by the rush to extend the EU by admitting economically weak candidates."

Elsewhere in Germany, a survey by the respected Allensbach Institute showed that support for the euro had slumped from 40 per cent at its launch to 31 per cent only 18 months later. Sixty per cent of the German population do not want to accept the new notes and coins in 2002 and 71 per cent said they had little or no trust in the euro. They expected it to fall further in value. Research published by the EC itself at much the same time revealed a similar, if not identical, fall in support for the euro in Germany. It also showed that only one German in three still trusted the EC, and only two in five Germans still thought membership of the EU was "a good thing".

The Allensbach Institute survey also showed that many Germans were bitter about their politicians telling them lies and making false promises. *Bild*, the biggest daily paper, was accused of a conspiracy to manipulate the public by failing to print any letters from its 12,000,000 readers who were anti-euro. Germans see foreigners as slow to invest in their highly-taxed economy while cash is flooding into Britain. The decision by Deutsche Telekom to plan the takeover of Cable & Wireless was seen as more than ample evidence of the trend that is damaging the German economy. But Deutsche Telekom was bullish, and confident. "If people have concerns about Britain not being in the euro, then we don't share them," commented one of the company's senior management in the media in July 2000.

Close observers of the economic scene in Germany have also drawn attention to other events recently. Up to three years ago the Bundesbank had held some $7 billion-worth of gold. For many years the quantity and value had been unchanged, subject to minor fluctuations only.

But by the end of 1999 that figure had suddenly risen to $33 billion-worth. Germany had acquired $26 billion-worth of gold in under two years. The Bundesbank claimed it was the result of revaluation, but the change in weight of gold held was not available to prove or disprove the claim.

Now why should the Bundesbank either buy more gold, or revalue? And why do it now, precisely?

Of course there was a fuss in Germany about revaluing gold when the countries joining needed to meet the Maastricht criteria. The revaluation of gold to reduce the level of public debt in that one critical year was one of the ideas mooted at the time. The public was outraged.

A few other facts add to the mystery. Many Germans did not want to give up the Deutschmark and join the euro; and the German government went into the euro "conditionally". The German constitutional court was asked to rule on the legality of entry. They said Germany could join conditionally. The agreement was never ratified in Germany.

So the question arises...what is now to stop the German Bundesbank saying one day: "Enough is enough, the euro is a disaster. We're relaunching the Deutschmark underpinned by our massive stores of wealth – gold."

The French and Italians would be scuppered, to say nothing of the Benelux countries nearby. They'd all have to join in a Deutschmark zone controlled by the Bundesbank. They would have little choice. And, hey presto, the Bundesbank gets what it's always wanted – control of monetary policy in the EU.

Meanwhile, there is another nightmare scenario to worry about. If the euro runs into even deeper trouble, and goes into freefall, are we going to see exchange controls reintroduced – among other things to prevent people from moving their assets abroad?

The EU might even declare a state of emergency and turn to the British for rescue. The logic would then be to enforce the terms of the treaties and compel the British to join, saying, in effect: "Sorry, there's no time for a referendum, this is an emergency after all, the pound is in, we need to prop up the euro and we need your assets."

Only Luxembourg qualified for the single currency under the terms of the Maastricht Treaty. All the rest fudged their accounts. Belgium and Italy had debt levels more than double the top limit, so Belgium redesigned its public sector deficit, and Italy introduced a special eurotax, 70 per cent of which was supposed to be repaid by 2000. It wasn't. Yet the special tax was still described as a lasting reduction in their deficit.

The French fiddled their telecom's pensions by making them state assets – but omitted to show the liability to pay pensions on the other side of the balance sheet. The Irish claimed that their EU contributions were the fruits of their own labour. And so it went on. Finally, as if by miracle, they all qualified. But they also displayed a blatant contempt for the rule of law, and a frightening indication of things to come. How can pension funds and national assets be regarded as sacrosanct in the hands of such people?

As Norman Lamont said at the time: "How can anyone believe in the impartial rule of law in the EU any longer?"

Maastricht said qualifying countries must have a debt-to-GDP ratio of under 60 per cent, "unless the ratio is sufficiently diminishing and approaching the reference value". Since then Germany's ratio had risen from 44.1 to 61.2, Austria's from 58 to 68.9, Spain's from 48.3 to 69.8, and poor old Italy from 108.7 to 122. Only Belgium has achieved a reduction, from 128 to 123.6, but that is still more than double the target.

The stability pact also provided for fines if countries failed to sustain these ratios – but it made no distinction between cyclical and structural deficits. In any case, if such fines were applied they would have the effect of making a bad situation worse.

The Exchange Rate Mechanism (ERM) fiasco at the end of the 1980s, and into the 1990s, cost Britain over 1,000,000 jobs and bankrupted over 100,000 businesses. That was the moment millions of Britons first fully realised what an error of judgment they had made in 1975 when they voted "yes" to stay in the then Common Market.

Today, we have largely recovered, but for many individuals there was and never will be any recovery. Those at the end of their working lives at that time have had to live with the consequences to this day. But, taken as a whole, the UK has recovered, and more. Today, the UK economy is buoyant, labour costs are far lower than most of euroland and so is unemployment.

When the euro was introduced in January 1999, British inflation was double that of the 11 eurozone countries. Within 18 months, euroland inflation was double that in Britain.

Maurice Fitzpatrick of accountants Chantrey Vellacott commented when that fact emerged: "I cannot see any features of sustainable convergence between Britain and euroland. If anything, there has been further divergence since the euro was launched."

Their economies were not only diverging from Britain's, but from each other's. Five of them already had serious inflationary problems from economies that were overheating.

Meanwhile, the euro itself had become the sick currency of Europe. It had few friends. The French hardly used it. Many people there considered it a monumental waste of effort. "Catastrophe" was the word used by a spokesman for one French retail chain that had spent vast sums converting its tills and accountancy systems to cope with the euro.

Successive new lows against the dollar (down over 25 per cent) and the yen (down a massive 40 per cent) revealed the foolishness of the ECB's policy of benign neglect and the inadequacy of its one-size-fits-all interest-rate policy.

In Eire, their central bank warned that inflationary pressures were building up rapidly against excess domestic demand and galloping growth. In the first year of the euro, the Irish economy grew by an unsustainable 8.25 per cent, and the same rate was expected for the following year. Workers were demanding 20 per cent wage increases on top of big increases already agreed, and backing these demands with strikes.

Inflation was rising so fast it was almost out of control, property prices were increasing at nearly 40 per cent a year, and local economists were saying interest rates should be more than double the current ECB's euroland rate of 4 per cent. The Irish press had long since been expressing serious doubts about the wisdom of their joining. They did so, of course, assuming the UK would soon follow – a big mistake. The Irish have been saddled with the wrong interest rates, raging inflation, and no means of addressing either. Local economists have estimated that Eire now needs interest rates at 14 per cent.

These calls for action have gone unheeded. The Irish have been left to fry in their own overheated juice. Restoring the competitive edge of the German economy has been regarded as far more important by the ECB, and low interest rates and a falling euro have been helping to achieve that overriding objective.

That brings us back to the issue of truth. The figures quoted earlier demonstrate the inescapable truth that the euro is not about economics. Britain is thriving outside the eurozone. The economic facts also prove that it would thrive outside the EU altogether. Strip away the spin-doctoring about the euro and it is as clear as day that the euro is ultimately about sovereignty.

Any country can remain independent only so long as it has control of its financial affairs. Leaving aside for a moment the huge issues of day-to-day management and fiscal control, the end-game is simple – how else can it protect itself? Who pays for the security of the nation when faced with an external military threat and the purse strings are held elsewhere?

Lose control of our financial affairs and the UK is no longer an independent nation.

Chapter Six

The Business of Business is Business

Monetary union was sold to the people of Continental Europe as a panacea. They were told it would reduce costs, reduce unemployment and create prosperity. The realities behind these wild and unfounded promises tell a different story.

Claims that monetary union makes it easier for buyers to compare prices are nonsense. Price discounting is a function of trade, not of monetary policy, nor currencies. The assertion that exchange costs are reduced is also nonsense. Exchange rates are a zero-sum game, as we shall see in a moment.

If travellers and businesses don't have to pay exchange costs they save less than 0.1% of GDP altogether – a sum that is barely measurable. And because UK businesses sell less than half their exports to EU countries, and we do not travel exclusively to them, we still have exchange costs and risks on the bulk of overseas sales and travelling.

It is not a problem to hedge currency risk. Many businesses generate a great deal of income by hedging and trading in currencies. If a currency is strong and getting stronger, the strategy is to buy now or forward. If it is weakening, wait. The people who complain about currency movements and risk simply don't understand them.

On the other side of each transaction is the bank that makes the deal. So when the trader wins, the bank loses, and vice versa. The net result is *always* zero.

In fact, for the banking and business sectors, the costs and losses caused by the introduction of the euro in the eurozone itself have been considerable – far in excess of any piffling savings.

Many companies and organisations have borne the huge cost of conversion already. One plc has admitted spending over £150 million.

Taking the larger companies as a whole it has been calculated that they are spending on average over £30 million each on conversion despite the fact that under ten per cent of the profits of the UK's top 100 companies come from the other EU countries. Many have no possibility of recovering that money from future euro-related business.

But that is not the whole story. Most UK businesses do not trade with Europe. Yet they all face the cost of conversion – with no chance of gaining any of the supposed benefits.

The total cost of converting sterling to euros has been estimated at £36 billion. This huge sum includes updating all computers, vending machines and cash tills, as well as staff-training and merchandising costs.

The government's own expenditure on conversion is put at £3 billion. Originally, Tony Blair told the House of Commons that the cost to the public sector was a vague "tens of millions", an error of several hundred per cent it later transpired.

Meanwhile, an ICM survey of 1,000 company chief executives early in the year 2000 revealed that 80 per cent of them were not prepared to authorise any significant preparations for a changeover from sterling to euros until they knew the results of a referendum. Opposition to joining the euro among the business community had grown to a swingeing 69 per cent by autumn 2000, having risen steadily since the euro was launched.

Looked at as a purely business decision we see a situation that should appal any responsible director. He or she is being asked to commit huge amounts of shareholders' funds just to meet some possible legal requirement years down the road. Furthermore, most investors expect this project to fail.

UK directors have a duty of care to their shareholders. Directors do not have the right to fritter away their companies' assets on highly speculative and questionable expenditure, to which the shareholders have not given their assent. The simple truth is that they have been invited to join a high-risk, unproven scheme, which offers a negative return, and to do so on the basis that they can never opt out, never de-merge, and never sell the shares. An absurd proposition.

If the chairman of a company squandered large sums of shareholders' funds on such an ill-considered, wasteful, inefficient, loss-making venture, he or she would rightly be removed from office for incompetence, barred from holding office as a director in future, and probably prosecuted for fraud or corruption.

No one knows better than the owner what is the best use of their capital – certainly no government. Capital investment can be maximised only by owners of capital. Every time government intervenes in that process, either by diverting that capital or by removing it in taxation, the economy and the potential for growth is damaged.

Neither parliament, shareholders, taxpayers, nor electors, have given their assent to the euro. It is increasingly unlikely they will ever do so. Meanwhile, in the unlikely event that customers or suppliers want to trade in the euro, or any other currency, British business people can do what they have always done – set their margins where they want them, buy or sell forward to cover the risk, and carry on as before. It really is that simple.

On the BBC's *Today* programme in February 2000, when asked how many British companies export to the EU, the chancellor of the exchequer plucked the figure of 750,000 out of thin air. This was not disputed by the interviewer. But Gordon Brown was exaggerating. His guess was 15 times higher than the truth.

Both the Institute of Export and the Bank of England estimate the total number of UK exporting companies at about three per cent of all companies in the UK. So, between 100,000 and 115,000 UK companies are involved in exports to some degree. The hard core is about 50,000 – and that is also about the number of exporters to the eurozone.

A damage-limitation exercise after the broadcast was mounted by the Treasury press office, who spun a web of further deceit by suggesting that Mr Brown had included all those companies that deal with companies that export to the eurozone – suppliers' suppliers' suppliers. They appeared not to notice the absurdity of such a notion.

Next, we are told the euro will help reduce unemployment. But employment is influenced by costs and demand. So long as social security costs on employment remain excessive in Europe, so will unemployment.

Employment has nothing whatever to do with monetary union, beyond being a pressure valve when other components of an economy get out of kilter. And there is another problem – a significant inflexibility of labour in Europe. Any solution to pan-European unemployment requires a ready movement of labour from place to place.

It happens in the USA – but it will not happen in Europe either now or in the foreseeable future. And if labour can't or won't move to the jobs and the jobs won't move to them, the problem remains insoluble. All of that has nothing to do with monetary union.

When the UK foolishly joined the ERM (a prelude to the euro) in the late 1980s, unemployment rose to 3,000,000, and the national debt spiralled upwards with it. The UK suffered five years of recession or no growth. Simultaneously, but for different reasons, on the Continent a recession was worse and lasted longer. Unemployment rose to over 20,000,000. Since the UK was ejected from the ERM Britain has created more jobs – nearly 3,000,000 – than the rest of EU put together. In the same period Germany has lost 2,000,000.

Today, unemployment is under 4 per cent in the UK, but averages over 11 per cent across euroland, when UK figures are included, and 13 per cent when they are not.

The USA has a population of about 270,000,000. In recent times it has been creating on average at least 2,000,000 new jobs a year. The EU has a total population of about 360,000,000. In 1998 it created 1.8 million new jobs, but even that total was exceptionally high by recent standards. So the figures speak for themselves – the EU has a population 25 per cent bigger than the USA, but generates fewer jobs.

In the USA, almost three-quarters of the population has a job. In the UK 71 per cent, in Germany 64 per cent, in France 59 per cent and in Belgium a mere 28 per cent work for a living. Those last three countries all have taxation levels and social security costs that positively discourage people from working.

Much of the new employment that has been generated in the EU, especially in France, has been in the public sector, which in turn has added to the tax burden. Civil servants in Germany and France make up nearly ten per cent of the workforce – double the UK figure. While the Banque de France and the Bank of England perform roughly the same function for countries with roughly the same populations, in Paris the Banque employs 16,000 people. In London, the Bank employs 6,000.

The Union of Industrial and Employers' Confederation in Europe (UNICE), in a 1998 report on European job prospects, co-signed by the Confederation of British Industry, said: "The EU's employment record is dismal. Since 1970 the US economy has created just under 50 million new jobs, whilst the EU has created just over five million. For every ten jobs created in the US, only one is created in Europe. Unemployment stands at 17 million in the EU – 10% of the workforce."

Dr Gerald Lyons, chief economist of DKB International, speaking in London on 17th November 1998, coined a new definition for EMU. He said: "This poor jobs performance in Europe has not been a short term development. It has been a sustained problem. This problem is not about to be reversed... . European monetary union will make Europe's jobs problem worse. EMU stands for Even More Unemployment."

There are nearly 4,000,000 companies in the UK, but only a third of them employ more than one person. Only 0.1 per cent of British businesses employ more than 500 people each. The other 99.9 per cent do not, yet they are responsible for well over half of all employment in the UK. Also, barely three per cent of them have any trade with the rest of the EU, either as exporters or importers.

So the scare-mongering claim that 3,000,000 UK jobs depend on EU membership is entirely false. A few thousand jobs would be directly affected if we left the EU, but only in the short term. An explosion of new activity and confidence would quickly replace them, and create many more. Only 87 MEPs, 2 commissioners and a few civil servants would be permanently out of jobs.

Finally, to the promise of more prosperity.

Freedom of choice is the dynamic of a healthy economy. It is the very anarchy – unpredictability – of freedom of choice that is the greatest strength of any economy.

Destroy that – by misguided so-called economic planning, by oppressive fiscal or irresponsible monetary policies – and you destroy the engine of wealth-creation. Economic planning is the fast route to the sick bed. The end-game is to plan the economy to destruction. It's been proved many times over from Lenin to Harold Wilson. And it's still going on in Europe today.

What was peddled as a "free market" is nothing of the sort. If anything, it has proved to be the exact opposite. That is why we should have none of it.

❖

There is not – nor ever can be – a commercially level playing-field, despite its being the dream of all left-wing politicians. Endless directives supposedly trying to equalise costs and obligations are absolutely certain to end in trouble. Either they regulate businesses out of business, or they create a hotbed of corruption, or both. The EU is already achieving both.

Bureaucrats simply don't understand that economies thrive on competition, on freedom of choice for consumers, on freedom to set prices and specifications for manufacturers and retailers, and on the right of all of us to make shrewd purchases – and to make mistakes. The freedom to make mistakes is an essential ingredient in a vibrant economy.

Prosperity is not a gift of government. It is the result of enterprise. The only contribution a government can make towards that is to encourage the conditions that allow enterprise to thrive. Broadly, that is best achieved by doing precisely nothing – except perhaps undoing much of the damage done in the past. What is needed is the exact opposite of the EU's present obsession with regulating everything.

The EU wants to gain control over our economy, to regulate our enterprises, to restrict our freedom to trade – except on their terms. They want to dilute our trading power with the rest of the world, to dominate us in a European environment that currently takes barely 15 per cent of our output.

During many encounters, French officials convinced Paul Knocker – an Englishman then working in Brussels – that they had three main reasons for promoting UK membership:

First, to reduce the UK's competitive advantage in world trade and the dominant position of the London financial markets. Second, that the UK was a significant net contributor to EU funds. Third, to keep the UK open to European goods and services and maintain the UK's net trade deficit with Europe. In brief, he became convinced that they needed us far more than we needed them.

Everybody knows that we trade far more with the USA than any other country in the world. We export more to the USA than to Germany and France together. Our economic cycle echoes the USA's, rather than Europe's. So does our pattern of taxation.

The US dollar is the most widely traded currency in the world. Like the US dollar, and unlike any European currency, sterling is a petro-currency.

The US dollar is the currency we use more than any other than our own. It is the currency we track. Our currency convergence is well established – with the US dollar. The euro is not going to replace that in the foreseeable future, quite possibly never.

We need to trade internationally just as we have always done.

Britain is a healthy and attractive commercial proposition for the rest of the world. English is the global language of business. Now add in our flexible – but increasingly threatened – labour laws, our level of labour and social security costs, and our levels of taxation, and what have we got? It may not be ideal, but the UK has the best trading environment in Europe.

The German entrepreneur Peter Dussmann wanted to open a bookshop in Berlin and keep it open until 10.00 p.m. He was taken to court by the local trade unions for breaking labour laws. More than 18 months later he won his case by reclassifying all his workers as senior management, including the cleaners.

In January 1999, the French government prosecuted the managing director of a private firm for allowing staff to work more than 35 hours a week. They wanted to work 46 to finish a job and meet a commercial commitment. What they did was commercially right and politically incorrect. Political incorrectness prevailed, and the penalty wiped out all the profits.

Lucien Rebuffel, who heads the organisation that represents 1.5 million small businesses in France, told an EU-wide survey that the 35-hour week there was "complex, rigid, costly, and little use [in] creating jobs. French companies face a serious handicap [from] increased costs".

Given such problems, and the situation in which they find themselves, is it any wonder that European business people are already finding the temptation to move here irresistible? In recent times, over 2,000 German companies have actively enquired of the Federation of German Industry about moving their businesses out of the country.

Many companies – not just German – are exporting themselves, lock, stock and barrel. Fed up with all the regulations and the cripplingly high cost of labour, they have simply moved their entire businesses to other countries. Some have come to Britain, others – especially those located in Germany – have moved east to the Czech Republic, Hungary and Poland, despite the risk that those countries may one day join the EU and they will have the same set of problems all over again.

Among the German companies seriously considering a move to the UK, Allainz, the country's biggest insurer, threatened to go. Sony moved some of its manufacturing from Germany to the UK to reduce costs. Dana Engineering took over a factory in Germany, changed its mind and moved to Leeds instead. The German electricity company RWE threatened to relocate to the UK to avoid taxes and costs.

Several big French companies have bought UK companies recently to diversify their interests and risks. Many others are considering a similar move. In 1998 alone, several major French companies bought UK companies. AXA bought the Guardian Royal Exchange, the French electricity supplier EDF bought London Electricity, Lafarge bought Redland, Imetal bought English China Clays, Artemis bought Christie's, and many other smaller deals were also completed. Indeed, tens of thousands of Continental companies have established a legal presence in the UK solely to avoid the regulations and taxation regimes that cripple enterprise there.

Yet more companies already in the UK – such as Rolls Royce – have said that they will stay in the UK provided that we do not join euroland.

Our politicians tell us how terrible life is outside the euro, talking down their own country in a disgraceful attempt to convince us that we must join, that it is somehow "inevitable". The facts say otherwise. Ever since it became known that we were not joining the euro, and that the British people were solidly against it, inward investment has been rising. Of course some companies and industries are having a hard time. That is what happens in the commercial world. Good management and poor management, strong demand and weak demand for the products and services they offer – these are the real factors at work, not membership of the euro or not.

Rover plant-workers were conned over the role of the euro when BMW pulled out in March 2000. The rush to find scapegoats was positively indecent. Everybody blamed someone else. The unions blamed management, the government blamed BMW, BMW blamed the weak euro, the eurosceptics blamed the EU. Not many blamed the lack of funding.

Yet a lack of capital was one of the key causes of Rover's problems. When BMW first bought the company, the British government offered £150 million in aid to support BMW's investment. This was vetoed by the EU's Italian competition commissioner, Mario Monti. Usually, EU objections to national subsidies for local industrial problems – including several in Italy

– are carefully timed to take effect after the benefits have been felt. The rules are upheld, but not so that they destroy jobs. The rescue of Air France was the classic case. With Rover, however, normal practice was ignored. The rules were enforced immediately and directly to the disadvantage of the UK.

Partially French-government-owned companies like Nissan have their puppet managing directors tell us that they will be closing down their car plant and switching manufacturing to elsewhere in the EU. But blaming it on the "strong" pound (equals weak euro) was a political statement, not a business decision. The company's poor commercial position was the real motivation behind the decision.

Meanwhile, many other foreign motor manufacturers were making precisely the opposite decisions at precisely the same time. When Nissan made that announcement, Ford announced a $3 billion investment programme in its UK operations over the next five years, while General Motors announced a £200 million investment in three major UK plants. Honda launched a £130 million modernisation programme to build a new four-wheel-drive model in Swindon. And Peugeot started working a seven-day week at their Wrighton plant, to meet demand for its 206 model.

All that happened within a month of the Nissan announcement – but hardly a word appeared in the British media.

And it was not just the motor industry that was doing well. Motorola invested £1.3 billion to buy and equip the Hyundai semi-conductor factory in Dunfermline, Fife. The French glassmaker Saint-Gorbain announced plans to open its first glass plant near Selby in North Yorkshire, an investment worth £65 million. Marconi announced the creation of 2,200 new jobs in Coventry from an investment of £100 million.

Little wonder that the Economist Intelligence Unit found that Britain was currently the second best place in the world to invest after the Netherlands. It was expected to retain this position for at least the next five years, regardless of the euro question. And the number of foreign-owned companies in Britain – almost 29,000 by the end of 2000 – was expected to go on rising by several hundred a year.

London and southeast England is now the wealthiest part of Europe. If it were a separate country, it would have the fifth largest GDP in Europe, and be among the most economically powerful in the world.

In 1998, over 400,000 citizens of the EU came to live in the UK. Contrary to popular perception, for every English person living in France, four French people now live in Britain. Over 250,000 French now live and work here, compared with 65,000 Britons living in France. Most French have come in recent years to escape high French taxation and to have more freedom in running their businesses. Well over 150 French companies have re-located here for precisely those reasons.

❖

EU regulations force the public sector to put contracts out to tender across all 15 member states. The Ministry of Defence in London placed a £5.5 million textile order for uniforms with a German firm knowing that our textiles industry was in acute crisis. How did the German firm win? By using cheap labour in Turkey.

Public sector regulations may be one thing. But, for tens of thousands of other businesses, the commercial environment in which they trade has deteriorated because of the regulations and costs generated from Brussels. During the 1997 election campaign the Labour Party promised to cut back on red tape. By 1999, it was issuing regulations faster than any other administration in history – over 3,200 in 1998 alone – that's 10 a day. While the USA and the rest of the Anglo-Saxon world is booming, the UK under a socialist government is now growing regulations faster than new businesses.

Much of this torrent is excused on the grounds that it comes from Brussels, and that ministers' hands are tied. Every single one of these new regulations adds costs to business, at the very least by absorbing management time in unproductive work.

The cost of the working-hours directive, introduced in 1999 and estimated by the government at £2.3 billion, was the most expensive legislation ever imposed in the UK. The cost of this to the NHS alone is over £100 million a year, to cover extra staff costs generated by the legislation and its impact on the calculation of holiday pay for nurses, which now includes overtime earnings.

Many businesses estimated that they would have to lay off up to ten per cent of their workforces to pay for it. Most have had to absorb or pass on a seven per cent increase in costs.

The Continental European bureaucrat's idea of free trade is to protect his or her own patch and prise open someone else's.

Try opening a new business in Italy. It is virtually impossible. In many cases, it's actually illegal to do so, because the Italians haven't passed the necessary legislation in their own parliament. Meanwhile the only options are to acquire or merge with an Italian firm, and overcome all the exhaustive compliance requirements still in place to obstruct outside competition, or become a supplier to one. Even Rupert Murdoch's vast and powerful media empire has been unable to get into the Italian market.

It is as closed a shop as the unions in Britain used to operate, with a Gordian knot of regulations, permits, licences and other approvals required before a newcomer can do business. It can have only one purpose – to keep others out. Much the same is true elsewhere in the EU. Holland is almost as bad.

In the UK it costs about £400 and takes a week to set up a new company. Some find it costs less than £100, takes one phone call and five minutes. In France it costs £3,400 and takes 15 weeks. In Germany, it costs £1,400, takes 24 weeks, and the applicant gets a free 1,000-page government manual on personnel management. Among many other things, it says that, as a German employer, you have to obtain written permission for staff to work on Sundays.

Even when a new business has been created, in some parts of the EU the cost of labour is cripplingly high. It costs 40 per cent more to hire a German than a Briton, and 30 per cent more to employ a worker in France, the Netherlands and Belgium. At least, it did before the Blair government introduced the EU's working-time directive and other employment costs. Even so, employment costs are still significantly higher elsewhere in the EU. Only Spain, and Portugal in particular, have lower employment costs than the UK.

Even when German labour costs were well known to be the highest in Europe, which probably meant the highest in the world, as the new German government took office in 1998, Oscar Lafontaine promised to "put more money in the pockets of the workers". Within a year, German workers were on strike in support of 6.5 per cent wage claims, with the prospect of German labour costs becoming even more uncompetitive. Herr Lafontaine resigned a few weeks later, his credibility shot to ribbons by the economic facts of life.

If the UK and Europe were two separate companies, what sane UK shareholder would accept a proposed merger with one with costs out of control, poor financial and trading performance, prospects that were even worse, and a suspect balance sheet constructed by the present desperate owners and never audited by competent accountants? The deal might be struck, but on terms that wrested total control, included the dismissal of all the directors, and imposed a completely different and infinitely more efficient and accountable system of management.

More realistically, from a business viewpoint, what can possibly justify being part of an organisation that puts up costs and reduces employment?

Chapter Seven

We, the People

A speech that might have been made from the floor of any recent annual conference of the National Farmers' Union (NFU), especially if the minister of agriculture were present, might have included these few choice words:

"Minister, agriculture is not about politics. Stop playing games with our industry and our lives. We are the yeomen of England, and you will not trample over us any more.

"This is a sovereign nation of nearly 60,000,000 people. We have some of the best farming land, some of the most hard-working, knowledgeable farmers, and some of the best agricultural research facilities in the world. Our livestock and our crops are as good as any produced anywhere.

"We do not need you to tell us what we may produce, nor in what quantities, nor to what standard, nor at what price, and all without regard for the needs of the marketplace. Such interference has already led to catastrophe. No one but politicians could have ruined so much for so many so quickly.

"If you and your masters in Brussels are not capable of allowing us to get on with the job of feeding this country and exporting our best produce, then all of you should go – and go now.

"You have a duty of care – like all elected representatives of the people – and we call you to account. The ludicrously lopsided CAP, the pathetically weak euro, the EU's hidden agenda, which seeks to concentrate agricultural production in other parts of Europe, and the endless interfering directives that we obey while the rest don't, have combined into a lethal cocktail that is killing us. Our produce has almost disappeared from the shops and the shopper unnecessarily pays more for the family's food. This is the logic of the madhouse. And last year alone more than 50 of us committed suicide because of what you have done to us, our families and our livelihood.

"We don't exaggerate. But if you think we do, then that opinion is itself a measure of the extent to which you fail to understand farming.

"You and your predecessors have destroyed Britain's fishing industry already, and you are now well on the way to destroying farming. Up and down the country, tens of thousands of other small businesses have been ruined as well.

"And all you ever talk of is Brussels, and what Brussels will or won't permit.

"Well, the time has come to tell Brussels where to go. And we are not the only ones. More and more people from all walks of life are reaching the same conclusion.

"We pay the EU £1.3 million every hour of the day and night, seven days a week. Less than half of it comes back here in the form of grants, and even that you withhold from us. Yet that money is ours twice over – in the first place as taxpayers, and secondly as farmers due payments under the CAP.

"Your inability to comprehend the scale of the problems you and the Brussels bureaucrats have created, and your abject refusal to act decisively on our behalf, leave us with only one answer – direct action.

"In the name of sanity, why should we tolerate for a single moment longer an endemically corrupt regime that has made it perfectly clear that it wants to destroy Britain's farming industry? And why should we tolerate for a moment longer a government that connives at such an objective? It matters not whether such connivance is based on ignorance or a hidden agenda – the result is the same.

"We must regain control over our own affairs. Our very survival depends on it. With the money we can save, and the freedom to make our own decisions, this industry might yet be saved in the short term, and inspired for the future. But we have to start right now.

"You and the EU are part of the problem, not part of the solution.

"Cromwell said it first, nearly 400 years ago. Those same words were used again in parliament in 1939. Today, they apply with equal force: 'Depart, I say, and let us have done with you. In the name of God, go.'

"Emmeline Pankhurst created another immortal line over 80 years ago:

'I incite this meeting to rebellion.' I incite this meeting of the NFU to follow her example."

Tragically, nobody has yet said all that, with or without the minister present. Perhaps next year – but by then the situation will almost certainly be much worse. Some who attended last year may not even survive until next year. Eventually, of course, words won't be enough. But, by then, who'll be listening?

The CAP was invented before we joined the EU. Essentially it was constructed to protect the interests of French farmers. It is irredeemably skewed in their favour, which is why the net contribution of the French to the running costs of the EU are virtually nil – almost all their payments come back to their farmers.

According to the government's figures for 1998, the CAP cost British consumers £6.7 billion in unnecessarily higher food prices, while a further £3.4 billion of taxpayers' money was wasted on funding the scheme.

But the effect of the CAP on British farmers has been far worse. The CAP has brought destitution and crippling misery to thousands of farmers and wrought untold havoc on British farming.

Today, some British farmers produce huge, unsaleable surpluses while others survive – if they can – in penury. Young farmers are now increasingly unwilling to start farming on their own, even if they are able to do so, as they see what has happened to their fathers' generation. So the old are encouraged to stay.

Interference from Brussels has also been an environmental disaster. It encourages the grubbing of hedgerows, the drainage of marshlands and the wholesale destruction of wild-life habitats. It has changed the British landscape. Much of our lattice-work of small fields has been turned into large areas of what look like mustard farms in the spring and nightmarish purple Gaugin landscapes in summer. Intensive, fertiliser-based methods of farming are positively encouraged by the CAP because that's what suits the rest of the EU. But the consequence here has been to pour chemicals onto our already most productive land, leaving much of the rest no longer farmed at all.

As the country with the best grassland in western Europe we find ourselves in the astounding situation of no longer being self-sufficient in the production of milk and dairy products. We are permitted by the EU to produce only 82 per cent of the dairy produce we require. Our meat industry has been crucified on the altar of EU legislation. And to add to this insanity, thousands of tons of good food are thrown away every year. They are not even given to the Third World.

Of course, elsewhere in the EU, the picture is very different. French farmers have never had it so good. They are as wealthy as they have ever been. By the mid-1990s, EU farmers had average incomes higher than their national averages everywhere except Britain. In Holland, farmers had average incomes 228 per cent higher than the Dutch average. In the UK, farm incomes have fallen by 90 per cent in the last five years. A farm that grossed £80,000 in 1995 could expect to receive £8,000 in the year 2000.

In such dire circumstances, why Britain continues to pour funds into this agricultural dungheap, knowing that little will return and much will disappear in corruption, is quite beyond rational comprehension.

Thirty years of the CAP have brought farming to its present sorry state. This was no accident, but the direct objective of the EU, whose policy has always been that EU agriculture should be concentrated in eastern Europe. The thrust east by the Germans in 1939 was as much about sources of food as it was about power. Today, for this reason, British supermarkets like Tesco and Sainsbury are buying large areas of farmland in eastern Europe.

How long do British farmers think they will last once the EU has the whole of eastern Europe under its control and low-cost labour is available to farm its bread basket?

Yet left to get on with earning an honest living in a free market, competing successfully against the rest of the world, and freed from the tidal wave of regulation and prohibition that has driven farming to despair, British agriculture can and will thrive again.

Christopher Gill, the Conservative MP for Ludlow in Shropshire, has been farming for nearly 30 years. He is also president of the British Pig Association. At the end of 1999, he wrote about the CAP in *Farmers Weekly*, referring to the "sheer idiocy of the beef and sheep regimes and the intolerable political interference that accompanies them. As with every other feature of EU life, so with farming. Every perceived 'problem' is solved by even more interference...greater bureaucracy, higher costs...a regime where the centre (Brussels) effectively tells the farmer what he may grow, in what quantities, to what standard and, to a degree, at what price. After twenty-five years within the CAP, we have now reached the situation in which there is, for the average family farm, hardly one aspect of British agriculture that is commercially viable.

> "...farmers have been encouraged to produce for a market which in many cases simply does not exist, the most glaring example being the production of fourth-rate tobacco in southern Europe, which nobody can smoke, at an annual cost to the taxpayer of close on £1 billion a year...I don't blame the farmer, I blame the system.
>
> I see an industry brought to its knees by the ruinous policies of the CAP. I see a breed of independent entrepreneurs forced into a bureaucratic straitjacket which pays no regard to the realities of the market. I see the yeomen of England and the owners of businesses in ancillary industries being forced to close...[by a] regime which is devoid of common sense and any vestige of morality. Repatriation of control over our own agriculture is a vital social, economic and practical necessity for the survival of our rural areas... ."

Any organisation that can pay farmers up to £360 per hectare a year for doing nothing with it, that can issue more than 26,000 words on duck eggs, or 2,000 words on the permitted length, circumference, curvature and crookedness of cucumbers, seriously needs its collective head examined.

But perhaps it is the meat industry that has suffered most of all from the interference of the EU. UK farmers may be forced to microchip about 20,000,000 lambs a year, at an estimated cost of £10 million, following a warning by Brussels that Britain faces heavy fines in the ECJ, and the loss of yet more meat export opportunities for failing to implement compulsory lamb traceability.

While we British import thousands of tons of meat and meat products from the EU, much of it is produced and processed in conditions that are not only cruel but also insanitary. Meanwhile, the UK obediently imposes all the EU's regulations on rearing and slaughtering animals and processing meat. As a result, our costs are extortionate and the industry is on its knees from over-regulation and falling profitability. Of course, other EU countries blithely ignore the regulations and – to add insult to injury – refuse to buy our meat and meat products.

The chaos and destruction caused in the meat industry is now truly staggering. On the Continent, governments pay the cost of abattoir hygiene inspections. In the UK farmers and abattoirs have to pay the costs themselves. Worse, we now have two inspection systems – one of our own and another imposed by Brussels, who send over their own, less qualified inspectors and demand payment of their costs from the farmers they are inspecting. In February 1999, when questioned in the Commons, the junior food minister, Jeff Rooker, didn't even know what was going on.

Today, UK meat-processing inspection is controlled mostly by Spanish veterinary officials charged with applying EU standards to abattoirs and meat traders. They already meet the cost of UK meat inspection, which is at least as thorough and has worked well for generations. As a result, costs have shot up. An organic meat processor in Wales used to pay £300 a year for inspection services. That same business now pays £18,000. A chicken pie and soup processor used to pay £2,500. That figure is now £80,000.

It later came to light that the UK's inspectors could have done this work in the first place. Instead, the UK government decided on an overly bureaucratic mixture of two schemes – UK meat inspectors would continue but they would in future be supervised by Continentals. It later emerged that most of these Spanish "vets" had received training on a course that lasted precisely one week. In the UK, a veterinary degree takes seven years.

British officials claimed to have fought against the regulations, but later admitted that no British objections had ever appeared on the agenda in over ten years of negotiations. As a result of this bungling, the British meat-processing industry is being destroyed as the Spanish so-called "vets" enforce regulations from Brussels. Eventually, more than 500 "vets" will be working in the UK under EU orders, all paid for by the British meat-processing industry.

So it is no surprise that nearly three-quarters of all meat-processing plants in the UK are under severe financial pressure as a result of the crippling extra costs they have to meet, just like the farmers who supply them. Just to add to these insults, back home, the Spanish themselves have got a three-year dispensation from Brussels to delay enforcing tuberculosis testing on cattle, because they don't have enough vets!

A letter to *The Scotsman* in July 2000 summed up the present chaotic state of the CAP – and the CFP – in uncompromisingly pithy terms. Malcolm Parkin wrote:

"EU policy puts the livelihoods of farmers at risk. It is ludicrous that the French government has just assumed the rotating role of presidency of the EU while France tops the list of EU countries that defy European directives (420 to date), including, of course, its enduring refusal to import British beef. But if that is not bad enough, the bias towards southern EU member states with regard to the CAP is now beyond belief.

For example, there has been a windfall increase in the CAP budget for 2001 of some 7 per cent due to currency fluctuations. Scottish farmers should note that all of this money will go to French farmers who suffered in the hurricane that struck parts of France last Christmas.

To add to our difficulties, the EC has decided that the Scotch whisky industry is a rich industry and not in need of subsidy, and, accordingly, has cut export refunds worth 19 million euros, while giving wine growers a whopping subsidy increase of 64.5 per cent and olive oil producers another 9 per cent boost to a subsidy already worth 2.5 billion euros.

Most shocking of all, the commission is giving a 2.8 per cent increase to French, Spanish and Greek tobacco growers, taking their subsidy to a staggering one billion euros. Tobacco products kill 500,000 EU citizens each year, and the commission pretends to be at the cutting edge of health policy!

Meanwhile, the UK milk sector, where dairy farmers face collapse, will get a funding increase of 0.3 per cent, while our sheep farmers will actually experience a cut of 2.1 per cent.

This one-way movement of taxpayers' money from north to south puts the livelihoods of our farmers at risk, and leaves our agricultural sector at an appallingly competitive disadvantage.

Even more astounding is the failure of the Common Fisheries Policy, which has been a straightforward disaster for Britain, and for Scotland in particular. British waters contain 65 per cent of the total EU resource, and yet the policy has resulted in dwindling North Sea stocks, the loss of thousands of Scottish jobs, and a UK fishing fleet a fraction of its former size. The quota system leads to two million tonnes of fish being caught and then discarded, dead, into the sea by fishermen without a quota to land this catch.

A system designed by EU bureaucrats to conserve fish stocks has achieved precisely the opposite effect. This shocking waste amounts to 25 per cent of all fish caught in EU waters.

What future can there be for an EU where blatant self-interest works in partnership with legislative lunacy?"

❖

As Mr Parkin indicated, to the great shame of our political leaders, farmers are not the only group of people to have had their lives ruined by the EU. It is an appalling truth, but fishermen have suffered at least as much, perhaps even more.

Certainly those in the fishing industry believe it has suffered worst of all. Today it is a mere shadow of what it once was. It has been virtually destroyed. And the damage started on day one of our membership of the EU when Edward Heath – to his eternal disgrace – deceitfully gave away the UK's fishing rights as a bargaining chip. He did so without consulting the industry, nor telling them what he had done. Heath did so without negotiation and much to the surprise of his Continental counterparts. They had asked for access to our waters for their fishermen and had no serious expectation that he would agree. Heath's ready willingness to concede without a murmur astounded them.

Since that time, of course, the British fishing fleet has been reduced to its knees, thousands of people have had their livelihoods ruined, and 3,000,000 tons of perfectly edible prime fish have been thrown back into the sea every year – dead! Meanwhile, the EU's ill-conceived and indefensible conservation policy goes on scoring two appalling own-goals. It is destroying what fish stocks are left. And it is enforcing the unnecessary destruction of huge quantities of perfectly good food, including species like coley, that are available in abundance.

The plight of the British fishing industry is now so dire that it may eventually disappear at a commercial level.

Since the UK fishing industry was sacrificed by Edward Heath in 1972, on the altar of the EU, as a supplicant's price for joining, the British fleet has lost more than 3,000 vessels and countless thousands of jobs. Today, we land barely 50 per cent of the white fish landed before the Second World War.

But, instead of spending public money attempting to improve the fishing industry, it is increasingly burdened with more controls. Today, the UK fisheries industry is ludicrously over-regulated. Britain currently spends £108 million per year enforcing government regulations on an industry worth £600 million – a bureaucratic on-cost of 18 per cent.

Over 40 per cent of fish landings are inspected and every year fisheries inspectors make 4,000 boardings of vessels for inspection purposes. Fishermen are turned into criminals for landing lobsters one millimetre too small – a difference so utterly insignificant that it was within the tolerances between different measuring devices. No matter – Lionel Minprize and Robert Turner of Scarborough, North Yorkshire, were fined £300. Other fishermen, with big trawlers, can be fined £50,000 for landing a single box over quota – a sum so huge it has put several out of business altogether.

UK fishermen fill in 170,000 logsheets a year, to be scrutinised by more than 150 port inspectors. Worse, as a direct result of the enforcement of the EU's quota regulations, fish stocks are still falling and the bureaucrats continue making savage cuts in fishing quotas, simply to deal with the consequences of their own folly in the first place.

And worse is to come for British fishermen. By 2004, foreign fishing fleets will be allowed to fish right up to Britain's shores, when Britain's 6- and 12-mile limits are to be abolished.

In early spring each year, Belgian fishing vessels are out in the Irish Sea by special permission from Brussels, scraping up cod swimming north to spawn, while the fishermen of Fleetwood, whose boats and nets are much smaller, are banned from putting to sea at all.

The lone voice of UKIP's MEP Nigel Farage, who joined the European parliament's fisheries committee, was unable to stop that committee endorsing a report saying that Britain had still not cut its fleet adequately and should lose more of its landings quota. It also applauded Spain for cutting its fishing fleet, which is already twice the size of any other member state's. Britain was forced to cut its fleet by 20 per cent while Spain got away with a 5 per cent cut.

We are surrounded by four-fifths of what the EU claims is a common asset – our fishing grounds. But we have one voice in nine on the committee. And a minority of one in nine speaking for 80 per cent of the asset is monstrous. The chairman and vice-chairman are Spanish. Two other members come from Spain, and the others from Italy, France, Portugal and Greece.

But British fishermen are not the only ones to suffer at the hands of Brussels.

Some years ago, the Indian delicacy Bombay duck – a firm favourite with British lovers of Indian food – was banned by the EU. As a result, tens of thousands of people lost the enjoyment of a favourite dish, one Billingsgate fish-market trader had his business destroyed and many small village communities in India were left destitute.

In theory, of course, the EU had "protected" us from a health risk. By establishing regulations of Byzantine thoroughness and setting absurd standards for future imports, they killed a trade which was no business of theirs to interfere with in the first place. Even at the time of their introduction, the EU knew perfectly well that no Indian village could meet the new standards. Result? Everyone lost. Benefit? None.

Happily, after an exhausting and costly battle with the bureaucrats, which lasted four years, a small group of enthusiasts finally had the importation of Bombay duck restored in late 2000.

❖

One of the worst features of the EU is its willingness to be selective and divisive. The unspoken agenda is almost always to gain advantage for one vested interest at the expense of another, while preaching endlessly about level playing-fields.

The evidence is everywhere. Air France was subsidised, blatantly in contravention of the regulations. The election of the ECB president was fiddled to avoid deadlock. Standards of chocolate-making are being enforced to suit the Continental market. New labour laws put up costs in the UK but not on the Continent. The Italian commissioner publishes lists of dirty beaches in the UK while Italy, Spain and Greece ignore the same directive. When they first emerged, the UK's BSE troubles were ruthlessly exploited for the benefit of Continental farmers. Proposed new EU copyright laws may make it illegal to view, let alone download, an internet site. And so it goes on.

Warfarin was banned for use as a rodent-killer by commissioners with little understanding of pest control in northern Italy and the UK – the two forestry areas with a grey-squirrel problem. When asked how landowners might now keep these pests under control, there was no response from Brussels.

The abolition of duty-free allowances for travellers was a political decision that had no commercial logic to it. If anything it was commercially perverse, since it removed a source of revenue from the airlines and airport operators that helped keep fares down. Its real purpose, of course, was to reinforce the ludicrous idea that Europe was now one country. None of that prevented the duty-free shop in Corfu airport carrying on as if nothing had changed. More than a year after duty-free was abolished, it was still selling duty-free goods to EU customers, and registering fictitious long-haul travel details on each transaction.

The fragmented sell-off of British Railways was dictated in large part by the 1991 EU railways directive. The result has been a disaster, with too many separate companies each responsible for little segments of the system, but no one accountable for the whole. As a direct consequence there is no clear responsibility for problem-solving. There are poorer services, more accidents, higher costs and labyrinthine contract arrangements, making effective and coherent management impossible. The only winners are the lawyers.

Now, by way of an encore, the EU wants VAT added to fares on public transport after the EU claimed in a green paper, produced by that British political failure Neil Kinnock: "The EU has an important role to play in setting the framework for policy and law. The UK cannot succeed in delivering an integrated transport policy in isolation from Europe." With his usual skill for avoiding the obvious question, Mr Kinnock does not say why.

It has been estimated that 200,000 UK small and medium-sized firms were adversely affected by the cost of the new national minimum wage introduced under EU employment regulations. But worse may be to come.

There are now suggestions of an EU employment pact — an ominous term that can mean only more bureaucracy, interference and cost, and ultimately perhaps more unemployment. Meanwhile, the enforcement of the EU's "working time" directive was already proving it to be one of the most devious of all. Introduced on a platform of "fairness" and "workers' rights", its effects are destructive and counter-productive. Now it's in place, the EU wants it applied to all workers — cab drivers and fishermen, doctors and train drivers, truck drivers and the self-employed who, they said originally, would be exempt.

Self-employed and small-business-owners are now obliged to take four weeks of paid leave a year, and there are no exemptions. Our gutless MPs defended this EU legislation as offering "workers' rights". But nobody asked me if I needed the "right" to be banned from earning a living for four weeks a year. Most self-employed are happy to have two weeks off and a few long weekends, working when the work is there. The EU has no business interfering.

Nursing homes have been particularly badly hit by EU regulations. More and more are going into receivership as the costs of meeting new stringent regulations spiral out of control. They affect all aspects of health care, including staffing levels, support, safety, and form-filling demanded by the new euro-led directives on health, safety and working hours. At the same time local authorities are cutting down on funding health care in the community. Advantage Healthcare had 78 homes for the elderly. Today, some have been sold, others closed and the company has gone into receivership after many successful years building up a £45 million annual turnover. Previously, the Healthcare Association and Grampian Care had also gone into receivership.

Yet another British success — the fine-art market — was sacrificed on the altar of EU political correctness, when our weak-kneed government predictably caved in to Brussels on *"droit de suite"* — not a phrase known to many people. But it is crucial to those working in the fine-art market in London. Essentially it is a four per cent tax levied every time a work of art is resold – supposedly for the benefit of the artists and their estates. Yet many living British artists are vigorously opposed to it.

It was estimated that between 5,000 and 8,000 jobs and ten per cent of our international auction business were endangered by the imposition of *droit de suite*. Inevitably the grateful Swiss and Americans will be sweeping it up, following the 20 per cent which disappeared in the same direction when VAT was imposed. Applied by the London art market, *droit de suite* will hand the rest of the Impressionist and Post Impressionist market on a plate to New York.

And what will our government do about enforcing the level playing-field this decision is supposed to produce? After all, we are told, *droit de suite* has been applied in Europe for many years. As with so much that emanates from the EU, closer examination shows that this is not so. Italy has never collected *droit de suite* since it was launched by Mussolini's fascist government in 1941. Not one single lira has ever been collected or paid in Italy – a classic example of Continental regulatory logic: first introduce the rule, and then ignore it.

And is this crazy idea now to be extended to others who make or own assets that last long enough to be resold? Is the house builder to get a second income when his buyer moves on? When a pension fund sells a block of shares will it get a cut if the next owner makes a profit? Is the car manufacturer to get a percentage when the second-hand salesman makes a sale? Am I, as an author, to get another royalty when a book of mine is picked up on a second-hand book stall? Is the cattle farmer to get another cheque when the butcher sells a joint of beef?

Those of us who make something that is capable of being resold agree a price for our goods, and the buyer takes the risk by investing his money in them. Any subsequent profit – or loss – is his, and his alone.

At the time of writing, the UK government is supposedly winning the fight to prevent the EU from imposing a 20 per cent withholding tax. Victory is far from certain. If the UK government eventually loses, the withholding tax will be levied on all interest paid on the international bond market. The USA unwisely tried something similar in 1963 and the whole market moved to London. When it was withdrawn in 1987 it was too late. In London, some 11,000 dealers are involved in the international bond market, to say nothing of the vast sums of money handled on a daily basis.

No matter where the torch is shone on the EU, folly and mischief come to light. The list of industries, sectors and businesses adversely affected by regulation from Brussels is long and alarming. In addition to those already discussed, the EU has had a powerful and negative impact on environmental planning, boat builders, distillers, hallmarks, public transport, hauliers, cheese makers, market gardeners, pheasant shooting, waste disposal and water management, to name but a few. This book could have been full of such stories, and many of them would have made depressing reading. Christopher Booker's column in the *Sunday Telegraph* every week is a well informed alternative source.

Here, just two examples will suffice: folly on postage rates and an assault on air traffic control.

The harmonisation of postage rates has resulted in the cost of a letter to any EU country increasing from the standard first-class rate of 26 to 36 pence. In 1998 the Post Office quietly raised the letter rate to Europe from 26 (a first-class stamp) to 30 pence. Disguising it with an advertising campaign, the PO replaced the price printed on the stamp itself with an imprecise "E" alongside the sovereign's head.

That provided the freedom to repeat the trick 18 months later, when an E-stamp suddenly rose to 34 pence. Later it went up by another 2 to 36 pence – a 40 per cent increase in under two years. These increases were blamed on a new invention of the EU's – the Remuneration for the Exchange of International Mail (REIMS). This is the mechanism devised by the 15 postal authorities to satisfy the EU that the prices they charge each other for handling euro-mail are not anti-competitive.

The Week is a magazine that sells all over Europe. Its costs of distribution have increased by 40 per cent directly and solely because of EU "harmonisation" rules. Previously, the 17 European countries covered by the agreements were divided into just three zones. Now they have been subdivided by weight, format and geography into 153 different categories, and for no discernible benefit the EU has vastly complicated the life of magazine distributors.

And as if that were not enough, the EC is soon expected to adopt a proposal to apply VAT to postal services, thus triggering another round of inflationary price hikes.

The EU's determination to take over everything and control everybody knows no limits. It is now planning to take control of our airspace. The idea is a single air traffic control system for the whole of western Europe. The EU's logic says that if borders have disappeared on the ground they should also disappear in the sky above.

But nobody has provided practical, operational, safety or other overwhelming reasons for Britain to give up control of our skies. For many years, Eurocontrol – which includes 13 non-EU countries as well as all 15 EU countries – has managed air traffic control over western Europe with remarkable success. It does not take much imagination to anticipate what might happen if the EU were to muscle in on such an arrangement.

Yet again, this appears to be centralisation and taking over responsibilities simply for the sake of it. The EU has no business interfering with the management of air traffic control, especially when it works very well already. The present system is a long-standing and outstanding example of international cooperation between professionals with highly trained, specialist skills. Politics has no place in it.

An organisation that has so successfully ruined our fishing and farming industries can only be expected to create damage and mayhem if it goes anywhere near air traffic control. It brings nothing but ignorance and arrogance to the table. It even had the nerve to describe the present air traffic control system as "antiquated", without offering a single shred of evidence. Not the kind of remark likely to endear it to the hard-working air traffic controllers it wants to take over.

Added to that, there are defence and security implications in such a change. Many non-members of the EU are members of NATO. There are times when the control of air traffic over Europe involves military as well as civil aeroplanes. Management of that airspace must be in the hands of the specialists on such occasions, not the politicians.

Taking over air traffic control looks suspiciously like an extension of the EU's military ambitions. Yet the EU's official line is that it wishes to "bring its management of the airways in line with its economic and political integration".

The EU's justification for these moves is simplistic in the extreme. It does little more than demonstrate the inadequacy of the thinking behind these proposals. A press statement said: "With more than one flight in three being delayed by over 15 minutes in 1999, the situation gives cause for serious concern. And even if some of the delays are due to airports operating at the limits of their capacity or to the airlines themselves, more than half are a direct result of Europe's airspace reaching saturation point."

It did not point out that saturation is saturation, and not even the EU can create more airspace!

It went on to describe the situation as "catastrophic" and then listed its proposed areas of interference. These included more transparency (whatever that was supposed to mean), more "collective management" and more working parties holding meetings to talk about the problems. A better description might have been "more bureaucracy". Of one thing we can be certain – if the EU gets control of air-traffic management, the delays are going to get far, far worse, and quickly.

❖

The Labour government is very keen to let "consenting adults" do what they like to each other – except when one person wants to sell a pound of apples or a pound of beef to another. Since 1st January 2000 that has been illegal, punishable by a £5,000 fine, or six months in jail – the same as a criminal receives for assaulting a police officer. At least, it would have been illegal if the government had got its act together.

The only problem is, this law is itself invalid. It was introduced under EU regulations without repealing an existing Act of Parliament that says that imperial weights and measures are legal. In this case, for technical reasons, the Act of Parliament prevails.

All the government has done is create chaos, generate millions of pounds-worth of unnecessary cost for traders and retailers, who have replaced old scales unnecessarily, and left trading standards officers and local authorities in disarray and confusion as they try to enforce two contradictory laws.

Ever since Edward Heath, the government of the day has been saying that metrication would be voluntary. It offers no commercial advantages, generates unnecessary costs, offends common sense, angers the vast majority of ordinary people, and achieves no discernible benefits. Compulsory metrication breaks pledges given by four successive prime ministers, including Margaret Thatcher.

So it was not surprising that the compulsory introduction of metrication was announced on the quietest day of the parliamentary calendar, just as MPs were leaving for the summer recess and a mere five months before it was supposed to come into force. The news was broken in a parliamentary written answer. Because the government knew the measure would be deeply unpopular throughout the country, and adversely affect over 60,000 retailers and market traders, they slid it into the public domain as surreptitiously as possible. Not even a press announcement was made. Nor did they offer any financial help with compliance. New scales were required, and the traders must bear the cost.

Worse was the attempt to ban imperial measurements except as a form of supplementary information. In the UK, everything is permitted unless it is specifically prohibited. On this occasion, in an attempt to obey their masters in Brussels, the government claimed that the EU had somehow "allowed" imperial to be used alongside metric measurements, so long as they weren't displayed in a larger format. This, in itself, is unconstitutional. While the EU might claim the power to tell the British government what it must do, it has no power to limit the rights and customs of the British people. Neither does it have the right to make criminals of those who prefer to use the systems of measurement we have used for centuries, and that – despite claims to the contrary – often have more common sense and advantages than the metric alternatives.

Indeed, the British Weights and Measures Association (BWMA) claims that the old measures originated in prehistory, and are far more consumer-friendly than the metric system, most of which was invented by scientists and bureaucrats in the aftermath of the French Revolution. It was then dragged across Europe by the armies of Napoleon. It met widespread popular resistance, which everywhere was quelled by force. To this day, in France, masons and carpenters calculate in pieds (feet) and pouces (inches), in livres (pounds) and onces (ounces) – beyond the reach of the metric police and their informers.

Britain's traditional weights and measures may not lend themselves so obviously to decimal points, but they are far easier to divide into fractions. They are also based on "human" measures, such as the length of the foot, the distance from nose to fingertip, the amount of water in two cupped hands, and the area over which a horse can pull a plough in a day.

And there's another point about the proposed switch from imperial to metric. By breaking the age-old link between cost and quantity, consumers do not know when they are being asked to pay more for less. The trend towards metrication in the supermarkets and elsewhere has been used to improve profit margins, just as was the switch to decimal currency in 1971. The pound imperial is exactly 453.59 grams. But cartons are not 453.59 grams. They have usually been rounded down to 450 grams. The old 20-ounce packet of crisps is not 56.7 grams – it has been rounded down to 55 grams.

Price confusion has proliferated, too. With units like a pint and a half-pint, a pound and half-pound, size options are limited. People know what they are buying. But not with grams. It might be the case that 100, 200, 250, 300, 325, 400, 410, 500, and so on, are all reasonable-looking numbers, while packaging and the quantities inside can be any size and appear sensible. But the customer cannot easily compare prices and value for money without a degree in mental arithmetic. One packet says 410 grams and costs £1.57. The alternative is 520 grams and costs £1.99. Which do you buy? Price increases have been possible by stealth as a result of this switch to metrication. On the whole, they have not dropped. Not surprisingly, in many cases prices have increased.

Added to that, the practicalities of marking up greengrocery, for example, with duplicate labels that change daily, makes the proposition utterly unrealistic. Only a pen-pushing bureaucrat could invent such an idea. The number of tickets doubles, the customer is confused, and the produce itself is more likely to get damaged. The real purpose of this "concession" was to be make the EU appear reasonable, knowing perfectly well that few traders would be willing to use it.

Of course the whole proposition is nonsense. We still buy a "bunch" of grapes or bananas, we drive distances measured in miles, use three-and-a-half-inch floppy disks, buy a quarter-pounder at the fast-food take-away, drink pints of beer, sleep in a king-size bed, print on A4 paper, pitch the stumps a chain (22 yards) apart, use graph paper squared off in tenths of an inch, measure our height in feet and inches and our weight in pounds and ounces. Even the arrival of Master Leo Blair was announced in pounds and ounces. Like most children still, one day he will ask for a "quarter" of sweets.

The building industry went metric several years ago. Today, we attempt to use metric-sized bricks and doors to repair and maintain buildings made with imperial-sized material. But we still buy screws at the ironmongers specified in imperial units – as indeed do Continental Europeans. British Standard fine threads come in sizes from a quarter, five-sixteenths, and three-eighths of an inch upwards, in larger sizes with Whitworth units and smaller sizes with 0, 1, 2, 3, 4, 5, 6, 7, 8, 9, 10, 11 British Association threads. There are no metric equivalents.

Now look at the continent of Europe itself. What do we find? In France, customers can legally buy a pound [livre] of apples. Across the continent, plumbing is measured in inches, or "thumbs". "Trois-quartres" (three-quarters of an inch) and "demi-gaz" (half an inch) are commonplace terms. The Dutch buy timber by the "thum". Everyone in Europe asks for three-and-a-half-inch floppy disks. Imperial units are commonplace, and nobody gives a tuppenny damn!

The introduction of metrication cannot possibly be about harmonisation and standardisation, at least certainly not in the UK. Our biggest single foreign market is non-metric. Most of our other major global trading partners are non-metric. The wealthiest retail chain operating in Britain is non-metric. The majority of our domestic trade, by far the largest part of our Gross National Product (GNP), is non-metric. Precious metals and precious stones are sold on the world market in non-metric units.

Computer parts are non-metric. The computer industry is dominated by the USA and Japan, where all measurements are imperial. Throughout the world all integrated circuits are made with pin spacings in fractions of an inch – typically a tenth, a fiftieth. That is never going to change so long as the industry is dominated by American and Japanese companies.

The modern Bible refers to gallons (St John, 2), while the King James version used "firkins". Our racehorses still gallop furlongs (ten chains). Sailors use knots, fathoms and cables. We may be obliged to buy petrol in litres, but we all know when prices reach £4 a gallon. Gas and water are still calculated in imperial units, and many industries still use and will continue to use imperial measurements with impunity.

If the law wanted to prove that it is an ass, there can be no better means of doing so. The admission by the DTI that "a common date for conversion...ensures that traders do not gain an unfair competitive advantage by delaying their changeover" is an open admission that traders who continue to use imperial will increase their business because they will be giving the public what they want.

The DTI also admitted earlier that "at present manufacturers in other member states have difficulty in competing with UK manufacturers in imperial units. For this reason alone it is unlikely that other member states would support an extension beyond 31 December 1999". So British firms won more business when they supplied goods in imperial units. From that we are invited to deduce that this advantage over their Continental competition must be stopped. Where is the sanity in that? And what happened to the idea of competition and freedom of choice?

As the BWMA pointed out after the introduction of metrication, it was ironic that the smart leaflets issued by the DTI as metric guides for retailers and shoppers offered copies in Welsh, of course, and also in Arabic, Bengali, Chinese, Greek, Gujarati, Hindi, Punjabi, Turkish, Urdu and Vietnamese. This was in deference to the cultures of the many immigrant minorities now living in Britain, while the purpose of the leaflet was to help destroy a vital part of our own native culture.

No public support for the switch to metrication was ever sought by any government, yet they still went ahead. All the opinion polls confirmed solid opposition. The lowest recorded level of support for imperial measurements was still over 70 per cent, and that was some time ago. By the end of 2000, support for imperial units was even higher.

In the ITV Teletext poll of Friday 4th February 2000, of 7,229 replies to the question "Do you support the new European law enforcing metric weights?", 97 per cent voted NO.

Happily there was also support from another, unexpected quarter. The law itself said that the compulsory switch to metrication was invalid. As the constitutional barrister Michael Shrimpton pointed out, in an opinion that is now known and understood by street traders throughout the country, the Weights and Measures Act, 1985, is still in force. This Act clearly and expressly provided for both imperial and metric measurements to be used in the UK.

More importantly, the regulations to enforce metrication were not themselves an Act of Parliament. They are what is known as secondary legislation, meaning that they were introduced under powers granted to ministers by an Act of Parliament – but the Act used was the European Communities Act, 1972. Since no parliament can bind its successor, an Act passed in 1972 – and regulations issued under it – cannot repeal an Act passed some 13 years later!

Also, secondary legislation cannot repeal primary legislation, either implicitly or explicitly. A regulation cannot contradict an Act. It is legally impossible to defeat the express purpose of an Act of Parliament by introducing mere regulations that purport to repeal it. Michael Shrimpton was categoric. If the government wanted to compel the use of metric units, they needed an Act of Parliament (not a regulation) that expressly provided for such a change.

The only way retailers and street traders could be forced to sell in metric units would be by passing another Act of Parliament, banning the sale of loose goods in imperial units. Meanwhile, it was argued, the Weights and Measures Act, 1985, actually repealed the compulsory metrication part of the European Communities Act, 1972.

After this confused state of affairs became apparent, and was explained with great clarity by Mr Shrimpton within a few weeks of supposed compulsory metrication, trading standards officers were in disarray. Any threats of prosecution, hefty fines, and confiscation of equipment, became little more than harassment, which is itself illegal under the Protection from Harassment Act, 1997.

It is also an offence under the Trade Union and Labour Relations Act, 1992, to compel someone to do something they are not obliged to do by law.

And to cap it all, the imposition of metric weights and measures flouts British rights under common law expressed with great clarity in Magna Carta and – if that were not enough – almost certainly contravenes the 1950 Convention on Human Rights, which safeguards freedom of expression. The British government might yet be embarrassed by a ruling on the matter by the European Court of Human Rights in the Hague. These illegal regulations seek to constrain a trader's right to express his heritage and traditions by selling to his customers in customary weights or measures.

The eastern region of the UKIP took up the cause of the retailers with great vigour. In a letter drafted for harassed traders to use in response to threats from trading standards officers, they pointed out:

1   Public opinion is strongly against this Regulation. According
      to a survey commissioned by the British Weights and
      Measures Association in January 2000, over 80 per cent of

people still think in imperial weights and measures and wish to buy and sell in them.

2   Metric units confuse the vast majority of customers.

3   Nearly all customers want to carry on using British weights and measures.

4   The alleged "crime" of selling in imperial units has no victim, except the EU itself. Since when did courts fine or punish people when no "harm" has been caused to someone else or to the public?

5   Such action would amount to a British magistrate fining traders simply for being British and expressing their Britishness.

Essex butcher Dave Stephens took up the cause with equal vigour. He risked a heavy fine or being jailed rather than change over to pricing his chops, sausages and mince in metric units. When a council official handed him a weights and measures order he tore it to pieces in public.

"I am a true Englishman and I don't see why we should have to put up with this euro nonsense. I have started a petition and so far everyone who has come into my shop has signed it. We have more than 3,000 signatures.

"We have lost so much to Europe, but I am determined to keep on with our traditional pounds and ounces. I feel so strongly about this that I am prepared to go to jail," he told the press.

On Tuesday, 11th January 2000, UKIP leader Jeffrey Titford MEP, several hundreds of other customers, and a gaggle of cameramen and reporters, assembled outside Dave Stephens' shop in Leigh-on-Sea, where they aided and abetted a substantial number of purportedly criminal acts. They purchased meat and meat products from Dave Stephens' Mandy's Chop Shop, all weighed and sold in pounds and ounces.

A public challenge was issued to the Southend-on-Sea Borough Council's trading standards department to observe these crimes being committed and to confiscate Mr Stephens' equipment.

Colin Gabell, head of trading standards at Southend Council, initially told the local newspaper that Dave Stephens was blatantly breaking the law. He was "doing things for publicity. But the time for publicity is over. My job is to enforce the law. Mr Stephens has got an unfair advantage over his competitors. Most are complying or are about to comply and Mr Stephens is obviously not going to comply".

Mr Gabell's remarks clearly imply that metrication was intended to stifle competition. Yet when the UK joined the Common Market it was supposed to be to open up markets and stimulate competition – the exact reverse of Mr Gabell's opinion. He also appeared to ignore the obvious fact that Dave Stephens' "unfair advantage" was merely offering customers what they wanted – the very essence of competitive trade.

Mr Gabell's comments also represented a stark admission that people preferred imperial measurements – otherwise there was no advantage in using them. He also ignored the fact that Mr Stephens would not have an "unfair advantage" – as he liked to call it – if traders were free to choose the measures they used. It had been generated solely by the regulators interfering in things that should not concern them.

Chairman of the BWMA, Bruce Robertson, set up a "Pound of Flesh" stall outside his Trago Mills food store in Newton Abbot, Devon, to sell apples, potatoes and English sprouts. Dressed in a prison uniform, he handed out receipts with names of the local trading standards officers and encouraged customers to report him, while a scoreboard kept a running total of his metric offences. By mid-afternoon, he'd broken the law 200 times.

Earlier, Mr Robertson had written to trading standards officers. He talked of the "unlawful imposition of these iniquitous regulations", and categorically stated that Trago Mills stores would continue to use imperial units of measurement after 1st January 2000, and for as long as the overwhelming majority of shoppers wished. "Metrication is neither necessary nor welcome. It is an abomination to our culture. We should be free to choose whether to use it or not at will," he wrote. In both these high-profile cases, the trading standards officers took no action.

But towards the end of 2000 there were clear signs that a test case in the courts was imminent. But not against one of the big guns in the retailing business, with money and clout. Trading standards departments showed no signs of prosecuting Tesco, which reverted to selling in imperial measurements when research showed that customers preferred them, nor McDonald's for selling quarter-pounders. Fast-food chains like Wimpy, Burger King, McDonald's and many others all sell quarter-pounders, and many restaurants sell steaks denominated in ounces – 8-ounce, 12-ounce, even 16-ounce steaks.

Distinctive product- or brand-names like quarter-pounder might raise even more tricky issues for weights and measures inspectors. Best to avoid them. A market trader was a much easier target. Make a criminal out of him.

But the threat of prosecution did not stop a butcher in Basildon, Essex, who erected prominent signs saying "No French beef sold here" and "Nothing French sold here". The police told him to take them down, after a French woman complained – another sign of the EU's corrosive attempts to control freedom of speech seeping into British life, undermining our rights and liberties, and giving official support to the lunacies of political correctness.

After the French refusal to open its markets to British beef, many thousands of traders and many millions of customers stopped buying and selling French products in quiet protest. That butcher merely gave expression to a reality. In any case, whatever the merits of his announcement, he had an absolute and unqualified right to make it, subject only to any local regulations about the size of display material.

And the very idea that an Englishman might be breaking the law by selling another a pound of apples was – is – anathema to most people. But to have it decided and enforced by unknown foreign bureaucrats was – is – widely regarded as intolerable.

Enforced metrication has brought the law into contempt – something the EU excels at – but it has also invited civil disobedience on a massive scale. In that, at least, it has succeeded. Without law there is chaos. But the law must be seen to be fair and reasonable. Ultimately, and at a practical level through the jury system, it is the people who decide what is law. If it is not fair and reasonable the law will be ignored, as in this case. Eventually, of course, they can decide to change the law by electing a parliament with a majority willing to repeal or alter the original legislation.

But enforced metrication has achieved even more than contempt for the law. It has undermined the relationship between the trading standards officer and the retailing community. On the whole, weights and measures inspectors do a good and necessary job in guarding against short measures, lack of hygiene, misrepresentation and so on. They are acknowledged for the work they do, and respected.

Of course in the case of metrication all this could have been avoided. There was nothing to stop the trading standards officers from advising the government of its concerns, and there was nothing to stop the government from taking notice. Instead, both caved in to EU pressure to introduce compulsory metrication, even when they knew it was entirely contrary to consumer interests, offered no practical benefits, caused confusion and expense for millions of people and was strongly opposed by the vast majority.

Not one trading standards officer, nor any local authority tasked with enforcement, had the guts to speak up against this wholly unwelcome and unnecessary legislation. Instead, they simply accepted the changes, cooperated with Brussels and set about trying to browbeat British traders and consumers into submission by threatening them with large fines, confiscation of equipment and even closure of their businesses.

Meanwhile, the government did not advise the local authorities or the trading standards officers themselves that the introduction of metrication was based on flawed legislation and would never stand up in court. They were left to find out the hard way when legal opinion was sought by the UKIP and published on the internet.

It is inconceivable that the government did not know that the legislation was faulty, and that it would fail at the first attempt to enforce it through the courts. Quite apart from the disgraceful contempt for the law itself that such an attitude displays, especially from our elected government, it was an equally dreadful piece of mismanagement.

The DTI estimated the overall cost to business of conversion at around £33 million, with most being spent on replacing or adjusting some 200,000 weighing machines. A machine costs between £60 and £150 to convert, and the price of new scales starts at about £450.

So the net effect was this: businesses were bullied, almost certainly illegally, into spending vast sums of money to purchase metric scales that they didn't want, to sell goods to customers in quantities they didn't like, to satisfy foreign bureaucrats they didn't elect. That is what the EU actually achieved.

As the dispute over the legality of metrication developed, it produced some curious side-effects. For example, the UKIP leader, Jeffrey Titford MEP, received a letter from a manufacturer of weighing machines. The business manager of Deben Systems Ltd wrote: "We are suppliers of weighing equipment and services to retailers throughout the country. We employ over 300 people. We are now finding that the failure to effectively implement (*sic*) and enforce legislation is having a significant impact on our business."

The manager pointed out that all major multiple retailers and about 60 per cent of independent retailers had converted to weighing in metric.

He went on: "However we are now getting stubborn resistance from our remaining customers largely due to the adverse publicity and campaigns run by pressure groups. We are also getting complaints from some of those customers we have converted that our advice was wrong and we have put them to unnecessary expense!

"Our trade association, the UK Weighing Federation [UKWF], has been in touch with the DTI to obtain clarification. Unfortunately, we can get no satisfactory reply; it appears that the major concern is about negative headlines and the creation of 'metric martyrs'."

He complained that the situation was becoming farcical, and that his company's reputation was being damaged. Furthermore, the company's capital was tied up in unsold stocks of metric scales and conversion kits.

He concluded: "The purpose of this letter is to draw the situation to your attention and to ask for your help in lobbying the government. We need them to issue clear and unequivocal statements on what the legal position is and what action will be taken against retailers who do not comply with the law."

It had not, apparently, occurred to the business manager of Deben Systems that he could sell his unsold items of equipment to the Europeans, who appeared to like them. He could make more dual standard and imperial units and sell them to the British retailers who now knew that the enforcement of imperial measurements was illegal. He could also sue the DTI for misleading him in the first place. His problem was actually a lack of commercial enterprise. He was also seeking the wrong help in the wrong place.

The UKWF's monthly statistics on the "progress" of metrication finally admitted after the first few months of supposedly compulsory metrication that the change-over was far from complete.

Of the 96,000 independent, non-supermarket, non-multiple retail outlets, 58,000 had converted to metric but 38,000 (just over 40 per cent) had not, and were still selling in imperial units.

At about £1,000 a time for legal costs, this rebellious disregard for so-called EU law left local authorities facing a bill of some £38 million if they attempted to enforce this flawed law, and the prospect of failing to secure a conviction in every case. Little wonder they funked it.

Chapter Eight

Back to the Future

Just remember what we've done.

Britons invented the computer, the jet engine, the hovercraft, the steam engine and railways, the telephone...and television. We invented mail services, and we discovered nuclear physics.

Over the last 250 years, British scientists and engineers have been responsible for almost four out of every five major inventions, discoveries and new technologies. Recent Japanese research revealed that more than half of all the world's most useful inventions since 1945 were made by Britons – not necessarily living in Britain at the time, but British all the same. The contribution from Americans was under 20 per cent. Given the size of our populations, that means the British are ten times more inventive. But both Anglo-Saxon nations together can claim three-quarters of all the world's useful inventions.

We may not have invented the printing press, but we were the first to develop a free press, the first to understand its importance in a democratic society and the first to seek to protect it.

The first man to sail round the world was a Briton, and so was the first to sail round solo. We invented football, cricket and rugby.

We spawned Shakespeare and Dr Johnson, Gladstone and Churchill, Gainsborough and Constable, to name but a tiny few in the glittering and lengthy catalogue of great Britons who have contributed so much to the world's cultural riches, its thinking and pleasure.

Today, we have far more than our share of creative people working all around the globe in advertising, the theatre and television, and in the film industry.

Over centuries, the British were among the first to understand that negotiation was better than war, that free and lawful trade was better than pillage, that the worker was worth his salt. And we were certainly the first to recognise that everyone had the right to a free and fair trial before his or her peers.

We gave the modern world the concept of "common law", the notion that the common people know the difference between right and wrong, the concept that certain rights belong absolutely to the people and that one of them is the freedom to enjoy their age-old customs and ways of doing things.

And having understood these things, we also understood that common law is not static. We know it is a living, vigorous phenomenon. It evolved. It still evolves. Custom and common sense constantly "improve" it. And parliament has no power to diminish or limit common law.

One of the most important, and oldest of our common law rights was – and still is – the privacy of a person's own home. As the Earl of Chatham pointed out in 1763: "The storm may enter – the rain may enter – but the King of England cannot."

As we saw earlier, the English political philosopher John Locke referred to an Englishman's home as his castle. Locke also pointed out that "the end of law is not to abolish or restrain, but to preserve and enlarge freedom. Man being...by nature all free, equal and independent, no one can be put out of his estate, and subjected to the political power of another, without his own consent."

People ask, "What is common law – where can I see it written down?" It has been suggested that common law can be encapsulated in the old proverb "do as you would be done by". Such an admonition applies as much to the individuals whom we elect to conduct our affairs and legislate in parliament as it does to everyone else.

Common law is the accumulated wisdom of centuries of case law, each being decided on its merits and on the principle that similar decisions should apply in similar cases. "Without the common law a court would, in each recurring case, have to enter upon its examination and decision as if all were new, without any aid from the experience of the past, or the benefit of any established principle or settled law. Each case...would in turn pass away and be forgotten, leaving behind it no record of principle established, or light to guide, or rule to govern the future." That was part of the judgment in Hanford *vs* Archer.

One of the priceless strengths of such a system of law is its integrity, its independence from government. Common law has the potential to withstand assaults from tyrannical and oppressive government, particularly government that seeks to draw all power to itself and to perpetuate its own unelected existence.

Common law is one of the essential British bulwarks against the ever encroaching EU.

We British were and are a force in the world…a force to be reckoned with.

Friedrich Hayek wrote: "British strength, British character and British achievements are to a great extent the result of a cultivation of the spontaneous." Not a quality much admired in the EU.

Some of these important differences between Britain and the continent of Europe have long been apparent, not just to us but to Europeans as well. Charles de Gaulle understood them when he prevented our joining the then Common Market in the 1960s. A hundred years earlier Alexis de Tocqueville wrote in *Journey to England*:

"England is the country of decentralisation. We have got a government, but we have not got a central administration. Each county, each town, each parish looks after its own interests. Industry is left to itself so you will not see an unfinished undertaking in England, for since everything is done with a view to private profit, nothing is undertaken without the necessary capital, and while the project is unfinished, the capital is idle.

In your country [France] industry is subject to endless interference; here it is infinitely free. I consider nothing is more difficult than to accustom men to govern themselves. There is however the great problem of your future. Your centralisation is a magnificent idea, but it cannot be carried out. It is not in the nature of things that a central government should be able to watch over all the needs of a great nation. Decentralisation is the chief cause of the substantial progress we have made in civilisation. You will never be able to decentralise. Centralisation is too good a bait for the greed of the rulers; even those who once preached decentralisation, always abandon their doctrine on coming to power. You can be sure of that."

The constitutional case for sovereign independence is overwhelming, and it was discussed at length earlier, based on the pamphlet *Defence of the Realm*. The full text forms the appendix to this book.

❖

But the economic case for the UK to restore its independence is equally overwhelming, contrary to the deceit served up by government ministers who seek to strut on the bigger stage in Brussels.

As Dr Martin Holmes, co-chairman of the Bruges Group, has pointed out, there are several good economic reasons for UK independence from the EU, any one of which would be sufficient by itself.

The UK's economy is structurally different from those of the countries on the continent of Europe. We have a petro-currency, they do not. The vast bulk of our international trade is denominated in US dollars, theirs is not. We have a home-owning population, they do not. This means movements in interest rates have a huge, direct and immediate impact on almost every family in the land. On the Continent, most families care little or nothing about interest rates. Apart from influencing job prospects, interest rates have scarcely any effect on their lives.

We have lower taxes as a percentage of GDP, although the Labour government has damaged that advantage over European economies. They want tax harmonisation, mainly to destroy our competitive advantage, which results from their extravagant spending on social welfare. In effect, they want us to pay for their profligacy. Worse, they want to carry on being profligate, and still be competitive within the EU.

By comparison with euroland, we have a flexible labour market. It is dreadfully sclerotic compared to the USA, but it is mobile compared to Europe. The same is true of trading and business regulations. We are poor against American standards, but way ahead of Europe. Again, the EU wants to destroy that competitive advantage, while sanity demands that we not only keep what we have but that we try vigorously to improve it.

We have a much bigger small-business sector than Europe. It does reasonably well. A few years ago it did much better, and the current unhealthy downward trend is directly the result of EU regulations. But we are still free to start and develop businesses as we like. In many parts of Europe aspiring entrepreneurs are not.

We have an economy that is oriented towards the rest of the world. Most of our trade is outside the EU. Trade with our so-called European trading partners is in permanent deficit – and the EU is the only area of the world where this is true. Leaving aside the political issues, in commercial terms alone we have tied ourselves closely to the one part of the world from which we benefit least. They import less than half our exports and sell us more than half our imports. Our worst trading partners are all in the EU, with Germany the worst of all. There, we have a deficit of over £3 billion a year. So much for trading partnership; more a one-way street in the wrong direction.

And that one-way street results in the imposition of all EU regulations on the 12 per cent of British companies that trade with non-EU countries, *and* the 80 per cent of British industry with no export or import activity whatsoever. All the pain inflicted by Brussels is directly relevant to barely eight per cent of our total economic activity and – if the government is to be believed – borne solely for their benefit!

For all these reasons, it is absolutely essential that the UK not only continues to manage its own economic and commercial affairs, but that it restores its freedom to pursue the policies that suit it. The tools must remain in our own hands – setting interest rates, setting monetary and fiscal policies, managing our own currency, and regulating our own businesses.

Moreover, the UK has several unique and buoyant industries that set us apart from the rest of the EU. We cannot expect the Europeans to understand their importance to us. Nor, sadly, can we expect them to view these sources of wealth with anything but envy. All these industries are unrelated to Europe and don't depend for their success on Europe. All of them generate high earnings outside Europe, and all of them are global operations. Each separately, let alone in combination, sets us apart.

We have an oil industry. They do not. We have a world-class financial services sector. They do not. We have a tourism market based on history and tradition, on pageantry and culture, on quaintness and craftsmanship, on big cities and sport. It is an essential source of inward revenue. Of course other countries have successful tourism markets, but ours is a unique mix and unique to us.

In recent years we have developed highly specialised manufacturing facilities. Yes, some of our older manufacturing industries have had a hard time, and many have sadly gone to the wall. But that is the nature of economic development. What worked yesterday isn't necessarily going to work today, let alone tomorrow. But our newer manufacturing companies, making products based on electronics, new scientific research and man-made raw materials, are replacing those old industries that are now redundant or unable to compete with low-cost production elsewhere in the world.

And then there is e-commerce and the internet. The British flair for enterprise and invention has seized this new technology and made something of it, fast. And, of course, like so much British enterprise, it has a global appeal. This is not a sector governments will be able to interfere with easily. Via cyberspace, e-commerce cuts across national borders, ignores regulation, and has no physical presence beyond the machines that hold the data. Here is the first industry, perhaps ever, that will maximise its potential at maximum speed simply because it is not vulnerable to government control.

It has been the Anglo-Saxon mind and economic environment, in the USA and Britain, that has grabbed this opportunity quickest and best. That is not an accident. It is a reflection of the similarities in thinking in the two countries. It also points up the fundamental difference in commercial attitudes between the UK and Continental Europeans.

None of these five industries and developments – oil, financial services, tourism, specialist manufacturing and e-commerce – is to be found to the same extent, or at all, across the Channel. They are ours, and ours alone, to protect and improve.

Finally, the UK is a global trading nation, as we have seen. But there is an important flipside to that coin. The Europeans are not. Only Germany has a genuinely international dimension to its trade that even remotely echoes ours. Most European trade is between the countries of western Europe. They largely trade with each other and lack a significant global dimension to their export activity. Their economic and trading mindset is inward-looking. That's why they are happy to set out a level playing-field for themselves. It suits them. But it does not suit Britain, where a trade and regulatory policy for 14 inward-looking economies is utterly inappropriate for an outward-looking global economy. One of the attractions we offered the EU when we joined the then Common Market was access to those world markets that had been beyond their reach for generations. Many still are.

But, when we joined, we threw overboard long established trading links with the rest of the Anglo-Saxon world, especially Australia and New Zealand, and with other countries – Argentina, for example. These ties meant nothing to our new partners in Europe. What we did was discard old friends, strip ourselves virtually naked, and walk off with new friends about whom we knew little and understood less. The consequences were inevitable. We have slipped away from the Commonwealth. Today we are at serious risk of becoming an insignificant part – a mere group of regions – of the EU.

What was left of our empire – the Commonwealth on which we turned our backs – reformed itself as a commonwealth of independent nations, which just might be the right template for a Europe we could all live with. But that is not a concept the rulers of the EU find appealing. They are marching firmly in the opposite direction – towards a totalitarian, single-party state – despite the fact that it is a discredited and antiquated political goal.

It was suggested earlier that the UK is already becoming Europe's very own offshore island – the Hong Kong of western Europe – despite government warnings that Britain will somehow be isolated if it is not a member of the EU. Britain is a country of nearly 60,000,000 people. It is utter nonsense to argue that we alone among all the other countries in the world would be isolated from European markets when we leave. Agreements brokered by the WTO and signed by almost every country on the planet are binding on all signatories and ensure that trade is conducted freely between them all.

We are one of the world's great international trading nations – the fourth largest in the world by GDP, and the second largest in the EU by GDP. Our most important trading partner by far is the USA, with the rest of the Anglo-Saxon world a close second. To this day, we have strong links with North and South America, Africa, Australasia, the rest of the English-speaking world and much of the Far East. As part of that huge free-trade area, where enterprise thrives, and with London as one of the great international financial centres of the world – what else do we need?

Our language is not only the language of over one billion people worldwide, but English is now also the world's leading international language for business and travel. It is virtually a compulsory second language for everyone on the face of the earth. If you speak English you can go anywhere and do anything. It dominates the internet, and that means it will dominate the future.

We are full members of NATO, the group of seven leading industrialised nations (G7), the WTO, the IMF, the World Bank, and a permanent member of the UN Security Council. How many of those seats and voices would remain if we disappeared into a superstate of Europe? The answer is probably none. Already the EU represents us at the WTO, while the ECB now claims the right to speak for Germany, France and Italy at world finance meetings, much to the annoyance of the national banks in those countries.

The loss of a distinctive British voice in world affairs would not be a problem only for us. The rest of the world listens when we have something to say. Our contribution to world affairs is as distinctive as it is valued. No EU spokesman can offer that, and certainly not in our place.

Sir Winston Churchill said in 1956: "If Britain must choose between Europe and the open sea, she must always choose the open sea." The great majority of British subjects instinctively know that is still right. Our political leaders may have been seduced, but we have not.

As we have seen, over 60 per cent of the British public want to leave the EU altogether, once they understand that our trade with Europe would continue as before when we leave. That is far higher a percentage than any political party has ever won of the popular vote to win an election and form a government. Usually British elections are won with barely 35 per cent of the popular vote.

The number of people positively wanting to stay in the EU is already down to less than a third of the population and falling. It is soft support, too. Every time a new crisis with Europe emerges support drops again. The British have had enough.

This trend was – astonishingly – confirmed by the EC's own survey in mid-2000. Despite couching their questions to maximise support, their "EuroBarometer" showed beyond all doubt that the British are not in favour of staying. Only 22 per cent were in favour of surrendering the UK's economy to control by the EU (asked as a question about wanting to join the euro). This was a six per cent drop in support in a year.

A poll conducted for the pro-EU magazine *The Economist* in October 1999 revealed that barely 16 per cent of the British identify with Europe. Only 21 per cent (one in five) felt some affinity with the EU flag. By end-2000, a EuroBarometer poll revealed that only six per cent of British people thought of themselves as "European".

Nor are we the only ones to feel as we do. In a recent opinion poll carried out by the Allensbach Institute, 76 per cent of Germans said they thought of themselves in the first instance as German; a mere 15 per cent thought of themselves as European. Over 200,000 Austrians have signed a petition calling on Austria to leave.

Life was very different when we first joined the Common Market. We suffered from years of economic mismanagement. The country had a chronic balance-of-payments problem and a weak pound. All the characteristic consequences of mid-twentieth-century socialism were self-evident. The pound was overvalued in the old fixed exchange-rate regime devised at Bretton-Woods after the Second World War, the trade unions and the government ran British industry, managements had neither the willpower nor entrepreneurial backing to take charge of their own businesses, shareholders were regarded with contempt, the products we produced were not what consumers wanted or deserved, and we were rightly regarded as something of a basket-case. "The sick man of Europe" was the phrase, more often used in sorrow than in anger.

It is – just – understandable why, in 1972–3, we sought protection in the then Common Market. But within a few years everything changed for the better. Not because of the Common Market but in spite of it. A rapid sequence of events set us free. Bretton-Woods collapsed, the pound found its true value, and Margaret Thatcher released management and industry from the shackles of trade union and government control. The rest, as they say, is history. But we have remained in what has now become the EU.

That is the new cross we bear. And we must throw it off. The financial savings alone are enormous.

The money we pay the EU is not based on budgets or need. It is not justified in any way. It is not calculated on a careful, professional and thorough analysis of priorities and benefits. The EU simply takes a percentage of our income. No government minister has to approve it, nor explain it to parliament. No debate on ways and means takes place at Westminster. There is no annual budget statement. Instead, the EU simply vacuums the money away without so much as a thank you. Later, we are expected to be grateful when we receive half of it back.

Customs duties collected at all UK ports of entry go directly to the EU. But this is not enough. They also take just under one per cent of all VAT revenue as well, and a third of one percent of our total GDP.

And the bureaucrats in Brussels are not required to explain or justify the need for a single penny of all these funds, nor their method of calculation and collection. All this cash simply disappears to Brussels because the treaties say so. No British parliament has voted on EU funding in years.

And because the UK economy has been doing well in recent years, Britain has had to pay more to the EU as the price of success. Our economic growth in 1998, for example, meant that we subsequently had to pay an extra £530 million to the EU.

But other economies were particularly weak, largely because of the self-defeating social and economic policies they followed. So they received massive rebates. In other words, our success was penalised to pay for their failures. Those failures that year – 1998 – resulted in £1.9 billion being handed back to other member states in the form of rebates, Germany getting the biggest bonus of £840 million, France £600 million and Italy £474 million. Apart from the UK, only Sweden paid more – in their case a mere £15 million.

Meanwhile, the cost of UK membership of this profligate club goes on rising. Today, the UK pays over £11 billion a year, directly in cash, into the EU, and bears substantially more in compliance costs.

The direct expenditure alone is equal to about £20 million a year per constituency of about 95,000 voters. If we assume that each constituency has some 35,000 houses then by leaving the EU each householder could have their council tax bills reduced by £570 a year.

Or we could simply say that £570 of the taxation paid by every household in the UK goes directly to the EU. The IOD puts the figure closer to £1,000 a year per family.

Who in their right mind would give, say, £100 a week to someone else, knowing that they would get back £60, and then only on condition that the other person could decide how it must be spent? Of the £40 lost, £32 would be spent on maintaining the stakeholder and benefiting his friends. And he would waste £8 through corruption. Now scale up the numbers, and – unbelievable though it might be – that's exactly what the UK's financial arrangements are with the EU.

At the time of writing, the last official figures were for 1999. The UK's Office of National Statistics *Pink Book 2000* shows that Britain paid £11.44 billion gross to the EU in 1999, or £220 million a week, or £1.3 million every hour of every day of every week of the year.

Eventually, about half of the UK's contributions to the EU comes back in the form of grants, of course. But the absurdity of that system more than matches any notions from the inventive minds of Gilbert and Sullivan. We apply for grants of our own money, and the EU then decides how our own money should be spent in our own country.

In 1999, we received back some £6.8 billion, after a fashion. We did not get value for money, and it meant that we were still squandering over £770,000 an hour on the EU. It simply disappeared – and is still disappearing – much of it down a black hole marked "corruption and waste".

Let's suppose we want to build a new bridge. We estimate the cost of the project and, if it is approved by the EU, we may be granted 50 per cent of the total cost. But the grant is not paid until the bridge is completed. So the funds to finance the project have to be borrowed on the money markets at commercial rates of interest. This significantly increases the cost. Indeed, depending on the length of time required to complete the bridge, it could easily double the cost.

Finally, the EU inspects the finished project, for it still retains the right to check that the original specification has been fully met. If it is satisfied the EU then approves the payment of the grant. Meanwhile, of course, the financial costs of building the bridge have further reduced the real value of the grant from the original 50 per cent to something less, possibly to nothing.

This is the financial management of the madhouse.

And while the UK makes a significant net contribution to the coffers of the EU, as indeed does Germany, most of the other nations do not. France, which is the driving force behind EU bureaucracy, has so arranged matters that its net contribution to the EU is almost nothing. As we saw earlier, virtually all of the French contribution immediately returns in huge grants to French farmers under the CAP, which was set up for their benefit in the first place.

According to an answer given in the House of Lords, between 1973 and 1998 the UK's net contribution to the EU budget was £31 billion, the equivalent of some £47 billion at 1998 prices. Of that massive total, 42 per cent was spent on expenses and non-UK projects, and 8 per cent (£3.76 billion) went "missing".

Meanwhile, our trade deficit with the other EU countries has been growing, too. So the total cost of our membership is substantially higher. We should add the cumulative deficits on UK trade with the EU over the same period, 1973–98, of £195 billion. Adjusted for inflation, that equals £359 billion at 1998 prices.

Together with the UK's direct payments to the EU, and with adjustments for inflation to the end of 1998, the total cost of UK membership of the EU is therefore equivalent to £406.5 billion, or £7,400 for every man, woman and child in the UK. This is roughly the same as the UK's national debt.

But look at the alternatives. Of course, no government would choose to put all its annual savings into one pot. But the sheer scale of options available underlines the immediate and massive benefit to the UK of keeping all that public money in this country and spending it directly on our own needs.

The cash we have contributed to the EU would have been at least enough to cut income tax by five pence in the pound, or cut the lowest rate in half. Alternatively, we could re-establish farming deficiency payments, increase old age pensions by at least £20 a week; or we could abolish petrol tax; or we could abolish capital gains tax, inheritance tax, insurance premium tax, air passenger duty and landfill tax, reduce vehicle excise duty to the levels of years ago – and still have enough left over to take a penny off the basic rate of income tax.

Here, too, is the answer to the problem of funding the NHS. It is staring us in the face. Up to £20 billion would be immediately available without adding a penny to taxation. By leaving the EU altogether, we would actually save much more than the £11 billion paid in cash into their coffers.

Because we have to meet the cost of financing each project supported by a grant, it has been calculated that all the new money available if we left the EU would actually total over £18 billion. To that, according to the British Chambers of Commerce, another £2 billion a year could be added by abolishing the 3,500 new regulations imposed in 1999 alone, by the Labour government acting on the instructions of Brussels.

At least some of that £2 billion would undoubtedly have been spent by industry on private health care for staff, and charitable donations to fund medical research. Both types of expenditure would have had a beneficial impact on the NHS's current problems, and both have been denied by the actions of government and its EU masters.

According to latest estimates, the £11 billion a year we currently give to the EU in cash would pay for 73 new 500-bed hospitals in one year alone – far more than we need to meet demand during even the worst of winters.

Or we could build over 1,100 new comprehensive schools – again, far more than we need to get class sizes down. Better still, the right combination of such large-scale, new capital investment in health and education would achieve a substantial improvement in both sectors, immediately and all at the same time.

And having built the buildings, today it costs about £100,000 a year to support a hospital bed, and just over £2,600 to keep a child in secondary education for a year.

This, too, could be funded from the additional money released by our exit from the EU. It would be more than enough to fund the training and support of all the doctors, nurses and teachers we need, and all the beds and classroom places.

❖

According to the IMF, the USA has seen its exports to the EU growing at 4.5 per cent annually since 1992. Ours have grown at 3.8 per cent a year over the same period. The USA is on the other side of the Atlantic and we are next door. They are not members and we are. In absolute terms, the USA now exports more to the EU than does Britain. Exclude British imports of American goods and the figures are even more startling. The remaining 14 EU countries together import only a fifth more from Britain than from the USA.

The reason for this extraordinary imbalance is simple. The Americans face a lower tariff wall. The details examined earlier proved that the cost of trading with the EU would actually fall if we left. With commercial freedom and flexibility, agreements with our long-standing trading partners in North America, Australasia and other parts of the Anglo-Saxon world would be revived and expanded, and all this new economic activity would feed back into a thriving Britain. Production costs would fall while opportunities for enterprise and employment increased.

The Institute of Economic Affairs says that withdrawal from the EU would set the UK back by about one per cent of GDP. Even that may be too high an estimate, as we would then be free to trade with the EU without current constraints. Even if the EU did attempt the illegal creation of obstacles to trade, those costs would be as nothing compared to the current costs imposed on all our industry by EU regulations. And they would fall only on exporters, not on everybody else as well.

When we leave, the EU dare not retaliate – we have a £9 billion trade deficit with them. Even if they did, we might have to pay the average GATT duty of 3.8 per cent on some 12 per cent of our total international trade – amounting to an extra cost of 0.04 per cent on GDP, which is hardly measurable.

By comparison, our contributions of £11 billion to the EU represent an effective tariff of about six per cent on our exports to the EU. Added to that, the costs to British businesses of conforming to current EU regulations makes the true total cost of membership infinitely higher.

In other words, even if the EU were foolish enough to impose maximum possible tariffs against us, and put their substantial trade surplus at risk, and even if the UK were foolish enough not to retaliate, the savings from being outside the EU and all its regulations would still be far greater than the tariff costs.

Of course, the ultimate goal of the WTO, in its succession of international talks, is to abolish all trade impediments between the world's nations. Such abolition will also abolish any remaining threadbare reasons for UK membership of the EU.

Thirty years ago when tariffs averaged 16 per cent there might have been one (and only one) good reason for a "common market" – but it has long since vanished. Today, the only way to benefit from low or zero tariffs is to be outside the EU, running our affairs as we wish, efficiently and competitively.

By leaving, in one bound we would be free of the mountainous 30,000 directives and regulations, free of the unnecessary costs on businesses large and small, free of the dead hands of bureaucrats, free of the CAP and CFP. Instead, that insignificant one per cent loss of GDP would be made up in months by the explosion in enterprise that would follow. Our new problem would be controlling growth!

Of course, when the government talks about our commercial relationship with the EU, it likes to refer to its being worth 60 per cent of our international trade. This is an excruciatingly careful use of words. It implies exports, but – actually – it is heavily dependent on imports for its validity. "International trade" in government-speak means traffic both ways. As we established earlier, we actually sell about 40 per cent of our exports to the EU.

Protection of the other 60 per cent of our trade, with the countries outside the EU, is vitally important to the UK. Some 80 per cent of our worldwide trade surplus is with the US alone. We don't need to become the 52nd state of the USA to trade with them. Whether or not we were to join NAFTA – which exists between the USA, Canada and Mexico – will not diminish that surplus, and might even increase it.

So the case to leave can be made on trade terms alone; never mind sovereignty. This is not idle speculation. It is confirmed by all the official figures.

Early in 2000, the National Institute for Economic and Social Research (NIESR) published a survey on the potential economic consequences of the UK leaving the EU. They found that some 2,000,000 jobs might be affected, but not lost. Companies would have to switch to other markets. And in any case we have established that the EU has every incentive to continue trading with the UK.

The NIESR report suggested that, short-term, there might be some 50,000 jobs lost in companies heavily involved in the EU, assuming some sort of trade war developed for a while. But that is so unlikely as to be near-impossible. There would be no trade war, no serious loss of jobs.

Exactly the opposite, in fact. Any losses would be far exceeded by new jobs created by the removal of EU regulations and directives. Britain would burst with activity – building a new fishing fleet, and expanding our fishing industry itself as fast as the boats were finished. Farmers would be free to expand milk and meat production. In the case of milk and dairy produce, in particular, the growth would be substantial. The slaughterhouses that have been forced to close down would spring to life again. And literally countless thousands of jobs and businesses would revive or be created from scratch as the bonfire of the EU's directives released new enterprise.

Of course there will be some job losses when we leave the EU – among civil servants, trading standards officers, meat inspectors sent from Spain and elsewhere, plus tribunal members and official busybodies of all kinds. But who's crying?

The commentator Robert Conquest wrote in his book *Reflections on a Ravaged Century* "The EU is…to an important degree a forced creation. It constitutes a bloc hindering the development of world free trade, being from a global point of view a large-scale special interest (or set of special interests). And it has proved inadequate to finding a joint foreign policy with the rest of the democratic world, or even as yet within its own councils.

"The 'idealism' of the sponsors of United Europe has the frequent faults of idealism: excessive devotion to an aim, disregard of legitimate public feelings, implicit falsification of particular moves… .

"Meanwhile, its divisiveness of the West and its runaway bureaucratism must surely be confronted as best we can not merely as unlovely in themselves but also as distortive – even corruptive – of the West's culture."

❖

Of the top 30 wealthiest nations in the world, 20 have populations of under 10,000,000. Virtually all of them are peaceful and democratic, as well as prosperous. The majority are not in the EU.

Norway and Switzerland are not in the EU and they are thriving. If there are benefits to membership, how is it that they cannot see them? Switzerland has the lowest unemployment in Europe and the highest wages. It also has the toughest immigration laws. Norway has kept control of its vital offshore oil and farming industries.

The tiny island of Iceland is independent of the EU. It is far from bankrupt. It boasts a total population of 275,000 people. It is a sovereign nation. It has its own currency, its own tourism industry, it controls its own fishing grounds, it has its own lifestyle and traditions, and it depends on no other country for support. It is thriving. Importantly, Iceland's fishing industry is doing well – which is more than can be said for the UK.

Having left, the UK would be free to continue as the offshore island into Europe for the rest of the world. There has been absolutely no slow-down in inward investment in the UK from all around the world since we decided not to join the euro. That is no accident. The rest of the economic world sees us for what we are – a good place to do business.

The UK has low inflation, low unemployment, a stable currency, a thriving economy and public finances that are under control.

Among eurolanders, there is rising inflation (Ireland's housing boom is rampant), devalued currencies (the German Deutschmark fell more than 15 per cent in the first year of the euro), endemic high unemployment and stagnating economies (just about everywhere), and public finances that are still out of control (Italy and Belgium).

In November 1999, the outgoing Lord Mayor of London, Lord Levene, said: "The City of London is thriving outside the euro. It has increased its share of business." A few days later, and more than once over the following months, the Governor of the Bank of England, Sir Eddie George, said much the same thing.

The City of London is bigger in terms of GDP than Switzerland, Sweden and Austria. It has grown faster and attracted even higher levels of inward investment since the euro was launched than it did before. The flexibility of being outside the eurozone suits it very well.

Our foreign exchange market is the biggest in the world, our bond market is one of the biggest, and our stock market is one of the big three – all of which are yet more reasons why the Europeans want us in euroland. The City of London handles a third of the world's foreign exchange. Daily market volume averages well over $750 billion, which is more than the combined average total for the next three largest markets – New York, Tokyo and Singapore.

London financial markets holdings are the largest of any single country in the world. Almost 40 per cent of the world's over-the-counter-derivatives market trade in London – double the USA figure. Over 60 per cent of the primary international bond market and nearly 80 per cent of the secondary market, a quarter of the world's marine insurance market and nearly 40 per cent of the aviation insurance market are all in London.

In 1999, the City of London totally dominated the issue of euro-denominated euro-bonds. More than two-thirds were issued from London, despite the UK not being in euroland.

The City – meaning finance, accounting, legal and consulting services – is now the UK's biggest and fastest growing economic sector – and now accounts for over a fifth of our national GDP (21 per cent) – the same as all our manufacturing industries combined. One in 5 (118) of Europe's biggest companies have their headquarters in London. All ten of the largest European law firms are in London.

That is probably why the City of London also handles 20 per cent of all international lending deals. In 1998, UK companies were responsible for almost a quarter of all international mergers and acquisitions, more than any other single country.

Furthermore, this vibrant sector, our cultural environment, and our comparatively low levels of personal direct taxation, have attracted many high-net-worth financiers, entrepreneurs and other wealthy individuals to the UK. How long will they stay if we put that environment at risk?

These are serious assets, which we have to protect. No one else will protect them for us – least of all the EU. Despite the present UK government's half-hearted attempts to "defend" the City of London from the potential damage of the EU's proposed withholding tax, the plain fact is that the EU can enforce it by redefining it as a "fair competition" measure. It is then subject to introduction by QMV, and the British veto will once again have been sidestepped. At the Helsinki meeting in December 1999 the EC admitted as much. Every country that has introduced a withholding tax on capital has simultaneously generated a flight of that capital to a safer haven.

And the EU has every reason to try to destroy these precious national assets – they want the jobs and opportunities that go with them. What possible benefit flows to France and Germany by our joining euroland other than the destruction of the great strengths of the City of London? Already the French and Italians are trying to destroy the London art market – for exactly the same reasons and motivation. They seek control over us, because they fear our strengths and envy our success.

So while Germany continues to subsidise its state banks, impose nationalist criteria on its pension funds' investment decisions, demands withholding taxes, and regulates every aspect of business life, the UK is still comparatively free to allow enterprise to flourish – and this is seen as unfair competition!

EMU is intended to disable some of the UK's most important financial operations and services to the direct (and hoped for) benefit of Frankfurt and Paris. EMU is intended to restrict the UK's ability to control its monetary affairs, change the regulatory climate under which it operates and remove the source of decision-making to a central bank that can permanently out-vote the UK.

We have abundant and inescapable evidence to show that the EU's agenda for the UK is to seize control of our assets and submerge our interests. This book is full of it. Yet we still stare in disbelief at our Continental neighbours, somehow hoping – even at the last minute – to convince ourselves that we have got it wrong, that they are honourable people. Sadly, they are not. As one of their own former employees, Bernard Connolly, put it: "They are liars. They are cheats."

❖

For the British, the EU has been a ghastly mistake. We ordinary people expected a successful and peaceful Europe to be a Europe of free people, and free nations, trading freely together, built on a sound system of accountable, divided and restrained government, dedicated above all else to the protection of liberty. As that great Anglo-Saxon president Abraham Lincoln put it: "…government of the people, by the people, for the people."

We British are slow to rouse. Too often, perhaps, we leave things to the last minute. We did so in the 1930s, and by 1940 we stood on the verge of ruin. But we also found ourselves carrying the torch of freedom. For a short and dire time the destiny of the free world lay in our hands.

We were alone. But we were also inspired. We did not flinch or waver then. We did not fail. Nor shall we now. Of those critical years, Winston Churchill later wrote:

> "…we have the confidence in our bones of a people unconquered for a thousand years. This nation has a free sovereign parliament, fairly chosen by universal suffrage, able to turn out the government any day but proud to uphold it even in the darkest days.

Parliament is supreme. That was one of the points in dispute with our enemy. And Parliament won."

Now it must win again. And it will, now that we, the British people, are finally roused. If we are fearless, defiant, resolute, unyielding, we can retain our liberty, our essential freedoms. We are the people. Society and its future is our responsibility. It is not the government's to give away. We cannot avoid that responsibility, nor can we allow that power to be removed.

It is non-negotiable.

Millions now know that we can and must leave the EU. Even the "inevitability" argument (of staying in the EU) has become threadbare. It is no longer credible.

Right now, millions of British subjects cry out for true visionary political leadership – statesmanship. They seek a politician who has the wisdom, vision, courage and sheer guts to make the unequivocal case for leaving, and take the short-term risks that go with such a statement. It is desperately to our shame as a nation that no such figure – no real statesman – can be seen on the stage of British politics today.

It is much better to face the truth. We have had more than enough of lies and distortions. There is really no reason why we, the people, should sink to the tawdry spin of the politicians who got us into this mess in the first place.

When the French lost patience with their ruling class they cut their heads off. In Germany and Italy they were hanged, sometimes upside-down. The Spanish garrotted or shot their leaders, and the Greeks put theirs in prison. We once cut off a king's head, but only once. This time, being the law-abiding nation we are at heart, a civilised examination of the facts in a court of law, based on charges of treason and misuse of public office, might suffice.

If the opinion polls are right, about 130,000,000 people in the EU (about 35 per cent) want it abolished. By the end of 2000, barely half the total population of the EU still supported it.

In 1939, Britain went to war to defend the independence of Poland. Six years later, both countries found themselves on the winning side. But Poland had finally been freed from Germany only to find a Russian yoke around its neck. As it was becoming clear that the USSR had no intention of allowing the Poles their independence, Winston Churchill told parliament:

"Are they to be masters in their own house? Are they to be free as we in Britain and the USA or France are free? Are their sovereignty and their independence to be untrammelled or are they to become a mere projection of the [Soviet] state, forced against their will by an armed minority to adopt a totalitarian system?"

Little did Churchill imagine that those same questions could be asked of Britain itself within half a century.

But the alternative is there, just waiting for us.

The UK has been behaving like a junkie towards the EU in recent years – dependent on it, and afraid to give it up. The EU has become an addiction. And the politicians have ruthlessly exploited this dependency.

They have been systematically adding to the doses, and injecting it increasingly against our will. They now endlessly repeat the suggestion – like some kind of crazed psychiatrist – that giving it up will be a terrible ordeal. They are trying to convince us that we are too weak to kick the habit of this dreadful toxin, and that breaking the habit is an experience to be feared.

We know what to do. Like any drugged child, we must escape the treatment before we can begin to feel better.

The EU is like bindweed – or a triffid. It gets into everything. Chokes everything. Swamps everything. Destroys everything.

It travels secretly along the ground, crawls up any strong support and squeezes it dry. Occasionally it throws out an attractive flower that smells and looks pleasing. But it's a trap. It's designed to stop you tearing up this weed. It's a bauble.

There is only one way to deal with a weed – pull it out, roots and all, and throw it away. Clear the ground. Weeds are fit only for the compost heap.

We could be out of the EU in ten minutes. Two privy councillors and a representative of the Queen could recall our ambassador with a phone call. That act alone declares that all treaties between the UK and the EU are null and void.

Parliament can repeal the European Communities Act of 1972. That has the same effect – it tears up the treaties, and the myriad of directives and so-called laws that have been based on it. They have no constitutional validity anyway, as they represent the giving away of powers that parliament had no right to give away. Meanwhile, all parties affected by them can consider them as repealed, effective immediately.

Just tear them up, and tell Brussels there will be no more cheques from us. We're selling all our euros as quickly as the market will bear. Our fishing grounds are now off-limits to up to 200 miles in all directions, effective immediately. Milk quotas and the CAP have been abolished in the UK, effective immediately.

We also tell Brussels that, effective immediately, we intend to set our people free, to work and organise themselves in an enterprise zone extending from one end of these islands to the other, bearing minimal taxation and regulatory interference from Her Majesty's government. Inventiveness and entrepreneurial enthusiasm will be encouraged vigorously, and British companies will be free to compete with the best and win against the best in the world.

In future, we tell them, we will happily work with you, but we will no longer work for you. And we shall compete with you on our own terms, not on yours. Here's the deal. Free trade between us, but if you impose duties on us we'll impose the same on you. We will not act first. You might care to ponder on these decisions and the fundamentals that lie behind them. You might even wish to allow the same freedoms to your peoples, unless you still believe that your way is best.

By the way, before we finish, please pension off Messrs Kinnock and Patten – at your expense, of course. And you can tell the other countries that we've left the prison gates open behind us.

❖

According to a posting on the internet in May 2000, Canada was at the time "seized by patriotic fervour as the result of a beer commercial". A video advertising Molson Canadian, the country's most popular beer, had become a national sensation. Known as the "Molson rant", it featured a young actor – Jeff Douglas – in a plaid shirt, praising his country. To the music of "Land of Hope and Glory" he mocked the ways in which Americans stereotype Canadians: "I'm not a lumberjack or a fur trader. I don't live in an igloo, eat blubber or own a dogsled. I have a prime minister, not a president. I believe in peacekeeping, not policing; diversity, not assimilation. I speak English and French, not American."

Then, as the music built to a climax and the maple-leaf Canadian flag filled the screen, he roared: "Canada is the second-largest land mass, the first nation of hockey and the best part of North America. My name is Joe and I'm Canadian."

The commercial quickly became so popular that many Canadians knew the words by heart, and it was even performed live to standing ovations at sporting events. Molson set up a website providing unlimited replays and commented: "It just seems to have tapped into a powerful undercurrent of feeling."

There is little doubt the same could happen in Britain, if the right company or organisation saw the benefits of lancing the boil of frustration currently felt by so many millions of Britons.

Ed Murrow, reporting on radio to the people of the USA a few months after the end of the Second World War, said:

"I doubt that the most important thing was Dunkirk, or the Battle of Britain, or El Alamein or Stalingrad. Nor even the landings in Normandy or the great blows struck by British and American bombers. Historians may decide that any one of these events was decisive, but I am persuaded that the most important thing that happened in Britain was that this nation chose to win or lose this war under the established rules of parliamentary procedure.

It feared Nazism, but did not choose to imitate it. The government led by Winston Churchill was given dictatorial power, but it was used with restraint, and the House of Commons was ever vigilant.

Do you remember that while London was being bombed in the daylight, the House devoted two days to discussing conditions under which enemy aliens were detained on the Isle of Man? Though Britain fell, there were to be no concentration camps here."

Since that time, we have taken our eyes off the ball. We have followed unworthy men down the wrong paths. We have permitted our standards to fall. We have compromised our beliefs, our customs and our traditions. We have endangered our rights and freedoms. Our present wounds are largely self-inflicted by neglect.

We – the people – have not been vigilant.

That greatest of speeches, delivered by John of Gaunt in Shakespeare's *Richard II*, concluded with the lines:

> "England, bound in with the triumphant sea,
> Whose rocky shore beats back the envious siege
> Of watery Neptune, is now bound in with shame,
> With inky blots, and rotten parchment bonds:
> That England, that was wont to conquer others,
> Hath made a shameful conquest of itself."

These words, written by one of England's greatest sons, captured one of the direst moments in our history. Now, across the centuries, those same words carry another message of uncomfortable truth.

But then, as now, all was not lost. That immortal speech started with words of inspiration. They can inspire us again:

> "This royal throne of kings, this scepter'd isle,
> This earth of majesty, this seat of Mars,
> This other Eden, demi-paradise;
> This fortress built by Nature for herself
> Against infection and the hand of war;
> This happy breed of men, this little world;
> This precious stone set in the silver sea...
> This blessed plot, this earth, this realm, this England..."

That is the call. Who's listening?

Appendix

Defence of the Realm

First published by the Magna Carta Society (a company limited by guarantee and now wound up), in April 2000. *Defence of the Realm* was summarised and updated in the autumn of 2000. Its full text follows.

❖

There is good reason to think that the Treaties of Rome, Maastricht and Amsterdam are illegal in the UK. Further, we argue that their ratification, the enactment of the European Communities Act 1972, and all consequential laws, directives, regulations and judicial decisions which purport to draw authority from that Act were and are illegal in this sovereign kingdom.

We argue that the signatories to those treaties on behalf of the UK exceeded their powers; that, since and including the passage of the 1972 Act, successive executives have systematically compromised the constitution of this sovereign nation and that all such actions are illegal and *prima facie* acts of treason.

Further, we argue that the UK's membership of the EU is null and void, that it can and should be so declared, and that all consequential laws, regulations, directives and judicial decisions fall with such a declaration.

Our justification for such awesome statements starts with Magna Carta, 1215, which gave sovereign recognition to already long-standing Anglo-Saxon common law, rights and customs. Some 150 years earlier William the Conqueror had made the first attempts to codify those rights and customs, which ultimately go back at least to the time of King Alfred and beyond.

Magna Carta is variously described as a covenant, contract or treaty. It is not an Act of Parliament. As we understand it, Magna Carta cannot be repealed by parliament. As a contract between sovereign and subjects, it can be breached only by one party or the other, but even in the breach it still stands. It is a mutual, binding agreement of indefinite duration. Any breach merely has the effect of giving the offended party rights of redress.

The present Queen referred to Magna Carta as a peace treaty in a speech in New Zealand in 1997.

So, Magna Carta is an affirmation of common law based on principles of natural justice. These principles – and the document itself – pre-date parliament.

To summarise our understanding of these principles and customs:

* Common law is the will and custom of the people.

* Statute law is the will of parliament. Statute can and does give expression to common law, but that common law cannot be disregarded by parliament, nor can it be repealed. It can only be extended – "improved" is the word used, but it is open to misuse.

* Parliament is made by the law, and is not above it.

* No parliament can bind its successors.

* Parliament is answerable to the people, is elected by the people to protect their interests for a maximum of five years, after which time power is returned to the people who may grant it to another parliament for a further five years – and so on *ad infinitum*. (Thus is the sovereignty of the people established over parliament.)

* No Briton, including members of the police and armed forces, is above the law. We are all subjects of the Crown first.

"The rights or...liberties of Englishmen...consist primarily in the free enjoyment of personal security, of personal liberty, and of private property... .To vindicate these rights, when actually violated or attacked, the subjects of England are entitled, in the first place, to the regular administration and free course of justice in the courts of law; next, to the right of petitioning the king and parliament for redress of grievances; and lastly to the right of having and using arms for self-preservation and defence.

And all these rights and liberties it is our birthright to enjoy entire; unless where the laws of our country have laid them under necessary restraints...so gentle and moderate...that no man of sense or probity would wish to see them slackened."

Blackstone (1723–80), *Commentaries on the Laws of England*

Magna Carta recognised that rights and customs were of equal importance to the people, and both were equally protected:

"And the city of London shall have all its ancient liberties and free customs...furthermore, we decree and grant that all other cities, boroughs, towns, and ports shall have all their liberties and free customs.

If anyone has been dispossessed or removed by us, without the legal judgment of his peers, from his lands, castles, franchises, or from his right, we will immediately restore them to him; and if a dispute arise over this, then let it be decided by the five and twenty barons of whom mention is made below in the clause for securing the peace."

Thus, Magna Carta recognised the authority of the House of Lords, established its constitutional role, and its composition for all time. A quorum is twenty-five hereditary peers:

"All fines made with us unjustly and against the law of the land, and all amercements, imposed unjustly and against the law of the land, shall be entirely remitted, or else it shall be done concerning them according to the decision of the five and twenty barons whom mention is made below in the clause for securing the peace, or according to the judgment of the majority of the same…provided always that if any one or more of the aforesaid five and twenty barons are in a similar suit, they shall be removed as far as concerns this particular judgment, others being substituted in their places after having been selected by the rest of the same five and twenty for this purpose only, and after having been sworn."

Article 61 of Magna Carta – the famous enforcement clause – specifically establishes majority voting, and requires four of the quorum of barons to take any grievances or petitions to the monarch, and admonishes the people to rise up against the monarch if and when such grievances are not corrected:

"Since…we have granted all these concessions, desirous that they should enjoy them in complete and firm endurance forever, we give and grant to them the underwritten security, namely, that the barons choose five and twenty barons of the kingdom, whomsoever they will, who shall be bound with all their might, to observe and hold, and cause to be observed, the peace and liberties we have granted and confirmed to them by this our present Charter, so that if we, or our justiciar, or our bailiffs or any one of our officers, shall in anything be at fault towards anyone, or shall have broken any one of the articles of this peace or of this security, and the offence be notified to four barons of the foresaid five and twenty, the said four barons shall repair to us…and, laying the transgression before us, petition to have that transgression redressed without delay.

And if we shall not have corrected the transgression…within forty days, reckoning from the time it has been intimated to us…the four barons aforesaid shall refer that matter to the rest of the five and twenty barons, and those five and twenty barons shall, together with the community of the whole realm, distrain and distress us in all possible ways, namely, by seizing our castles, lands, possessions, and in any other way they can, until redress has been obtained as they deem fit…and when redress has been obtained, they shall resume their old relations towards us. And let whoever in the country desires it, swear to obey the orders of the said five and twenty barons for the execution of all the aforesaid matters, and along with them, to molest us to the utmost of his power; and we publicly and freely grant leave to everyone who wishes to swear, and we shall never forbid anyone to swear. All those, moreover, in the land who of themselves and of their own accord are unwilling to swear to the twenty five to help them in constraining and molesting us, we shall by our command compel the same to swear to the effect foresaid. And if any one of the five and twenty barons shall have died or departed from the land, or be incapacitated in any other manner which would prevent the foresaid provisions being carried out, those of the said twenty five barons who are left shall choose another in his place according to their own judgment, and he shall be sworn in the same way as the others. Further, in all matters, the execution of which is entrusted, to these twenty five barons, if perchance these twenty five are present and disagree about anything, or if some of them, after being summoned, are unwilling or unable to be present, that which the majority of those present ordain or command shall be held as fixed and established, exactly as if the whole twenty five had concurred in this; and the said twenty five shall swear that they will faithfully observe all that is aforesaid, and cause it to be observed with all their might. And we shall procure nothing from anyone, directly or indirectly, whereby any part of these concessions and liberties might be revoked or diminished; and if any such things has been procured, let it be void and null, and we shall never use it personally or by another."

Although the Magna Carta predates parliament by some 50 years, it was subsequently enacted in 1297 with the passage of Edward I's Confirmation of the Great Charter Act, which included the words:

"And we will that if any judgement be given henceforth contrary to the points aforesaid by the justices or by any other [of] our ministers that hold plea before them against the points of the charters it shall be undone and holden for nought."

The text later includes words to the effect that the "charter of liberties shall be kept on every point".

This admonition was repeated at the coronation of the young Henry III:

> "…it shall be lawful for everyone in our realm to rise against us and use all the ways and means they can to hinder us…that each and every one shall be bound by our command…so that they shall in no way give attention to us but that they shall do everything that aims at our injury and shall in no way be bound to us until that in which we have transgressed and offenced shall have been by a fitting satisfaction brought again in due state…this having been done let them be obedient to us as they were before."

Bracton's great constitutional work written some time between 1235 and 1259, said:

> "…the law makes the King. Let the King therefore bestow upon the law what the law bestows upon him, namely dominion and power, for there is no King where will rules and not law."

Sovereignty

Sovereignty must – by definition – be absolute and unqualified. It is like the concept "unique" – it cannot be limited. Either a country is sovereign or it is not. Either a monarch is sovereign or not. The title, rank and style "King" is recognition of the physical embodiment of the nation's sovereignty. It bears no compromise.

In the context of today's issues, we can either have the Queen as the constitutional head of a sovereign country, or we can have a president of the EU. But, by definition – and despite John Major's claim after Maastricht that the Queen was henceforth a citizen of Europe – we cannot have both.

The 37th of the 39 Articles of Religion passed during the reign of Elizabeth I, which still have legal force, and which can be seen in any book of common prayer, says:

"The Queen's Majesty…is not, and ought not to be, subject to any foreign jurisdiction."

Clause 4 of the Act of Succession confirmed the power of the sovereign, the role of parliament, the common-law rights and liberties of the people, and the relationship between them. It said:

"IV. And whereas the Laws of England and the Birthright of the People thereof and all the Kings and Queens who shall ascend the Throne of this Realm ought to [in the sense of 'must', throughout] administer the Government of the same according to the said Laws and all their Officers and Ministers ought to serve them respectively according to the same The said Lords Spiritual and Temporal and Commons do therefore humbly pray That all the Laws and Statutes of this Realm for securing the established Religion and Rights and Liberties of the People thereof and all other Laws and Statutes of the same now in Force may be ratified and confirmed. And the same are by His Majesty by and with the Advice and Consent of the said Lords Spiritual and Temporal and Commons and by Authority of the same ratified and confirmed accordingly."

The Act of Supremacy 1559 went even further. It included the words:

"…all usurped and foreign power and authority…may forever be clearly extinguished, and never used or obeyed in this realm. …no foreign prince, person, prelate, state, or potentate…shall at any time after the last day of this session of Parliament, use, enjoy or exercise any manner of power, jurisdiction, superiority, authority, preeminence or privilege…within this realm, but that henceforth the same shall be clearly abolished out of this realm, for ever."

The Act of Supremacy is now largely repealed, but its central intentions live on through the use of almost identical words 129 years later, when the Declaration of Rights of 1688 was written. This, too, is a settlement treaty, and not an Act of Parliament. It too, therefore, cannot be repealed by parliament.

The Convention Parliament which drew up the Declaration was called when the Bishop of Salisbury invoked Clause 61 of Magna Carta, and demanded the attendance of 25 barons to address his grievances – evidence that Clause 61 has teeth, and that there is a precedent for such action today.

The Declaration was engrossed in parliament and enrolled among the rolls of chancery. It has never been listed, however, within the chronological tables of Acts of Parliament – a fact which might be significant.

The Bill of Rights, December 1689, incorporated all the essential clauses of the Declaration of the previous February, and may be argued to form an entrenchment of the Declaration, severely limiting parliament's ability to make changes. Indeed, it could be held to be doubly entrenched.

Clause 13 lays specific responsibilities upon members of parliament to protect the best interests of the people who elected them:

> "And they do claim, demand and insist upon all and singular the premises as their undoubted rights and liberties, and that no declarations, judgments, doings or proceedings to the prejudice of the people in any of the said premises ought in any wise to be drawn hereafter into consequence or example."

The Bill of Rights includes an unequivocal and entrenching statement from the Declaration of the previous year. Its intention was:

> "…for the ratifying, confirming and establishing the said declaration and the articles, clauses, matters and things therein contained by the force of a law made in due form by authority of Parliament, do pray that it may be declared and enacted that all and singular the rights and liberties asserted and claimed in the said declaration are the true, ancient and indubitable rights and liberties of the people of this Kingdom, and so shall be esteemed, allowed, adjudged, deemed and taken to be; and that all and every the particulars aforesaid shall be firmly and strictly holden and observed as they are expressed in the said declaration, and all officers and ministers whatsoever shall serve

their Majesties and their successors according to the same in all times to come."

The Bill of Rights included the Oath of Allegiance to the Crown, which was required by Magna Carta to be taken by all Crown servants, including members of the judiciary. Specifically…they were required "not to take into consequence or example anything to the detriment of the subjects' liberties". Similar words are still used today as Crown servants swear or affirm that they "will be faithful and bear true allegiance to Her Majesty Queen Elizabeth the Second, her heirs and successors, according to law", and that they "will well and truly serve our Sovereign Lady Queen Elizabeth the Second…and will do right to all manner of people, after the laws and usages of this realm without fear or favour, affection or ill will".

Members of the armed forces swear equally unequivocal oaths of attestation which commit them to "protect her from all enemies and to uphold her in her person, dignity and crown".

None of these oaths mentions parliament, which clearly indicates that parliament cannot interfere with the relationships or duties established by them. That brings us to one of the pivotal issues of our case – the direct, indisputable and irreconcilable conflict between the oaths sworn by privy councillors, who subsequently swear oaths on appointment as EU commissioners.

Privy councillors swear:

> "I will to my uttermost bear faith and allegiance unto the Queen's Majesty; and will assist and defend all jurisdictions, pre-eminences, and authorities granted to Her Majesty and annexed to the crown by Acts of Parliament or otherwise, against all foreign princes, persons, prelates, states and potentates. And generally in all things I will do as a faithful and true servant ought to do to Her Majesty. So help me God."

EU commissioners swear:

> "To perform my duties in complete independence, in the general interests of the communities; in carrying out my duties, neither

to seek nor to take instruction from any government or body; to refrain from any action incompatible with my duties."

It is impossible to comprehend how privy councillors who subsequently become EU commissioners live with the contradictions inherent in these conflicting promises. By definition, one oath or the other must be broken. But the legal consequences of such breaches has – to the best of our knowledge – never been put to the test in a court of law or anywhere else, despite Lord Denning's confirmation that anyone swearing an oath of loyalty to the EU should immediately resign from any public office that was held on an oath of allegiance to the Crown.

"A man cannot serve two sovereigns."

Lord Denning

We detect an horrific prevailing mood in the highest offices in the land, that mere words don't matter any more.

In times past, words and their meaning had value and were fully respected. Sir Robert Howard, a member of the Convention Parliament, and of the drafting committee for the Bill of Rights, wrote:

> "The people have always had the same title to their liberties and properties that England's kings have had unto their crowns. The several charters of the people's rights, most particularly the Magna Carta were not grants from the King, but recognitions by the King of rights that have been reserved or that appertained unto us by common law and immemorial custom."

In other words, any attempts to reduce the rights, freedoms and liberties enshrined in the constitution would be *ultra vires*.

(Few people have ever seen the whole of the original document known as the Declaration of Rights, which is housed in the records office of the House of Lords.

Until very recently part of it had been rolled up for what may have been many generations. Now, the entire document – including the engrossment

– has been photographed and transcribed verbatim, possibly for the first time in centuries.)

The Declaration of 1688 first declared the throne vacant, and went on to clarify and confirm the future governance of England. It established that the Crown, both Houses of Parliament and the people are parts of a permanent single entity, and also made clear that abolition of the structure or responsibilities of parliament in part or in whole would be illegal. The Bill of Rights, 1689, spelt out the details:

> "…the said Lords…and Commons, being the two Houses of Parliament, should continue to sit and…make effectual provision for the settlement of the…laws and liberties of this kingdom, so that the same for the future might not be in danger again of being subverted. …the particulars aforesaid shall be firmly and strictly holden and observed…and all officers and ministers whatsoever shall serve their Majesties and their successors according to the same, in all time to come."

So, neither Magna Carta nor the Declaration of Rights can be repealed, nor did they make any grant of freedom. They both proclaimed what were taken to be self-evident freedoms that exist by right. Equally, both were based on a concept of permanence.

Indeed, in 1661, one of His Majesty's justices of the peace told a grand jury:

> "If Magna Carta be, as most of us are inclined to believe …is…unalterable as to the main, it is so in every part."

The oaths sworn by William and Mary subsequently locked those rights and that parliamentary structure into a constitutional framework that could not later be undone by parliament itself or by the monarchy.

William wrote to parliament to this effect:

> "…restoring the rights and liberties of the kingdom, and settling the same, that they may not be in danger of being again subverted."

The historian G M Trevelyan writing (in the early 1920s) of these turbulent times some 300 years earlier, said:

> "In the Stuart era the English developed for themselves...a system of parliamentary government, local administration and freedom of speech and person, clean contrary to the prevailing tendencies on the continent, which was moving fast towards regal absolutism, centralised bureaucracy, and the subjection of the individual to the State."

Is Constitutional Change Treason?

The celebrated judge Sir Edward Coke said in 1610 that the Crown cannot change any part of the common law. Indeed he went further and said that the Crown cannot create any offence by proclamation (nowadays, by statute) that was not previously an offence under common law.

So in England – in a nutshell – since it was established that new rights can be conceded, but existing rights cannot be taken away, so it is arguable that any subsequent attempts to overthrow the laws and constitution of the UK must be treason.

Treason has been defined as any action which "attempts to overthrow or destroy the constitution". The defining words used in the Treason Act of 1795 were put to the test in the case of R V Thistlewood in 1820. On the face of it, such a definition would appear to rule out any referendum on the adoption of a foreign currency, since it must, *ipso facto*, deny us our constitutional rights of self-government. Indeed, the previous referendum on what was then called the Common Market may also have been unconstitutional, since the executive of the day and their legal advisors have subsequently admitted that they knew then that the true purpose of the Common Market was not free trade but full political union.

That brings us to the Treaty of Union with Scotland, and the obstacles placed in the way of a Catholic attempting to ascend the throne. These were most recently and clearly spelled out in the Declaration of Rights and also in the Bill of Rights. Such an event was held to be inconsistent with the safety and welfare of this Protestant kingdom.

The authority for this is not the Act of Settlement, but Article 11 of the Treaty of Union of 1707, which embodies the substance of the Act of Settlement of 1701.

Once again, this treaty was not incorporated into statute law and therefore cannot be repealed by an Act of Parliament – yet another inconvenient fact that's been forgotten by this present government.

The Statute Law Revision Act, 1867, attempted to take common law into statute and then repeal it. But, as we have argued earlier, this cannot happen, since common law is above statute law and predates it. In any case, both Magna Carta and the Declaration of Rights specifically reject any such attempt to amend or abolish them.

We can find no supporting evidence for Halsbury's claim that only Clauses 1, 9, 29 and 37 of Magna Carta still stand today. Blackstone and Dicey make no such claim.

Coming to more recent times…

In 1913 (Bowles *vs* Bank of England) it was ruled that:

> "The Bill of Rights still remains unrepealed, and practice of custom, however prolonged or however acquiesced in on the part of the subject, cannot be relied on by the crown as justifying any infringement of its provisions."

The case of Chester *vs* Bateson, 1920, held that "common law is not immune from development or improvement". It does not talk about "limitations" or "destruction".

So the issue then turns on what is "improvement". The word is open to a considerable latitude of interpretation, and some future undemocratic tyrant or despotic government might – would – argue that certain freedoms and rights were dangerous and should be "improved" by abolition.

That's the perverse logic used in the communist and fascist worlds of years ago. Indeed there are alarming signs of exactly that deviousness of interpretation among our present executive. And it represents a serious risk that cannot be ignored.

The erosion of one single right – however alluring the apparent logic and reasonableness might be – and all rights are then exposed. That's why the right to bear arms is so crucial, despite the aftermath of Dunblane.

One of the researchers to this document, Mike Burke, went to the Court of Appeal on 8th March 1999 in support of his case based on Clause 7 of the Declaration of Rights, 1688, and the Bill of Rights, 1689, permitting him to bear arms in self-defence. The appeal was rejected.

Despite further extensive enquiries and research, he still awaits an answer to the question: where exactly did the learned judges in the High Court and the Appeal Court discover authority for the removal of our right to arms, and the repeal of at least one clause in the Bill of Rights?

Of equal concern is the fact that subsequent searches of legal records have so far revealed no trace of the judgment rejecting his appeal. Yet the case raised an important constitutional right, embedded in legislation that has not been repealed and that – we have argued above – cannot be repealed.

That such a case should not be recorded at all in legal records raises yet more important questions about the suppression of rights by stealth, and this time apparently with the connivance of the judiciary or their administrators.

It must be of some concern that the last time Britons were forcibly disarmed of weapons held for self-defence, the result was the American War of Independence.

> "What of the militia? It is the whole people. To disarm people is the best and most effectual way to enslave them."
>
> George Mason

We can put it no better than the great political philosopher John Locke:

> "The right of self-defence is the first law of nature. When the right of the people to keep and bear arms is, under any colour or pretext whatsoever, prohibited, liberty, if not already annihilated, is on the brink of destruction."

The legal status of the Parliament Act, 1949, may also have an important bearing on our case. Some respected constitutional lawyers believe that it is not valid. It purports to enable legislation to be enacted after a year despite the opposition of the House of Lords. But, as Professor Hood Phillips pointed out over 50 years ago, the Act cannot be valid because it was rejected by the House of Lords and no power of amendment was conferred on the House of Commons by the Parliament Act, 1911.

Indeed the Parliament Act of 1911 offers no authority to the House of Commons to amend primary legislation at all. And if the Parliament Act of 1949 is invalid, so must be much European-led legislation, including most recently the European Parliamentary Election Act, 1999.

Of course, in recent times, the House of Commons has frequently attempted to interfere with the constitution. Worse, the courts appear to have given up legislative supremacy to parliament, and this trend has been compounded by the fact that no one has gone before the courts and claimed his common law rights.

Those rights are clear, and they have been enshrined in documents for generations. Today they may be hidden and forgotten, but they are still there. The common law rights of the people cannot be subverted by ministers and other servants of the Crown. They have only the same powers and rights as the people who elected or appointed them.

Indeed it can be argued that the only means by which the constitution and the rights it protects can ever be changed is by revolution, because all Crown servants would have to be "persuaded" to take a new oath of allegiance to a new sovereign state. Their forebears were appointed specifically on condition that they would respect and defend the rights, freedoms and customs of the people. Nothing has changed the substance of that commitment since then.

An attempt was purportedly made to repeal Magna Carta in 1969, when the Statute Laws (Repeal) Act was sneaked through parliament during the moon landings.

It repealed Edward I's Confirmation of the Great Charter Act of 1297 – but it did not repeal Magna Carta itself. Yet again, as we understand the legal position, a repeal of a statute which gives effect to common law does not repeal the underlying common law itself.

The gap between the two events might extend to hundreds of years, but the effect is always the same. The original common law remains untouched.

If parliament could be held to have repealed Magna Carta it could also be held to have acted unlawfully in that, by definition, parliament must have exceeded its powers on that occasion.

On 21st July 1993, the speaker of the House of Commons issued a reminder to the courts. She said:

"There has of course been no amendment to the Bill of Rights…the house is entitled to expect that the Bill of Rights will be fully respected by all those appearing before the courts."

Lord Wilberforce, speaking in the House of Lords in 1997, said:

"Perhaps I may remind noble lords of what our essential civil rights, as guaranteed by common law, are: the presumption of innocence; the right to a fair hearing; no man to be obliged to testify against himself; the rule against double jeopardy; no retrospective legislation; no legislation to be given an effect contrary to international law — an old principle that has been there for years; freedom of expression; and freedom of association…firmly secured already by the common law of this country, and not intended to be superseded or modified by new inter-state obligations…"

Once again, John Locke distilled the issue:

"A ruler who violates the law is illegitimate. He has no right to be obeyed. His commands are mere force and coercion. Rulers who act lawlessly, whose laws are unlawful, are mere criminals."

Parliamentary Limits

Ironically, it seems that the power parliament has most interest in exercising nowadays is the manufacture of criminals, by making more and more conduct illegal, regardless of the effect on our essential rights guaranteed under common law. If government, any government, "believes it can do as it wishes without the constraint of a constitution which is enforceable then no one and nothing is safe". These are the views of a lawyer who has made a special study of the EU's *corpus juris* proposals.

"A government above the law is a menace to be defeated."

Lord Scarman

Parliament cannot do as it wishes. There are a great many things parliament cannot do. It cannot sit for more than five years, it cannot permit anyone not elected to speak in its chamber, nor anyone who has not sworn an oath of allegiance, it cannot dissolve itself and it cannot legitimately depose the Queen.

No parliament can bind its successors. This principle is itself a maxim of common law, and has been often restated:

> "Acts derogatory to the power of subsequent parliaments bind not."
>
> Blackstone and Halsbury

Neither can parliament legislate in contravention of the treaties which established the constitution and sovereignty of this nation – a point central to our case. Furthermore, parliament has a duty of care to preserve and protect the rights and freedoms of the people who elected it.

Nor can parliament complete the passage of a bill without the royal assent.

The sovereign, on the other hand, can dissolve parliament – with or without the advice of ministers – and can withhold the royal assent. Only the sovereign can call for new elections, and only the sovereign can sign treaties. Those powers are the embodiment of the sovereign's supremacy over parliament. They may, from time to time, be delegated.

Because the sovereign is constitutionally bound to respect the provisions of the Bill of Rights, such royal prerogative has restrictions:

* It cannot be used in an innovatory way. (If this were not so, the executive could dispense with parliament and the judiciary and become an unlimited tyranny. Any future attorney general could claim that an edict was part of a treaty and it would become unquestionable.)

* It may not be subversive of the rights and liberties of the subject. (The case of Nichols *vs* Nichols, 1576, stated "Prerogative is created for the benefit of the people and cannot be exercised to their prejudice".)

      *   It may not be used to suspend or offend against statutes in force. (This comes from the Bill of Rights and the Coronation Oath Act which specifies the following form of words. Archbishop: "Will you solemnly promise and swear to govern the peoples of this Kingdom of England and the Dominions thereto belonging according to the statutes in Parliament agreed upon and the laws and customs of the same." Prospective Monarch: "I solemnly promise so to do.")

The limitations of royal prerogative are clear. Sir Robert Howard again:

"No prerogative may be recognised that is contrary to Magna Carta or any other statute, or that interferes with the liberties of the subject. The courts have jurisdiction therefore, to enquire into the existence of any prerogative, it being a maxim of the common law that the king ought to be under no man, but under God and the law, because the law makes the king. If any prerogative is disputed, the courts must decide the question of whether or not it exists in the same way as they decide any other question of law. If a prerogative is clearly established, they must take the same judicial notice of it as they take of any other rule of law."

Thus, we argue, while sovereigns have, over the centuries, at times devolved the royal prerogative to sign treaties to plenipotentiaries to act on their behalf, such devolved power is strictly limited, and cannot be used to remove the freedoms and liberties of the people by imposing foreign government and foreign law on them.

In other words, the signatories to the European Communities Act 1972 exceeded their powers under the royal prerogative.

We further argue that the subsequent claims made by government ministers and officials that European law is "supreme" in the UK is wholly ill-founded. At least one lawyer has suggested that anyone making such a claim is either ignorant, or lying, or bluffing, or admitting illegalities, or perpetrating a combination of all four follies.

Blackstone pointed out that English law was superior to that of other nations because liberty under the law was the purpose of the constitution:

"A right of every Englishman is that of applying to the Courts of Justice for redress of injuries. Since the law in England is the supreme arbiter of every man's life, liberty and property, Courts of Justice must at all times be open to the subject, and the law be duly administered therein."

The *Cambridge Law Journal*, 1955, referring to (now Professor Sir, QC) William Wade's *The Basis of Legal Sovereignty*, said that:

"sovereign legislation depends for its authority on (what Salmond calls) an 'ultimate legal principle', i.e. a political fact for which no purely legal explanation can be given. If no statute can establish the rule that the courts obey (the UK) parliament, similarly no statute can alter or abolish that rule. It is above and beyond the reach of statute...because it is itself the source of the authority of statute."

In other words, the relationship between parliament, sovereign legislation and the courts of law in the UK is unalterable.

It is surprising to us that the so-called "supremacy" of the ECJ has not been tested in the courts on this point already. If Wade is right, the UK courts are supreme in this jurisdiction.

An attempt was made to bring these and other matters to court in 1971 by Raymond Blackburn, who challenged the government's right to join the Common Market on the grounds that it could do so only by surrendering sovereignty. A year later, Ross McWhirter invoked the Bill of Rights to show that the government did not have authority to give away the right and liberties of the people. Tragically, he was assassinated before the matter was decided. His brother Norris made a similar attempt to question the legality of the Maastricht Treaty in 1993. Summonses were issued against the then foreign secretary for treason.

The attorney general used a purported power to take over the case and then drop it as "not in the public interest". Yet the Bill of Rights prohibits "suspending laws or the operation of laws". His action was also contrary to natural justice because the attorney general was sitting in judgement in his own cause.

To accept that the only remedy lies with the body that perpetuates the abuse is to admit that there is no remedy. That must be wrong, both morally and constitutionally.

In January 1977, John Gouriet asked the attorney general to declare illegal the proposed boycott of all communications with South Africa by the Union of Post Office Workers on the grounds that it would be a criminal breach of the Post Office Act. The attorney general refused to uphold the law, claiming that he was the sole arbiter, and Mr Gouriet issued proceedings against both the law officer and the union.

Summing up in the Court of Appeal, Lord Denning quoted the great 18th-century attorney, Sir Thomas Fuller:

"Be you never so high, the law is above you."

Lord Denning added:

"When the Attorney General comes…and tells us that he has a prerogative by which he alone can say whether the criminal law can be enforced in these courts or not – then I say he has no such prerogative. He has no prerogative to suspend or dispense with the laws of England. If he does not give his consent, then any citizen of the land – any one of the public who is adversely affected – can come to this court and ask that the law be enforced."

This judgement was overturned in the House of Lords on the grounds that Mr Gouriet did not have the necessary *locus standi*. Within a year, Lord Denning had helped introduce new rules which now permit an application to the courts even if the applicant can demonstrate no more than "sufficient interest".

Lord Hailsham later described Mr Gouriet's case as the most important constitutional case since 1689.

Applying the principle of Pepper *vs* Hart (1992) (the interpretation of statutes by reference to the debates in parliament during passage of the bill), the following statements during the passage of European enabling-legislation are relevant:

"The house as a whole may therefore be reassured that there is no question of this bill [the European Communities Bill 1972] making a thousand years of British law subservient to the Code Napoleon."

Mr Geoffrey Rippon, chancellor of the Duchy of Lancaster, *Hansard*, 15th February 1972, p270

"Our sovereignty cannot be bartered away by the Solicitor General, or even by the Prime Minister, because it is not theirs to give. I speak not only of the sovereignty of this house, but also of the higher sovereignty of the British people."

Mr Alfred Morris MP, *Hansard*, 17th February 1972, pp727–8

Government statements made during the time of national debate on the question of the UK joining what became the EU can be described at the very least as deliberately misleading, and at worst as barefaced mendacity by ministers who had received expert legal advice to the contrary and knew the full facts:

"There is no reason to think that the impact of community law would weaken or destroy any of the basic rights and liberties of individuals under the law in the UK."

The lord high chancellor, Command Paper 3301, 1967, on the constitutional implications of the UK joining the European Community

"...no question of any erosion of essential national sovereignty."

White paper on joining the Common Market, issued by the Heath government in July 1971

Three years later, writing in support of the "Yes" campaign in the 1975 referendum, Roy Jenkins was equally misleading:

"The position of the Queen is not affected. English Common Law is not affected."

On the other hand, if the government's statements of 1967 and 1971, and Roy Jenkins' remarks of 1975, were correct, these statements now support our case for declaring that all EU legislation is unconstitutional in the UK and therefore null and void.

The inescapable fact is that successive governments have acted as if such statements and commitments did not exist. They have simply been ignored.

That brings us to the trustworthiness and honesty of the elected representatives of the people, to whom they have a duty of care. Furthermore, a government that has introduced in something short of three years a score of Bills and Acts of Parliament that deal with various aspects of the constitution, needs to be reminded that it has no right to exceed the powers vested in it. We, the people, own the rights to our own property – in this case Britain.

Every five years we might be said to "lease" its care to "tenants" (parliament), who have an obligation to look after our property and act in our best interests as the ultimate owners.

Those same "tenants" do not own the title to our deeds, nor any right of ownership over the property itself. They merely own the right of abode, and duty of care, for a maximum of five years. They are caretakers, if you like. They have no right to sign away those title deeds. They did not own them in the first place.

> "In all tyrannical governments the supreme magistracy, or the right of both making and of enforcing laws, is vested in one and the same man, or one and the same body of men; and whenever these powers are united together, there can be no public liberty.... But where the legislative and executive authority are in distinct hands, the former will take care not to entrust the latter with so large a power, as may tend to the subversion of its own independence and therewith of the liberty of the subject.
>
> With us therefore, in England, this supreme power is divided into two branches; the legislative, to wit, the Parliament, consisting of the King, the Lords and the Commons; and the other, the executive consisting of the King alone."
>
> Blackstone (1723–80), *Commentaries on the Laws of England*

"Whoever would overthrow the liberty of a nation must begin
by subduing the freeness of speech."

Benjamin Franklin

The modern disproportionate dominance of the elected House of
Commons over the sovereignty of the people, and the erosion of
constitutional checks and balances, were first given serious encouragement
by Lord Mansfield, a Scottish Jacobite who became lord chief justice of
England in the 18th century. Despite Blackstone's observations, he had no
problem with an executive operating within the legislature.

The institutions and practices which have grown up since that time –
collective cabinet responsibility, organised political parties, career politicians,
and a whip system that denies politicians the freedom to vote according to
their conscience – are not based on legislation, nor on common law, nor on
the law and custom of parliament.

Sir Ivor Jennings pointed out in *Law and the Constitution* that these
conventions had never been formally recognised by parliament or the courts.
The courts recognised a constitution based primarily on the Bill of Rights.

To explain away this perversion and destruction of our legal constitution,
politicians like to suggest that we have an unwritten one, consisting of
"conventions" that they themselves have devised to regulate and give an
appearance of legality to activities that, according to Walter Paley's
book *Political and Moral Philosophy*, are unconstitutional and therefore
illegal.

Returning to the present time, and the central issue we have raised
about the condition, status and validity of Magna Carta and the
Declaration of Rights, we come to the case of R V Witham, 1997. This
addressed the "doctrine of implied repeal", and Mr Justice Laws demolished
it:

> "Access to the courts is a constitutional right: it can only be denied
> by the Government if it persuades parliament to pass legislation
> which specifically – in effect by express permission – permits the
> executive to turn people away from the court door."

He explained the basis of his conclusion thus:

"What is the precise nature of any constitutional right such as might be...[beyond] the power of government...to abrogate? In the unwritten order of the British state, at a time when the common law continues to accord a legislative supremacy to parliament, the notion of a constitutional right can...not be abrogated by the state save by specific provision in Act of Parliament, or by regulations [that]...specifically confers the power to abrogate. General words will not suffice. And any such rights will be the creatures of the common law, since their existence would not be the consequence of the democratic process but would be logically prior to it.

The common law does not generally speak in the language of constitutional rights, for the good reason that, in the absence of a sovereign text, a written constitution which is logically and legally prior to the power of the legislature, executive and judiciary alike, there is on the face of it no hierarchy of rights such that any one of them is more entrenched by law than any other."

That brings us back finally to the meaning of words, respect for their meaning, and acceptance of the force, obligations and commitments they carry. The Alice in Wonderland language – "words mean what I want them to mean" – adopted increasingly by the executive in modern times is at the very heart of the UK's current political scepticism, as governments blithely ignore almost anything that is inconvenient to them, prefer political correctness to substance, and spin-doctor their way around every obstacle.

If the words used in the Witham judgment have any meaning, legal or otherwise, the logic of the case we have argued in this document is overwhelming. Whether those in or close to the executive, the legislature or the judiciary will recognise the force of our case sufficiently to find the courage to lend support, is altogether something else.

Sovereign Authority

We have already argued that the ultimate powers of sovereignty remain in the sole possession of the monarch. Indeed, it is the unique covenant between sovereign and people that stands as the bulwark supporting our constitution and rights.

The sovereign is the court of last resort, the only person who can stand finally between the people and renegade politicians. Indeed, we would go further. It is the sovereign's sworn duty, as laid down in Magna Carta (see above).

The coronation oath is a contract for life between the sovereign and the nation. The original form of the oath was stated earlier in this document, and still has the force of statute law. However, at the coronations of both the Queen and her father George VI, the words of the oath were changed to meet the needs of the statute of Westminster, 1931, which granted autonomy to the dominions. The words used at these coronations did not have the force of statute law behind them, having been merely agreed between the leaders of the Church of England and the government of the day in each case. Both oaths were illegal, as *The Times* newspaper pointed out on both occasions. In any case, parliament has no power under the Bill of Rights to interfere with the coronation oath as first enacted during the reign of Charles II.

Despite the huge constitutional issues raised by these events of 1937 and 1953, the essential words in the oath sworn by the Queen were:

"...to govern the peoples of the UK...according to their laws and customs."

She also swore to preserve for the people...

"all rights and privileges as by law do or shall appertain to any of them".

The coronation oath is not a contract between the sovereign and parliament. It is a contract between the sovereign and each individual subject. It cannot be broken by a vote in parliament. It can be broken only by the sovereign or by the individual.

Like all contracts, if one party to the contract believes the terms are at risk, the other party can be called to account.

As we have indicated already, today just as for nearly a thousand years, if an individual believes his freedoms, rights and liberties are at risk, the sovereign can be called upon to protect those rights as promised in the contract.

Likewise, the sovereign can call individuals to arms to protect the realm.

We know of two occasions in modern times when the covenant between sovereign and subjects first established in Magna Carta, and renewed in every coronation oath since, has been put to the test by one party to the contract or the other. Conveniently, the two examples come from opposite sides of the covenant.

In 1975, in Australia, the governor general, acting on behalf of the Queen, dissolved the Australian parliament and called new elections, when the then government attempted to pass legislation that was held to infringe the rights of all Australians.

In 1982, we saw the sovereign's call to arms to prepare and despatch a task force to rescue the Falkland Islanders, whose rights and sovereignty were threatened by war.

Actions of this kind enhance the status and strength of the monarchy, and reaffirm to the nation's subjects that their rights and freedoms are being preserved. They also demonstrate in a modern context that Magna Carta and the Declaration of Rights are alive and well.

The sovereign is the ultimate protector of the nation and guarantor of the rights of each individual, and those responsibilities are the sovereign's, and the sovereign's alone.

At least one constitutional commentator agrees with us:

> "For parliament to develop or improve on a fundamental right is one thing. But to enact legislation which expressly removes an already existing fundamental right, and to have that enactment blindly upheld by a court, is quite another.
>
> If there is one thread which runs through the whole turbulent history of British constitutional development, it is the belief that we (parliament and the courts) are the servants of fundamental constitutional rules which were there before us and will be there after we are gone."

Allott, *The Courts and Parliament*, 1979

The Ultimate Test

Despite all those rights, freedoms and protections, established over centuries, today our common laws, rights, freedoms, liberties and customs are being demolished with the speed and thoroughness of a team of statutory bulldozers.

Long ago, Magna Carta dealt with the problem of a sovereign acting above the law. Later, the Declaration of Rights confirmed the estates of the realm and their relationship to one another – a series of checks and balances. Today, that relationship has been seriously undermined. We now have a House of Commons acting above the law, plainly contemptuous of the (remaining) powers of the Queen and the House of Lords.

Such an overwhelming concentration of power in the hands of the executive, especially one with a huge parliamentary majority, means that we are currently faced with an extreme example of what Lord Hailsham famously called "an elective dictatorship".

Writing in *The Sunday Times*, in July 1970, he said:

> "It is the parliamentary majority that has the potential for tyranny. The thing that the Courts cannot protect you against is parliament – the traditional protector of our liberties. But parliament is constantly making mistakes and could in theory become the most oppressive instrument in the world."

Others had agreed with him in the past.

> "A political system resting on professional party politicians is clearly fatal to all liberty and national well-being. It represents a total destruction of our historic Parliamentary constitution behind whose forms, institutions and ceremonies it has disguised itself whilst at the same time rendering them meaningless.

> The full meaning of Parliamentary supremacy is now lost to us by the constitutional corruptions which the professional politician has fomented by their appeals to an alien and fraudulent political ideology. By clearly identifying and correcting these corruptions we can recover the enduring qualities of strength and freedom

of our parliamentary constitution for which generations of Englishmen have for centuries been ready to sacrifice their lives and their possessions."

Richard Crossman (1907–74), Introduction to Bagehot's *The English Constitution*, 1867

Ben Greene pointed out in his book *The Restoration of the English Constitution* that Bagehot was quite open about the deception by which the English people were deprived of their great constitutional heritage. The English monarchy had been reduced to an "act of disguise" for a *de facto* republic. Its role enabled the executive to effect change without people realising it. This "ancient show", as the monarchy was called, covered the clandestine introduction of "a new reality".

John Locke once more. He had no doubts. The people remain sovereign:

"…there remains still in the people the supreme power to remove or alter the legislative when they find the legislative act contrary to the trust reposed in them."

Winston Churchill expressed clear views about our relationship with Europe and about our sovereignty as enshrined in Magna Carta.

"We are with Europe, but not of it. We are linked, but not combined. We are interested and associated, but not absorbed. And should European statesmen address us in the words which were used of old: 'Shall I speak for thee to the King?', we should reply with the words of the Shunamite woman: 'Nay sir, for we dwell among our own people'."

Churchill was confident of the safeguards contained in Magna Carta. Writing in his *History of The English-Speaking Peoples*, he said:

"…and when in subsequent ages the state, swollen with its own authority, has attempted to ride roughshod over the rights and liberties of the subject it is to this doctrine that appeal has again and again been made, and never, as yet, without success."

The Magna Carta Society, and tens of thousands like us, believe the time has come – indeed, is overdue – to put the great principles and rights enshrined in Magna Carta and the Declaration of Rights to the test once again.

Eventually, the issue of the EU's right to rule over the UK must be tested in the highest court in the land and – given the speed and comprehensiveness of present EU legislation and its destructiveness – that test must be made as a matter of the highest priority.

Already faced with the most fundamental concerns for the structure and protection of this nation's constitution, it now appears that the battle over the EU has developed a second front – the dismantling of our parliamentary institutions and the most cavalier disregard for our constitution and rights.

Under the terms of Magna Carta, the House of Lords has an obligation to hear petitions brought by free men, and take them to the Queen, who – equally – has an obligation to hear them.

That is the ultimate consequence of the unique contract first established with Magna Carta and renewed at each coronation.

To those in government and the judiciary who might try to argue that we no longer have the right of petition and appeal to the Queen, there are serious questions to answer:

When do they claim that right was taken away? By whom? And how? On whose authority? And by what right? As it happens, the House of Lords' Records Office confirmed in writing as recently as September 2000 that Magna Carta, signed by King John in June 1215, stands to this day. Home Secretary Jack Straw said as much on 1st October 2000, when the Human Rights Act came into force. Halsbury's *Laws of England* says: "Magna Carta is as binding upon the Crown today as it was the day it was sealed at Runnymede."

(The last monarch to receive and act on a petition was Queen Victoria. There appears to be no evidence of any attempt to prevent or hinder any such petition subsequently. Nor does there appear to be any legislation which attempts to defy the contract made between sovereign and subjects in Magna Carta and the coronation oath.)

However, it has become custom in the last few years for petitions to be passed to ministers of the Crown for action, but that is not to say that the monarch can no longer act in her own right. Indeed, in current circumstances, the ministers themselves are party to our complaint, and cannot therefore deal with the matters complained of.)

In any case, the sovereign cannot be absolved from her obligations, responsibilities and duties to her subjects, and certainly not on the mere advice of ministers. Otherwise the coronation oath would be meaningless.

We believe a petition should be submitted to the Queen, based on the following terms:

> "We the undersigned seek to draw attention to and seek redress from the imposition of foreign laws, directives, regulations and judicial decisions by and from the EU and its institutions, to the detriment and prejudice of your sovereignty and to our rights and freedoms as defined in Magna Carta, the Declaration of Rights, and by the customs of your people, and which you, our sovereign, swore to uphold and preserve inviolate in your coronation oath of 1953."

If Magna Carta stands, her subjects have a right to enter such a petition.

If it does not, this kingdom stands in dire peril, the executive has some momentous questions to answer, and all free people of this kingdom should hear the call.

Future Action

The objective of *Defence of the Realm* has been to make a case for the constitutional repudiation of the UK's membership of the EU.

There are, of course, other means by which the UK's membership of the EU may end – the government of the day might withdraw its ambassador and void the treaties with the EU; the EU might collapse or throw us out (equally unlikely); parliament might vote for repeal of the 1972 Act; private prosecutions of government ministers for treason might be successful. Any one of these events would have much the same practical effect as we seek.

Whichever event prevails, we argue that there are other actions, legal and otherwise, that need the urgent attention of those in a position, and with the knowledge, to take them.

1   Determine how best to test in the courts the claim that European law is "supreme" in the UK. This is the first step towards ultimately proving the illegality of EU law in the UK.

2   Examine the direct conflict between the oaths sworn by privy councillors and EU commissioners. At the very least, we advocate that those who have taken the EC's euro should be publicly stripped of their status as privy councillors.

3   Examine the constitutionality of the three separate attempts currently being made by parliament, acting under instructions from the EU and the European Court of Human Rights, to interfere with the oath of attestation made by all members of the armed forces. The first involves the setting up of an embryo European army, and passing command to a foreign power, the second proposes giving the "right" to junior ranks to sue their commanding officers, and the third interferes with the setting and interpretation of standards of behaviour likely to be detrimental to the efficiency of the forces. In all these actions parliament appears to be exceeding its authority and compromising the sovereignty of the Queen.

4   Examine the issue of citizenship (Article 8 of the Maastricht Treaty – "Citizenship of the union is hereby established"). British citizenship (we prefer the term "subject of the Crown") is a birthright. Citizenship is not in the gift of a self-appointed foreign institution, which in any event is unaccountable to the British electorate and, we argue, has no standing here.

The notion of dual citizenship, implied under this treaty, is nonsensical. Across the world, applications for dual citizenship are entirely voluntary. Furthermore, the EU is even now only an association of sovereign nation states. It is not in itself a state, much as it might like to pretend otherwise. It is impossible to be the citizen of a non-state. At the very least, therefore, that legal anomaly needs to be disputed in the courts, with the outcome providing individual subjects with a practical and effective means of rejecting so-called citizenship of the EU, and all its pathetic paraphernalia – passport covers, driving licences and the like.

5   Examine the constitutionality of the 1975 referendum and the referendum proposed on the euro, both of which concern changes that appear to have been forbidden under our constitution and, if possible, instigate proceedings to have them set aside.

6   Investigate the case against all the plenipotentiaries acting under the royal prerogative and who signed the Treaties of Rome, Maastricht and Amsterdam on behalf of the UK, and who may be held to have exceeded the powers granted to them.

7   Test the legality of all new EU legislation, directives and regulations, as attempts are made to introduce and enforce them. To date, insufficiently vigorous opposition has been applied. There are major battles ahead, including: the euro and tax harmonisation, weights and measures, a European defence force, Europol and *corpus juris*. As the EU attempts to enforce its policies and law on the UK, contrary to Magna Carta, the Declaration of Rights, and common law, each and every one must be disputed to the utmost of our resources and willpower.

8   The restitution of the constitution will release an avalanche of cases of maladministration, involving whole industries (fishing, for example) and many thousands of individuals and businesses, going back over many years.

The desire for an immediate and gigantic bonfire of EU inanities will need to be balanced with an equally important desire to achieve rapid but orderly abolition of (now) illegal regulations. An immediate moratorium on enforcement seems the most practical and desirable first step.

The vital issue of making good the damage suffered by the people will come a close second. This might perhaps be addressed in much the same way as restitution and re-instatement was handled after the Second World War, with the state leading a programme of national rebuilding. What redress do the people whose livelihoods have been damaged or destroyed over the last 30 years have against government ministers and enforcement agencies past and present? And how can it be delivered quickly and fairly, without time-consuming and expensive civil proceedings? It is possible that justice itself will demand that the state foots the bill.

We urge that a powerful independent body be set up as a matter of the highest priority and charged, primarily, with determining the best means of achieving rapid and equitable redress for all those affected by the enforcement of EU law, regulations, directives and judicial decisions in the UK since 1st January 1973.

9   Investigate the constitutionality of actions and decisions concerning the EU taken or authorised by all the prime ministers, their administrations and enforcement agencies, since 1972. Consider what legal response is now appropriate.

Further examine the past actions of ministers and officials who exceeded or may have exceeded the authority delegated to them by the people, and who attempted to defy the clear intentions of the constitution of the UK. The investigation should specifically consider what liability attaches to all or any of these people who, like all of us, are subject to the law and not above it, and whose past actions paid no proper attention to the common law.

10 The people are sovereign. The monarch is the embodiment of that sovereignty. So it was and still should be. But these tenets of the constitution have been seriously threatened by the erosion of the checks and balances between the sovereign, the Houses of Parliament and the people – an erosion which has been insidious, lengthy and allowed to thrive by the negligence of the people, who have failed sufficiently to exercise vigilance.

It was 473 years after Magna Carta that a further treaty became necessary between sovereign and people. Today, 312 years have passed since the Declaration of Rights.

Events of recent years, and the momentous issues raised in this document, convince us that a new and historic reaffirmation of the rights of the people is now essential – a confirmation of liberties between the monarch and the people. It should restate the true relationship between sovereign, the two Houses of Parliament and the people, re-establish the checks and balances between them, and reaffirm the covenant between sovereign and subjects.

A Declaration for the next thousand years based on the rights, freedoms and customs of the British people for the last thousand years. Nothing else will do.

Index